THE CULT OF OSAMA

The Cult of Osama
Psychoanalyzing Bin Laden and His Magnetism for Muslim Youths

Peter Alan Olsson, M.D.

PRAEGER SECURITY INTERNATIONAL
Westport, Connecticut · London

Library of Congress Cataloging-in-Publication Data

Olsson, Peter Alan, 1941–
The cult of Osama : psychoanalyzing Bin Laden and his magnetism for Muslim youths /
    Peter Alan Olsson.
        p. cm.
    Includes bibliographical references and index.
    ISBN: 978–0–275–99989–6 (alk. paper)
1. Bin Laden, Osama, 1957—Psychology. 2. Terrorism—Psychological aspects. 3. Muslim youth—
Psychology. 4. Charisma (Personality trait) I. Title.
HV6430.B55O47 2008
363.32501'9—dc22   2007028008

British Library Cataloguing in Publication Data is available.

Library of Congress Catalog Card Number: 2007028008
ISBN: 978–0–275–99989–6

First published in 2008

Praeger Security International, 88 Post Road West, Westport, CT 06881
An imprint of Greenwood Publishing Group, Inc.
www.praeger.com

Printed in the United States of America

The paper used in this book complies with the
Permanent Paper Standard issued by the National
Information Standards Organization (Z39.48–1984).

10 9 8 7 6 5 4 3 2 1

Every reasonable effort has been made to trace the owners of copyright materials in this book, but in
some instances this has proven impossible. The author and publisher will be glad to receive information
leading to more complete acknowledgments in subsequent printings of the book and in the meantime
extend their apologies for any omissions.

I dedicate this book to Vamik Volkan, M.D., who not only taught me about applied psychoanalytic approaches to psychohistory, international relationships, and psychobiography but also has been a mentor, valued colleague, and friend. Volkan's work is an inspiring contribution towards the noble but illusive ideal of world peace. Vamik Volkan has furthered progress in the domain referred to by Freud in this passage from his famous correspondence with Einstein entitled "Why War?"

Anything that encourages the growth of emotional ties between men must operate against war. These ties may be of two kinds. In the first place they may be relations resembling those toward a love object, though without having a sexual aim. There is no reason for psychoanalysis to be ashamed to speak of love in this connection, for religion itself uses the same words: "Thou shalt love thy neighbor as thyself." This, however, is more easily said than done. The second kind of emotional tie is by means of identification. Whatever leads men to share important interests produces this community of feeling, these identifications. And the structure of human society is to a large extent based on them. (Freud [1933] 1958, 22:212)

CONTENTS

ACKNOWLEDGMENTS

I am very grateful for the excellent editorial help and astute suggestions I have gotten from Susan Peery and Randy Miller. Debbie Carvalko at Praeger/Greenwood has a wonderful sense of humor and has been ever upbeat, pragmatic and encouraging. Megan Chalek, Nicole Azze of Greenwood, and Matthew Van Atta of BeaconPMG have been consummate professionals.

My son Nathaniel Olsson (the lawyer), and my old and dear friends and colleagues Bob White, M.D. and Roger Hansen, M.D. have provided valuable feedback and have been tireless proofreaders. My valued psychoanalytic colleagues Dr. Althea Horner, Dr. Martin Stein, and Dr. Ron Turco have been persistent in their encouragement of my work. My daughter Shannon Sweet did excellent photography that helped me look scholarly for book covers and my Web site. Shannon and her husband Mike Sweet were very helpful in setting up my Web site. My son Andrew Olsson used his computer skills with search engines to find hard-to-find materials. The love of my life, Dr. Pam Olsson, has been patient with that "hunt and pecker" hiding out in his study for all those long hours.

Introduction _____

WHY STUDY THE MINDS OF OSAMA BIN LADEN AND ISLAMISTS?

Who is this terrorizing and martyrdom-seeking murderer bin Laden? Why does he want to hurt and kill Americans? Osama has inspired and authorized the deaths of more than 3,000 people, and he and his Al Qaeda franchises are constantly planning more operations! What goes on in his conscious mind? More importantly, what goes on in Osama's *unconscious* mind? He is merely a man, and yet he can't be simply labeled as a psychotic or only a cruel criminal. How did his personality and character, or lack of character, form? Are there common themes in his life pathways and trajectories and those of his terror cult leader colleagues?

Why did some Muslims and Arabs cheer and rejoice when they saw the World Trade Center and Pentagon's flames of destruction? Why do young Arab and Muslim men and women blow up themselves and innocent people in the name of God and at Osama bin Laden's or a jaded Muslim Imam's bidding? How do even young Americans succumb to the twisted pied piper mentoring music of Osama and company? These questions inspired the writing of this book.

Many terrorism "experts" do not grasp the following idea, which is one of the core ideas developed in this book. Adolescent and young adult individuals and groups need mature adult leaders that care about them and present them with worthy and noble ideals, goals, and spiritual values. An inseparable corollary is that middle-aged and older adults need to be admired by youths so they can imagine good things for the future of their community and the world. These two domains are genuinely spiritual in nature and transcend the importance of personal wealth, power, or prestige. Many young people will live for and/or die for such causes. They are one of the key forms of the power of Love, or in Erikson's term for this one, generativity.

Do homicide bomber martyrs really seek death as a lonely project? Or are they ultimately reaching out for admiration and acclaim from somewhere and someone? Often they feel assured of God's special love for them and prosperity for their surviving family. We know that since his boyhood and early school years, Osama bin Laden has been deeply devoted and committed to Wahhabism (Coll 2005, 50–61; Volkan 2004, 300n341). As we explore the mind, motives, and psychology of Osama and his colleagues, it is cogent and heuristic to keep in mind their fantasies of martyrdom and heroic commitment to Islamic fundamentalism. The Islamic fundamentalist commitments of Osama and his colleagues have remarkable resonance with millions of Muslim youths. Osama uses a pied piper appeal to recruit in-betweener youths and their Muslim communities to his perverted *jihadi* cause. How do radical Islamists use the normal adolescent need to rebel and separate psychologically from their families to spread their perverted appeal to religious idealism in Muslim youths?

Many political, diplomatic, military, economic, and intelligence experts and journalists are writing about Osama, Islamism, and Al Qaeda. However, an in-depth psychological attempt to understand Osama and a social-psychological grasp of the power his group wields around the world are also important. This monograph represents an effort to form psychoanalytic hunches and to follow trails of applied psychological data toward an understanding of Osama bin Laden and his colleagues' minds.

Osama and his colleagues, like other destructive cult leaders, would shun knocking on the door of a psychoanalyst or psychotherapist's office. Although we do not have data obtained from the analytic couch or consulting room, we do have books about him, his videotaped statements, and his writings. They are a means to make inferences and speculate about Osama's mind and motives. Of particular applied psychoanalytic interest in this respect is the poignant poetry that Osama has written. In addition, the biographies about Osama and his colleagues offer some important psychobiographical data. Such data allows psychodynamically informed inferences about their minds and motives.

It is, of course, fascinating for a psychiatrist, psychotherapist, or psychoanalyst to imagine how Osama would react to a well-documented and well-timed interpretation of his destructive acting-out behavior. We can assume that his well-fortified narcissistic defenses and religious rationalizations would provide him with staunch protection at such a hypothetical encounter. He rejected even his own mother's effort to reason with him (Bergen 2006, 151).

PRAGMATIC EFFORTS TO DIAGNOSE OSAMA AND PREDICT HIS BEHAVIOR—AND THE "SCIENCE," PHILOSOPHY, AND POLITICS OF A PSYCHIATRIC DIAGNOSIS

This author's 2005 study of destructive/apocalyptic cult leaders and their followers raises the issue of applying psychiatric diagnoses and psychodynamic concepts to these individuals (Olsson, 2005, 24–28). "Malignant Pied Pipers" is my term for destructive cult leaders like bin Laden and his colleagues. Because of their particular bent of personality and cultural/religious stances, they are unlikely ever to voluntarily seek psychiatric or psychotherapeutic help. Their rigid fundamentalist mentality requires everyone to think and believe exactly as they do, or die. For radical Islamists, some Jewish fundamentalists, and American Christian fundamentalists like Pat Robertson, it is their way or the highway. They become the godlike final judges, juries, and executioners of others.

A PSYCHIATRIST DIAGNOSTICIAN OF HITLER: MY ROLE MODEL FOR THIS BOOK

Psychiatrist and psychoanalyst Walter Langer did a secret report during World War II called *The Mind of Adolph Hitler.* Because of the urgency of the study but the impossibility of Hitler's direct collaboration, Hitler thus became Langer's *subject* of study rather than his patient. However, Langer did remarkably good psychodynamic diagnostic work and made many accurate behavioral predictions via secondary and tertiary sources of data about Hitler. *The Cult of Osama* is about Osama bin Laden and his radical Islamist colleagues, and their Islamo-fascism. It is intended as a similar effort to Langer's work about Hitler and his Nazism or fascism. Like many would-be world conquerors who malignantly blend utopianism with potentially apocalyptic methodologies, Osama and his Islamofascist colleagues and their recruiters of Muslim youth must be understood and stopped. A core thesis of this book is that ideas and truth are more important than bullets or rockets in the effort to stop terror cults.

Writers and journalists like Peter Bergen (2001, 2006) have done extensive interviews with Osama and those who know him well. Jessica Stern (2003) describes her skilled interviews with violent fundamentalists that included Islamist terrorist leaders and homegrown American terrorists. Bergen and Stern's perceptive interview-based observations have provided helpful data for the applied analysis of this study.

THE CLINICAL ART AND SCIENCE OF DIAGNOSIS

The usual work of a psychiatrist involves seeing the patient for several inter-views. The psychiatrist sends for records of previous psychiatric treatment and may speak over the phone with previous therapists and psychiatrists.

The clinician may also consult with the patient's general physician about physical symptoms the person may have that can mimic psychiatric disorders. Psychological testing may be ordered in some situations. If the psychiatrist is unclear about the diagnosis and/or treatment plan after the evaluation sessions, he or she might request a second-opinion consultation with a respected colleague. The central purpose and priority is the well-being and best care of the patient.

This psychobiographical study is *not* a clinical case report about Osama and his colleagues, but rather what is called Applied Psychoanalysis. Applied analytic studies can be useful, but they are not by their nature as accurate or in-depth as the results of psychotherapy with a person. The author has not personally interviewed Osama bin Laden as Bergen had the opportunity to do. That fact limits the strength of this study's conclusions about Osama's mind, but it has not deterred the efforts at using key secondary and tertiary sources in order to proceed with the analysis. In addition, some psychoanalysts such as Kohut and Kernberg have worked with highly charismatic-messianic individuals and have provided compelling observations and theories to shed light on a personality like Osama's.

The applied psychoanalytic diagnostic conclusions and speculations in this study are founded on a depth and density of thoroughly studied secondary sources. Many exploitive cult leaders like Osama, Zawahiri, and Zarqawi, et al., love to talk, write, be videotaped, and/or be interviewed. During their sermonizing, pontificating, and "inspired" writing, they sometimes become quite emotional, autobiographical, and self-disclosing about their attitudes, passions, and motivations.

COUNTER-TRANSFERENCE, A VALUABLE TOOL OF APPLIED PSYCHOANALYSIS

Reading Osama's poetry, writings, and biographical material and viewing videotapes of him inevitably stir intense inner feelings (anger, rage, fear, and sadness, to name just a few). In a therapeutic relationship, the complicated personal emotional reactions that therapists have toward their patients as the patient discloses painful, cruel, or vivid emotions are called counter-transference. These reactions on the part of the therapist usually stem from unresolved problems of the therapist or problems that have been resolved by the therapist during his or her own personal analysis. They indicate profoundly painful yet important areas of the patient's/subject's conflicts that would never be explored or resolved if it were not for the therapist's refusal to be frightened off from such heuristic but challenging therapeutic work. This domain of counter-transference data collection adds an additional source of applied psychoanalytic information. Rather than a true scientific instrument, counter-transference is an invaluable clinical tool of the psychotherapist and can be used carefully by a researcher in applied psychoanalysis. It is, of course, preferable if the researcher him or herself has had a thorough psychoanalytic experience, because of the subtlety inherent in this area of exploration. A somewhat analogous tool is used by good biographers who value trusted colleagues to read their manuscript and are asked to have the integrity to bring up areas of potential bias, blind spots, and possible distortions. Such collegial relationships have inestimable value to psychobiographers.

At times a reader can feel profound loathing for Osama and his colleagues; at other times we can wish empathically that they had been in therapy as boys so that they could have resolved their grief, loneliness, shame, wounded narcissism, and hate, instead of taking the road to becoming terrorist leaders. Examination of counter-transference in applied analysis work is complicated, but it has been helpful in the process of forming hypotheses as I have read Osama's writings and poetry; listened to his pronouncements on tapes; examined his body language and nonverbal behavior; and read descriptions of Osama by those who have actually interviewed him. My counter-transference reactions to Osama have helped me to intuit beyond Osama's charismatic soft-spoken exterior. Beyond his unconscious denial and rationalization, is, I am convinced, the realm of Osama's unresolved grief/depression, loneliness, and narcissistic rage. My experiences with highly messianic/charismatic personalities in psychotherapy work, and similar observations made by Kohut and Kernberg, have helped me make important inferences about Osama and his colleagues' narcissistic rage and acting out. Denial of unresolved grief and rage often tend to find ultimate expression in violent actions rather than appropriate sublimation, via political processes or professional career activities. I am also convinced that narcissistic wounds are common and overdetermined threads among radical Islamist leaders' psyches.

Second-opinion consultation-collaboration with experienced colleagues about these counter-transference-generated hypotheses is particularly important. (Consultation with my colleague Bob White, M.D., who is a psychiatrist experienced in individual psychodynamics and a national expert in group psychotherapy, has been of particular value in this regard.) Group process can mobilize powerful forces for good or evil that is greater than the sum of a group's members.

REMARKABLE SIMILARITIES OF OSAMA'S LIFE TRAJECTORY AND THOSE OF DESTRUCTIVE CULT LEADERS

Biographical details about Osama bin Laden's childhood and early family history reveal some similarities to the psychological dynamics and personality patterns that occur in destructive cult leaders like Jim Jones or Charles Manson (Olsson 2005, chap. 4, 7). The available psychobiographical information about Osama bin Laden is incomplete and at times contradictory, but there is enough density of biographical data to form psychoanalytic hunches and some solid conclusions about important aspects of bin Laden's personality and psychological agendas. An in-depth psychological understanding of Osama bin Laden is just as important as an understanding of the financial, theological, military, political, tribal/cultural, religious, and media factors behind his power.

SHOCK, AWE, AND THE UNCANNY: A DEFINITION OF TERRORISM

Many people who saw the World Trade Towers hit by airliners on 9/11 said things like, "It was surreal!" or "It looked like a Hollywood movie." In fact, effective horror film writers and directors exploit the same experience of "The Uncanny" that the terrorist does. The intuitive and/or calculated impact of the terrorist act comes from our human tendency to regress psychologically to magical, black-and-white, superstitious, or primitive thinking under stress or shock. Our shocked nervous systems and minds become more fragile and vulnerable for a period of time. Osama and colleagues even had issued threats and warnings months before his terror cult's actions. This gave a prospective and retrospective magical, grandiose, and prophetic quality to the 9/11 events.

Freud, in his fascinating paper "The Uncanny," sets the scene of where we all are susceptible to regress during the aftermath of a terror attack when he says:

> Our analysis of instances of the uncanny has led us back to the old, animistic conception of the universe. This was characterized by the idea that the world was peopled by the spirits of human beings; by the subject's narcissistic over valuation of his own mental processes; by the belief in the omnipotence of thoughts and the technique of magic based on the belief; by the attribution to various outside persons and things of carefully graded magical powers, or mana; as well as by all the other creations with the help of which man, in the unrestricted narcissism of that stage of development, strove to fend off the manifest prohibitions of reality. It seems as if each one of us has been through a phase of individual development corresponding to this animistic stage in primitive man, that none of us has passed through it without preserving certain residues and traces of it which are capable of manifesting themselves, and that everything that strikes us as "uncanny" fulfills the condition of touching those residues of animistic mental activity within us bringing them to expression. (Freud [1919] 1958, 17:240–41)

By way of introduction then, and in light of Freud's perspective on the uncanny, I offer this composite definition of terrorism: Terrorism is an act or threat of violent action against noncombatants with the objective of exacting revenge, or intimidating, influencing, or shocking an audience. It is executed in order to threaten a society, a political hierarchy, an economy, a peace initiative, or an international agreement. One objective is the shock value of an action that is novel, symbolic, unsuspected, and strategically damaging in its pragmatic scope and painful victimization. Modern TV media provides a unique worldwide cybernetic reverberating psychodrama stage of visual imagery and propaganda for terror events (Stern 2003, xx; Fields 1986, 2; Olsson 2005, 149).

Radical Islamist terrorists have honed their skills in the conducting of terror events on the worldwide psychodrama stage! Their creativity in staging terror is truly uncanny.

GROUP PSYCHOLOGY AND COMMUNITIES WHERE TERRORISTS RECRUIT

It also seems important to try to understand the related and uniquely chilling social-psychological fit between the religiously flavored charismatic leadership of a man like Osama bin Laden, and the group psychology of communities where he and his colleagues and mentors recruit devoted terrorists. It is a serious mistake to glibly label and dismiss bin Laden as simply a mass murderer, thug, or criminal. In painful truth, he is a Robin Hood–like figure and a spiritual hero for many people in the Muslim world. He is someone we must try to understand because of his impact on our society. Since some of the power of Osama's attacks have involved psychological domains, it is important for us to understand the intrapsychic dynamics as well as the group psychology that can help in our recovery and in the prevention of future attacks. As ancient martial arts and warrior codes point out:

1. Hasty declaration of war inflates the status and grandiosity of the enemy;
2. Contempt fuels the enemy's outrage; and
3. Incorrect and dangerous assumptions are easily made about an enemy one has only contempt for and scant knowledge about.

In essence, if one knows one's enemy and oneself in depth, one will rarely suffer defeat and often may not need to fight. If one only knows one's self, one will lose half of the battles (Sun Tzu [500 BCE] 2002, 51).

This book, then, is an effort to know our enemies, Osama bin Laden and his colleagues and minions. We will approach them from an applied psychoanalytic, psychobiographical, and social-psychological perspective. The psychological view is obviously not the only lens through which to understand Osama et al., but it is an important one. In addition to a density of childhood experiences of loss, separation, unresolved grief, shame, humiliation, and disappointments in parental figures, we can also detect in bin Laden's life trajectory evidence of what are called *dark epiphanies* in destructive cult leaders (Olsson 2005, 18, 38–39, 148). Destructive cult leaders usually encounter these life experiences when they are young adults. Such dark epiphanies reify and magnify their earlier, and still unresolved, painful molding experiences. In adolescent or young adult life phases, antiheroes are often chosen to compensate for or counteract disappointment or humiliation/shame experiences with parental figures. Islamists naturally will object to this interpretation because they would favor more noble interpretations of their behavior.

WHY BIN LADEN'S AL QAEDA IS SIMILAR TO A DESTRUCTIVE APOCALYPTIC CULT

Al Qaeda and its metastatic subsidiary franchises have many similarities to destructive and apocalyptic cults (Olsson 2005, chap. 7). Zarqawi's and bin Laden's cyberspace fund-raising and recruitment; their charismatic, *Koran*-distorting, religion-flavored recruitment techniques; and their disdain for their homeland communities if they are friends of America all seem remarkably similar to the core personality and group dynamics in many destructive/exploitive cults. Osama bin Laden, like most destructive cult leaders, seems to this psychiatrist and psychoanalyst to harbor unresolved and exponentially escalating resentment about his painful childhood experiences (Olsson 2005, 17–18, 37–41). Osama's poetry in particular captures this domain of his pain. Osama, like many political and cult leaders, seems to identify with, fuse or merge with, and even become one with "his people." Osama, like David Koresh of the Waco apocalypse and Jim Jones of the Jonestown Guyana group suicide/homicide, audaciously and grandiosely defines "the cause" of his religion, Islam, as he sees it. He even seems to identify with the prophet Mohammad himself. Miliora's analysis of Osama (2004) concludes, and this author agrees:

> I suggest that bin Laden came to see himself as walking in the steps of Mohammad, the warrior-prophet whom he idealized, to liberate and restore Islam as a potent force in the world. Indeed, I suggest that bin Laden is captivated by a narcissistic fantasy of immense proportion with regard to his self-image as a warrior prophet, in the image of Mohammad, and participating in a divinely conceived mission to achieve an Islamic revolution. (132–33)

Like many charismatic/messianic leaders with narcissistic personality patterns, Osama entwines his personal past of childhood narcissistic injuries with that of "his people." He purportedly "feels their pain." Miliora (2004) cites Osama's stark vengeful statement about 9/11 that was broadcast on U.S. television in October 2001:

> What the United States tastes today is a very small thing compared to what we have tasted for tens of years. Our nation has been tasting this humiliation and contempt for more than eighty years. (132)

Do many experts underestimate the power of the religious imagery that Osama and colleagues use and abuse? In the process of his terror cult's Pied Piper music, Osama seems to be seeking a sense of spurious inner restitution and revenge as he leads his followers away from their families and countries of origin to join in his *jihad* (armed struggle) of *acting out*. He in this sense is the ultimate Malignant Pied Piper seeking his payback from his disappointing Saudi father figures.

Acting out behavior is the attempt by an individual to resolve an internal, unconscious struggle through external action. One recognized dimension of this term is that the acted-out behavior was appropriate in a previous (childhood) situation that a recent situation is a reminder of and symbolically represents (Abt and Weissman 1965, 3). This book will examine the hypothesis that Osama, among several dynamics, acts out his unconscious grief, disappointment, and anger at his father. He displaces his hatred onto the dictatorial Saudi rulers who rejected him and also onto their American "friends." Osama and his radical Islamist colleagues all seem ambivalent and rigid about authority and sexual/aggressive impulses. We will explore this more in the next chapter.

THE PARANOID AND APOCALYPTIC TEXTURE OF OSAMA'S EPISTLES AND SPEECHES

Like many other destructive cult leaders, bin Laden's outlook is paranoid as he alleges a conspiracy by Israel and the CIA against Islam (Berman 2003, 4). As early as 1994, Osama had condemned Israel in detail for stealing Palestinian territory; he also blamed Arabs who signed the Oslo accords, implying destructive compromises with Zionists (Lawrence 2005, 9–14). In October 2002, Osama issued a detailed indictment of American morality, behavior, and policies that provides his rationale for *jihad* and lethal attacks on all America's men, women, children, military, allies, government, and way of life (Lawrence 2005, 160–75). Israelis and we Americans are no angels, but we hardly deserve all of the ire that Osama directs at us. Osama and Al Qaeda are certainly not angels in terms of the killing of innocents.

Bin Laden's shadowy Al Qaeda network does not sharply define "in-group, out-group" boundaries the way some Western cults have done. However, he and his colleagues seek to establish a worldwide fascist-Islamist utopia of the Caliphate (Wright 2006, 58–59). I use the term "Islamist" here to indicate the most radical Wahhabi Muslims. "Islamists call the unified pan-Islamic state that rules the entire hub of Islam, and ultimately the entire Muslim world, the *Khilafah* (Caliphate)" (Bodansky 1999, 19). This "state" is arrived at by *jihad*, an armed struggle that I consider to be a world war based on Osama's own pronouncements and the exponential growth of his following. Osama's vintage of *jihad* and caliphate fits the definition of fascism.

Roham Gunaratna explains Al Qaeda's operational strategy in these terms: "As defined by Osama, Al Qaeda has short-, mid-, and long-term strategies.

Before 9/11, its *immediate* goal was the withdrawal of U.S. troops from Saudi Arabia and the creation there of a caliphate. Its *mid-term* strategy was the ouster of the 'apostate rulers' of the Arabian Peninsula and thereafter the Middle East, and the creation of true Islamic states. And the *long-term* strategy was to build a formidable array of Islamic states—including ones with nuclear capability—to wage war on the U.S. and its allies." Listen to Osama in an August 1996 edict from Afghanistan: "It should not be hidden from you that the people of Islam have suffered from aggression, iniquity, and injustices imposed on them by the Zionist-Crusader alliance and their collaborators to the extent that the Muslims' blood has become the cheapest in the eyes of the 'world,' and their wealth has become as loot, in the hands of their enemies" (Gunaratna 2002, 119–20).

Osama then cites as evidence with colossally broad strokes what he calls the "massacres" in Palestine, Iraq, Lebanon, Tajikistan, Burma, Kashmir, Assam, Phillipines, Fatani Ogaden, Somalia, Eritrea, Chechnya, and Bosnia Herzegovina. Osama grandiosely insists that all of these troubled locations fit his idiosyncratic pronouncements and fabric of vengefulness. Osama speaks as if his voice is *the voice* for all devout Arab Muslims in the whole world!

Bin Laden continues to extend his grandiose diatribe:

[A]ll of this—and the world watched and heard and not only did they not respond to the atrocities, but also, under a clear conspiracy—between the USA and its allies, under the cover of the iniquitous "United Nations"—the dispossessed people were even prevented from obtaining arms to defend themselves. The people of Islam awakened, and realized that they were the main target for the aggression of the Zionist-Crusader alliance. And all the false claims and propaganda about "human rights" were hammered down and exposed for what they were, by the massacres that had taken place against Muslims in every part of the world. (Gunaratna 2002, 120)

Further detail about these issues will be referred to in subsequent chapters and can be found in Lawrence's cogent and detailed book, *Messages to the World: The Statements of Osama bin Laden.*

OSAMA'S APOCALYPTIC VISION OF MARTYRDOM

Osama's call to all Muslims for *jihad* against Israel, America, and American allies becomes inherently apocalyptic. This is because with an asymmetric war between America's global military and nuclear power and jihadists' suicide bombings, insurgencies, and terror tactics, the net result is not a victory for either side, but ongoing misery or perhaps terrifying increments of destruction. It is at this point that Osama's hero-warrior leadership merges with and exponentially crescendos into the realm of martyrdom and the death-politics of fundamentalist mentality. The only winners are death and destruction.

MARTYR PSYCHOLOGY AND FUNDAMENTALIST MENTALITY: THE TRAGIC FLAW IN THE THINKING OF FUNDAMENTALISTS AND SUICIDE BOMBER-MARTYRS

In a tragic sense, fundamentalists and suicide bomber-martyrs are gods unto themselves. Whether Christians, Jews, Muslims, Sikhs, or Hindus, fundamentalists see their way of thinking and believing as the one and only way. It is "my way or the highway," as the saying goes. The fundamentalist, no matter how sweet, kind, or pious he or she acts on the surface, is convinced of having *the* superior moral, ethical, theological, epistemological, and spiritual truth. There is no room for doubt or debate. The radical fundamentalist is willing to condemn to hell or kill those whose beliefs are different. The radical fundamentalist is the final judge, jury, and executioner. He even declares the content of Heaven and Hell and the pathways to either spiritual location.

The fundamentalist's devastatingly concrete, rigid, and grandiose way of thinking is more readily embraced at times of severe social turmoil, rapid social change, and economic suffering. Experiences of oppression, such as in refugee camps, provide potential psychosocial soil and roots for fundamentalist mentality. Often, fundamentalist mentality can gain momentum in an atmosphere of ignorance, arrogance, fear, hatred, insecurity, or bigotry. Fundamentalist thinking actually ignores the core meaning of what faith is really about. In Kierkegaard's term, genuine faith involves a "leap of faith." Faith also respects mystery. Genuine faith requires humility, reverence for life, and a realization of mankind's smallness in a big universe. Faith seeks God and his meaning in the world in worship and service to others, and never grandiosely takes over God's role via TV caveat and sound bite. A student of mine once heard a rabbi's sermon during which he said that to use God's name to support a man's or group's aggressive, destructive, or self-serving idea or action is a violation of the fourth commandment of God's Ten Commandments:

> You must never use my name to make a vow you don't intend to keep. I will not overlook that. (Deut. 5:11)

DEFINITION OF MATURE MENTALITY

If fundamentalist mentality involves black and white thinking, mature mentality involves flexibility of thought. Mature mentality implies both a thorough educational and maturational process that allows the mature person to listen carefully and respectfully to another person's ideas and beliefs. The mature person reaches his own independent conclusions that may agree completely, in part, or not at all with the other person. Mature mentality demonstrates the positive results of a person's ability to transcend pathological narcissistic states like vengeance, blind narcissistic rage, and viciously sadistic humor. When these lower transformations of narcissism are successfully resolved, the maturely developed human being comes to possess what Kohut called the "Higher Transformations of Narcissism," i.e., wisdom, humor, and creativity (Kohut 1971, 326–28). Kohut says that *wisdom* is:

> A cognitive and emotional position the attainment of which might be considered one of the peaks of human development, not only, narrowly, in the analysis of narcissistic personality disorders but in the growth and fulfillment of the human personality altogether. (Kohut 1971, 326)

At the close of his famous book, *The Analysis of the Self*, Kohut describes the atmosphere of maturity and wisdom that best surrounds the graduation phase of a successful analysis.

> And finally, patient and analyst may, upon the termination of the treatment, share in the acknowledgement of the fact that the analysis itself has of necessity remained incomplete. In a jointly held attitude of soberness and wisdom, yet without sarcasm or pessimism, analyst and patient will admit as they are parting that not all has been resolved and that some conflicts, inhibitions, and symptoms, and some old tendencies toward self-aggrandizement and infantile idealization remain. These frailties, however, are now familiar and they can be contemplated with tolerance and composure. (Kohut 1971, 328)

A successful psychoanalysis is not the only road toward mature mentality. A good education with the good fortune of having the presence of wise and mature mentors is another road. When parents are unavailable to a bright and curious young person, a clergyperson or teacher can provide a crucial role model or a vehicle to avoid lower transformations of narcissism and fundamentalist mentality.

POLITICAL POWER AND THE DENIAL OF DEATH

The social psychological framework offered by Ernst Becker (1973) can help us to begin to understand the social self-psychology of suicide bombers, terrorists, and martyrs. Becker writes, "The social hero-system into which we are born marks out paths for our heroism, paths to which we conform, to which we shape ourselves so that we can please others and become what they expect us to be" (82).

Becker (1973, 5) articulates this thesis in more detail earlier in his Pulitzer Prize–winning work, saying,

> It doesn't matter whether the cultural hero-system is frankly magical, religious, and primitive or secular, scientific, and civilized. It is still a mythical hero-system in which people serve in order to earn a feeling of primary value, of cosmic specialness,

of ultimate usefulness to creation, of unspeakable meaning. They earn this feeling by carving out a place in nature, by building an edifice that reflects human values: a temple, a cathedral, a totem pole, a skyscraper, a family that spans three generations. The hope and belief is that the things that man creates in society are of lasting worth and meaning, that they outlive or outshine death and decay, that man and his products count.

Many suicide bombers, martyrs, and terrorists seem to be participating in a social hero-system as described by Becker. They seem to fantasize that they are building a spiritual edifice for their peoples' future and an immortal paradise for themselves. All this, with God's blessing in eternity. They are mythical hero legends in their own minds. Ultimately, they are pitiful and sad human beings.

If anyone on earth should understand how oppression, economic marginalization, and political persecution in refugee camps could empower and create suicide bomber-martyrs, it is the Jews and Israelis. The new ghettos in Gaza and the West Bank should stir collective holocaust memories and profound empathy in Israel's collective consciousness. Unfortunately, too few Israelis gain such a perspective.

Throughout human history there has been no better psychosocial soil for the growth and development of recruits for martyrdom, insurgency, and terrorism than refugee camps, where young people witness the daily devaluation, despair, and persecution of their parents. Young people in these ghettos of group woundedness and narcissistic injury are ripe for the seductions of terror cult recruiters and folk heroes like Osama bin Laden, Hamas leaders, violent right-to-life radicals, violent Likud radicals, and fundamentalist Islamic clerics preaching sacred hatred and vengeance. We will examine this issue in detail in chapters 3, 4, and 5.

THE UNIQUE VULNERABILITY OF MANY MUSLIM ADOLESCENTS AND YOUNG ADULTS TO TERROR CULTS

It also seems important to try to understand the related and uniquely chilling social-psychological fit between the religiously flavored charismatic leadership of a man like Osama bin Laden, and the group psychology of communities where he and his colleagues and mentors recruit devoted terrorists.

DESTRUCTIVE CULT RECRUITERS' EXPLOITATION OF "NORMAL" ADOLESCENT REBELLIOUSNESS AND SEARCHES FOR INDEPENDENCE

Like other Malignant Pied Pipers, bin Laden's appeal has a unique "fit" for or appeal to magnify and expand normal adolescent rebelliousness and search for independent identity. Anna Freud (1936, 137–38) observed that adolescents become enthusiastic about community activities at times and at others they long for solitude. They can be submissive to a chosen leader or defiant to any authority. They can be extremely self-absorbed or materialistic, and simultaneously very idealistic.

What would be "normal" adolescent rebellion and protest for some adolescents become terrorist actions through the tutelage of a malignant leader like Osama bin Laden. As we will discuss later, there are even significant numbers of American adolescents that experience Osama bin Laden and Al Qaeda's magnetism (Jose Padilla, Adam Gadahn, and others). In other words, Al Qaeda recruiters, by intuition or design, take advantage of a normal adolescent stage of transition typically marked by striving for independence, rebellion, and searching for identity. In many instances it takes little recruitment effort because some adolescents seek out the Al Qaeda gurus. The turmoil in the Middle East and many parts of the Muslim world creates many young adults who are in the phase of what psychoanalysts call "prolonged adolescence." Siegfried Bernfeld (1923, ix) described a specific kind of male adolescent development called "the protracted type." Osama himself seems stuck in a protracted destructive adolescent acting-out pattern of behavior (even as he passes 50 years of age). "Protracted adolescence" extends far beyond the usual time frame of adolescent characteristics and is epitomized by intensely creative work that is bent towards idealistic aims and assertion of intense moral and spiritual values.

There are uncanny similarities in "follower psychology" between Al Qaeda recruits and recruits in many other destructive cults. The followers are not all poor or uneducated young people. And bin Laden's lieutenants and Al Qaeda leader colleagues are well educated and collectively dedicated to the ideal of *jihad*. Radical Islamists like bin Laden seem to recruit by using personal charisma and manipulating the *Koran* to form attractive mixtures of theology turned into starkly articulated radical political-action ideology.

In Arabic, "Al Qaeda" means "the base" (as in military base, or base of an architectural structure). In addition to enlisting well-educated youth, radical Islamists also recruit poor and less-educated Muslim "foot soldiers" through religious Madrassah schools and young-adult mosque programs and activities. Osama's *jihad* appeals particularly to disaffected or idealistic Arab and Muslim youth. These adolescents and young adults have often suffered while watching their parents being humiliated, oppressed, and impoverished in countries ruled by wealthy dictators who are perceived as puppets of America. They idolize Osama and resonate with his life journey and heroism during the defeat of the Soviets in Afghanistan and his claims of victory in Somalia and the bombing of the USS *Cole* in Yemen. When he condemns American violence and calls us cowards, "Methinks the man protesteth [and projecteth] too much!" Osama's personal rebellious identity has led to a peculiar status as anti-American, anti-Western, anti-Jewish pied piper and Robin Hood–like mythic hero.

Many Madrassah-type "schools" offer economic advantages and spiritual inspiration to families and Muslim communities that have few alternatives. Even many affluent Arab or Muslim young people latch on to radical Islamist propaganda because it seems to represent a sacred, idealistic, even utopian cause that is brighter than and superior to mundane business, agricultural, or professional life. The farewell videotapes made by the suicide bomber martyr/murderers are filled with grandiosity and the glow of notoriety, not to mention financial rewards and allusions to sexual rewards in paradise.

In his recent best-selling book *The Earth Is Flat,* Thomas Friedman describes some remarkable interviews he conducted with three young militants in the West Bank town of Ramallah. Friedman (2005, 467) described how the young men vowed they would turn the area into a violent cauldron if Israel killed Yasser Arafat (who was still alive at the time and clearly their hero). Yet they showed Friedman pictures of their loved ones, for whom they wanted to live.

In one interview, Friedman describes a young militant, Anas, who grew emotional. He was the only one of the three who was in college. After fierce talk about being willing to die for Arafat, Anas shifted to eloquent talk about his desire to study engineering at the University of Memphis, near where his uncle lived. Unfortunately, he told Friedman, he could not get a visa into the United States. This episode described by Friedman captures both the fluidity of identity and the hero-hunger of adolescents. It shows us that we must apply an accurate knowledge of practical psychology to our foreign policy and diplomacy. It also illustrates our peril if we remain isolated in an American fortress. Visiting students in our country learn more than math, science, and technical skills. There is opportunity for us to share our values and especially our friendship with foreign students. In fact, in the long run, friendship in its many genuine forms may offer more powerful protection against radical Islamic terrorists than rockets and "smart" bombs.

The recruiting techniques of Al Qaeda and its metastatic subsidiaries are clever, creative, and diverse in their applied theology. Exploitive cults in the West seek to alienate young people and older recruits from their families and communities of origin. Al Qaeda, often through the Madrassahs, woos local Muslim families and communities for its own ends. Especially in Pakistan, many Madrassah students and their families see membership in Al Qaeda and participation in *jihad* as a high calling. Al Qaeda recruits whole communities with its pied piper music of *jihad.*

Jihad
A holy war undertaken as a sacred duty by Muslims.
Any vigorous, emotional crusade for an idea or principle. (Webster's College Dictionary 2001, 712)

The likes of the 9/11 suicide pilots Mohammad Atta, 33, and Marwan al-Shehhi, 23, fit a common pattern. They grew up in middle-class Arab families. They were educated and went to study further in Europe, where they lived on the fringes of society. They were radicalized by Islamist clerics at local prayer groups in mosques. Their loneliness, transitional status, and search for deeper meaning in life left them vulnerable targets for terror cult recruitment (Friedman 2002, 13). We will never know if Mohammad Atta might have changed the destructive trajectory of his life if he had been befriended by a kindly German university professor who might have helped influence him toward a more moderate worldview.

Osama and his followers. The leader and the led. What are the psychological roots and soil of their thirst for blood and death? We will start with an examination of Osama's life journey. It allows us to see many common psychological states, traits, and patterns common among the members of the cult of Osama.

Please note that this book contains a good deal of psychoanalytical terminology, which at least some readers may find unfamiliar. For the benefit of these readers, a glossary is available in the back of this book to aid in this and other terminology.

IN SEARCH OF HIS MOTHER/FATHER/ HIMSELF: OSAMA'S EARLY LOSSES AND NARCISSISTIC WOUNDS, THE STUFF OF ISLAMIST LEADERS' CHARISMA

Forgive me, son, for nothing do I see
In our terrain but a declivity.

—Osama bin Laden (Rohde 2002, 16)

OSAMA'S FATHER: MOHAMMAD BIN LADEN

Mohammad bin Laden, Osama bin Laden's father, was born about 1930 into a poor Yemeni family. He emigrated as a laborer from Yemen to Saudi Arabia in the late 1950s. His son Osama was born in Saudi Arabia on March 10, 1957, in Riyahd. Osama means "Young Lion" in Arabic. Mohammad bin Laden had boundless ambition, worked hard, became a skilled engineer, and started a construction company. He gained the enduring respect and favor of both King Saud and his successor, King Faisal. Mohammad was a trusted confidante of King Saud. King Faisal gave Mohammad bin Laden the contract to rebuild the Islamic holy sites at Mecca and Medina in 1973. He became a multimillionaire through these and other construction projects. Mohammad bin Laden grew to be a complicated and powerful man who tried to have his spiritual cake and eat it, too. He became enormously successful by standards of extravagant "Western materialism" and in the eyes of Saudi families who identified with the West. There is evidence that though Osama deeply admired his father's vast financial success, he despised his tendency to serially marry then quickly divorce young women.

Osama shared his disdain for his father's promiscuous polygamy with Jamal Khalifa, who was his best friend at King Abdul Aziz University in Jeddah (Bergen 2006, 17).

However, in addition to accumulating great wealth in a true western capitalist way, Mohammad bin Laden also hypocritically remained a devout fundamentalist Muslim in the Wahhabi tradition. As we will see, his son Osama has come to identify with his father's rigid Wahhabism and boundless and grandiose ambition, but I believe there is profound ambivalence in Osama's mind and soul regarding his father. His father died when Osama was about 10 years old.

OSAMA'S MOTHER: HAMIDA (ALIA) GHANEM

Mohammad bin Laden had more than 20 wives during his lifetime; Osama has more than 50 siblings. Mohammad bin Laden himself would get confused about which children were the offspring of which wife (Bergen 2001, 47). Osama's mother Hamida (according to Robinson 2001), or Alia (Bergen 2006) Ghanem, is Syrian, and Osama is the only son of her marriage to Mohammad bin Laden. She comes from Latikia, a resort town in Syria that the Bin Laden Group helped develop. She is described as beautiful, liberal in her Muslim beliefs and dress code, and independent-minded. Hamida (Alia) refused to accept the traditionally passive female role in the marriage (Robinson 2001, 39). Bergen says that Alia Ghanem and Mohammad bin Laden divorced soon after Osama was born. Sharp conflicts over his authority led Mohammad to banish Hamida (Alia) to another town (Tabuk). She eventually married Mohammad al Attas and had three sons and a daughter with him. Her destiny has been more modest financially, but happier without Mohammad bin Laden's lingering shadow.

After his mother's remarriage and his father's death, Osama moved into his mother's compound in the Musharifa neighborhood of Jeddah, where his mother lives to this day. Osama, already of low family rank as the 17th son, thus had lost his mother for years while she lived in a separate household in Tabuk. Osama was raised in that interim by his stepmother Al Khalifa, another woman of strong personality whom Robinson says Osama eventually respected, despite the loss of his real mother on a day-to-day basis (Robinson 2001, 39–40).

When Osama was reunited with his mother in 1967, they both struggled unsuccessfully to reconnect emotionally. People who knew Hamida (Alia) say that she is a warm, kind, and good soul who was as much a victim of Mohammad bin Laden's complex shadow as Osama was and still is (Robinson 2001, 56–58). There is evidence that Osama holds a high degree of unconscious ambivalence towards his mother, as he does toward the memory of his father. Although commissioned by and obviously biased toward the bin Laden family who has disowned Osama, Robinson (2001) offers this perspective on Osama immediately after his father's death when he was 10:

[H]is grief was deeper than simply the loss of a loved one. Beneath the surface, he had long repressed (see glossary) a deep gouge in his psyche. This was caused by the partial loss of his mother and a relationship with his father shared with so many siblings, a handful of wives, and the pressures of a vast business empire. Before his tragic death, Osama's interest in strict Islam had drawn him closer to his father. It was a paternal relationship he craved, yet Mohammad's sudden death had robbed the youngster of a chance to enjoy anything other than fleeting moments of satisfaction. (55)

The family recalls that Osama reeled emotionally and withdrew into himself.

Bergen (2006) provides some intriguing vignettes about the conscious attitudes of Osama and his Al Qaeda colleagues towards women, and particularly about Osama's behavior towards his mother. Bergen interviewed Osama's childhood friend and neighbor from Jeddah, Batarfi Khaled, who has kept close touch with Osama and his mother Hamida (Ali). Khaled said to Bergen:

He's always a very obedient son, more than any of his brothers. I mean very obedient. He never raises his voice to her face. And he was always smiling, kissing her hands, and he was kissing her feet. It was a kind of an I-am-your-slave thing. And always calling her—always. Asking her about the smallest of things: what she was cooking today and what she did and where she went. [An unconscious effort to retrieve a feeling tone of long-lost childhood days with her? That is purely this author's speculation.] And that's why she loves him, but she doesn't subscribe to his line of thinking or what he does. So I guess it's tough. (240)

Osama's behavior as described in Bergen's interview is suggestive of intense reaction formation, in addition to the ambivalence mentioned previously.

It is questionable in my opinion as to whether Osama holds any intimate respect or affection for his mother, and especially for her ideas and morals. And here lies a crucial issue in any in-depth effort to understand the "hearts and minds" of so many Arab and Muslim men and women. Every one of us resides in our mother's body for nine months, and we are dependent on our mother for food and comfort. All of us are also under her authority in our childhood. Most men push away forcefully from their mother's authority.

Fundamentalist men have a particularly powerful way of reversing any power and control over them that their mothers had. In this respect, Osama's attitude is typical of the deep unconscious gynophobia and defensively domineering behavior towards women that is characteristic of most fundamentalist men (Muslim, Jew, or Christian). This pervasive hostility is couched in religious dogma and condescension, even though their outward behaviors seem affectionate or "devoted."

Osama's affection for the gynophobic and woman-debasing Taliban is well known. Mullah Omar, the fugitive leader of the Taliban, took one of Osama's daughters as one of his wives. I strongly suspect that Osama's daughter had no say in the matter of her own marriage. Let us detour briefly into the topic of Islam and Islamists' view of women. This is a crucial topic in our trying to understand the unconscious dynamics within the mind of Osama and most Islamist terrorists and their potential recruits. This is a difficult issue to confront about Christian, Jewish, Islamic, or any radical fundamentalist without sounding judgmental—but I will try.

THE ROLE OF WOMEN IN FUNDAMENTALIST RELIGIOUS HOMES AND THE MOTHERING OF BOYS: A PROFOUNDLY IMPORTANT PSYCHOLOGICAL FOOTNOTE

Dr. Althea Horner has observed that it is likely that the mothering behavior of a woman with negative attitudes towards males will be tinged with envy and resentment, if not downright hostility, towards a son. Strict fundamentalist Islamic law gives fathers and brothers and husbands and sons the right and duty even to kill a woman if she wounds their narcissism or that of their family and community. Especially if a male is embarrassed in a public way, a so-called "honor killing" is deemed appropriate and good. Since the *Koran* and particularly radical Islam in this sense view women as essentially the possessions of men, as the cultural background for the rearing of male children, it is likely that the mothering of boys, by more women than not, will carry overtones of the envy, resentment, and even fear they feel toward the domineering male, be it their fathers, their husbands, or their sons (Horner 1992, 599–610). There are, of course, very similar severely problematic psychodynamic problems in the child-rearing situations of fundamentalist Christian, Mormon, Jewish, and other religious fundamentalist homes.

As a result of these deeply embedded cultural and religious child-rearing attitudes and their emotional atmospheres, there is an experience of unconscious maternal rejection. The sons grow up with a reservoir of primitive insecurity and rage that will find its outlet in rigid detachment, hostility, and domineering behavior towards women. This gets rationalized as religious doctrine or "law" by fundamentalists.

Professor Daniel Pipes, in his perceptive book *In the Path of God: Islam And Political Power*, has a fascinating section of his chapter titled "Muslim Anomie," subtitled "Male-Female Relations." Pipes points out that unlike the traditional and Victorian Western view that women do not or should not enjoy sex, Muslims actually believe that women's sexual desires are more powerful than men's. Sexual desires and needs make women potentially unreasonable, evil, and agents of the devil. Pipes concedes that this conception might be related to women's greater physical capacity for sex (multiple orgasms?), or it might go back to Mohammad's sexual experiences. Regardless, Pipes summarizes this complex area well:

> But whatever its origin, female sexuality is thought of as being so powerful that it constitutes a real danger to society. At the same time that Islamicate civilization

encourages sexual satisfaction, it also considers unrestrained females the most dangerous challenge facing males trying to carry out God's commands (for it is the men who have the far heavier religious burden). [Supreme, fundamentalist rationalization, perhaps?] In combination, their rampant desires and their irresistible attractiveness give women a power over men which rivals God's.

Left to themselves then, men might well fall victim to women and abandon God. *Fitna* would result, that is, civil disorder among believers. Just as distress over the *fitna* between Muslim rulers characterized Muslim attitudes to politics, so did the fear of *fitna* dominate private life. (Pipes 1983, 177)

In this sense, there is no problem between men and women or with sexuality for a Muslim fundamentalist, as long as women are under strict control. Pipes says that in Arabic, *fitna* also means "a beautiful woman" (Pipes 1983, 177). This psychological, cultural, and religious process of externalization and projection leads to intense fear among men and boys that female lusts might bring on anarchy.

A well-analyzed and/or mature Western person would see the control of sex, love, and lust as the responsibility of each individual man or woman. Each individual, when confronted by a romantic, erotic, or sexually tempting situation, would be responsible for his or her own actions. The individual's moral, ethical, marital, and religious convictions would come into play. A mature person might enjoy a pleasant sexual fantasy but stop short of sexual acting out. Even a modern Helen of Troy or Anna Nicole Smith could not dissolve the strength of character and ego ideal of mature men. Nor could a modern Don Juan or Brad Pitt do likewise with women of solid character and maturity.

Often young men raised with radical fundamentalist views of women turn with intense devotion toward older bearded Imams, fundamentalist preachers or rabbis, and other male clerics for succor and direction. Mohammad Atta, the alleged 9/11 attack leader, left careful notes about how his dead body should be handled, and he rigidly stated that no woman was to touch or see him. Atta was overprotected by his mother (Sageman 2004, 86). Maternal overprotection is another source of grandiosity and subtle pathological narcissism in men. If the mother of Osama bin Laden or Mohammad Atta had begged her son to halt 9/11 plans, it seems unlikely that either of them would have taken the request seriously. The same would be true of radical fundamentalist antiabortionist bombers like Eric Rudolph in America. The psychological reality is that many strict fundamentalist men like Osama and their recruits like Atta cannot be comfortably intimate with women; they fear collaboratively intimate sexuality and look to shallow polygamous relationships or virgins in the next world for delusion-based pleasures that will sadly never come to fruition.

Peter Bergen begins his absorbing book, *The Osama Bin Laden I Know,* with a section called "Dramatis Personae." It is, unsurprisingly but revealingly, an annotated list of 58 people. Only one, Alia Ghanem, Osama's Syrian-born mother, is a woman! Bergen mentions that she visited Osama several times in the mid 1990s to try to persuade him to return to Saudi Arabia. She also attended Osama's son Mohammad's wedding in Afghanistan in 2001.

Bergen (2006) quotes Mohammad Atef, Al Qaeda's military commander:

> Sheikh bin Laden has a lot of respect for the women. There is a misconception that we don't have any soft corner for women. Sheikh bin Laden – he is always very, very careful for his mother and he is in constant touch with his mother. I was present in that meeting in Khartoum: Sheikh bin Laden told his mother, "I can sacrifice my life for you, but right now what you are talking to me is against Islam. I'm fighting against the enemies of Islam and you want that I should announce a cease-fire with the enemies of Islam." And his mother said, "Okay, I will not repeat my demand again." (151)

Soon after his mother's return to Saudi Arabia with his answer, Osama's citizenship was cancelled. His black sheep/Robin Hood status in Saudi Arabia was assured. And his mother's pleas for moderation were ignored. Perhaps Robin Morgan's thesis (1989), that the vast majority of wars and terrorist acts are testosterone-saturated creations of men, is true! Horner hypothesizes, and I agree, that the promised polygamous group of virgins waiting for the (male) Wahhabi suicide bomber in heaven can be seen as a sexualized, idealized, fanta-sized/magical repair of a lifelong defective view and experience of women by these radical Arab and Muslim men. These sadly misguided terrorists believe they will finally be rewarded in the next life with a combination of an idealized, perfect, and guilt-free but sexually gratifying Oedipal mother that only Sophocles and Freud could fully appreciate.

With such empathic deficiencies running rampant in the fundamentalist Muslim child-rearing cultural atmosphere, ego maturation and development in its fullest sense is compromised. Life and character structures thus become dominated by a brittle, rigid gender identity, with lessened capacity for empa-thy in crucial aspects of marriage and family relationships—or, I might add, in the tragic disregard that Osama has for the innocent women and children that his suicide bombers kill. Beneath the surface of espoused respect and affection for women by fundamentalist men lies a discounting, devaluing, and conde-scending attitude towards women. Jewish, Muslim, or Christian women who tolerate and stay subservient towards this remain undeveloped spiritually, intel-lectually, and psychologically.

FATHER HUNGER AND PSEUDOHOMOSEXUAL DYNAMICS IN RADICAL ISLAMIST YOUNG MEN

A corollary of the radical Muslim man's view of women just described is the intensification of father-hunger (Herzog 2001) in these men. The latent homosexual, really *pseudohomosexual,* issues described by Lionel Ovesey prevail in father-hungry, unconsciously women-mother-disrespecting, lonely young Muslim men. Ovesey (1969) described men attracted to men out of dependency and power-submission needs, rather than sexual gratification per se. Radical clerics tend to dominate young Arab/Muslim men at mosques. When these Imams preach radical hatred of the United States and the West, a destructive, culturally ignorant chemistry prevails. Apparently, few if any Muslim young men stand up in mosques to question or challenge any teachings of these biased Islamists, even when they preach the advocacy of murder in God's name. Such radical Islamist fundamentalist propaganda feeds the rigid, insecure, mother-father-hungry Muslim boys a psychological diet of hate. The angry enemy within becomes projected onto the American, British, and Israeli enemies out there.

OSAMA BIN LADEN'S LOSSES, NARCISSISTIC WOUNDS, AND UNCONSCIOUS SHAME

Osama's father Mohammad spent his time making hundreds of millions of dollars for his Bin Laden Corporation. Some quality time for Osama and his father occurred during an annual weeklong "male-bonding" hunting vacation in wild desert regions of the Saudi Kingdom. Osama blossomed during these brief trips with his father and his royal friends. Osama apparently outshone his less adventurous half-siblings. Mohammad was impressed with Osama's prowess in the desert and probably recalled his own boyhood adventures in the Yemeni desert. Bergen describes a lengthy interview with Jamal Khalifa, who became Osama's closest friend at King Abdul Aziz University in Jeddah. Jamal said that he and Osama were very conservatively religious in their late teens and early twenties. Jamal describes their adventures in jeeps in the desert and mountains. He said that the bin Ladens had a retreat in the desert between Jeddah and Mecca called Bahra. Osama referred to it as "our land." Jamal kidded Osama, saying, "Who is the crazy person who came to this place and owned the land?" Osama said, "My father." Jamal said about Osama,

> He likes his father very much. He considered him as a model. He was not with his father very much, because his father died when he was ten years old. And also, the father didn't meet his children much. He was very busy—a lot of children, a lot of houses, so he just met them officially. There are fifty-four children [25 sons and 29 daughters] and he had twenty-plus wives. Osama's mother is Syrian; he's the only child from his mother and Mohammad Bin Laden.
>
> Osama heard a lot about his father. He's a person who built his company from nothing. He was not a person who sits down behind the desk, and gives orders. Similarly, Osama when he used to work with his brothers in the company, he used to go to the bulldozer, get the driver out and drive himself. (Bergen 2006, 17)

Clearly Osama identified with, or introjected, his father. However, Jamal also describes how critical he and Osama were about the way their fathers practiced their polygamy, saying:

> We found that they were practicing it in a wrong way, where they are married and divorced, married and divorced; a lot of wives and sometimes they don't get equal justice between all of them. (Bergen 2006, 17)

Jamal states that he and Osama practiced polygamy "the Islamic way" and although Osama was divorced only once—because the woman did not adapt her life to his (!?)—they both were fair and just, and gave each wife what was enough for her. He says they helped solve a social problem (not just fun), because there were more women than men in their society. (Perhaps a smug rationalization?) "Osama, I'm sure that he doesn't have any problem with his wives. You imagine, now they are with him in his situation, so it means that he is really practicing this polygamy well" (Bergen 2006, 18).

Osama also excelled in Islamic studies, which drew positive attention and praise from his father. Sadly, this time was far too brief, and I agree with Robinson's implication that it left a profound father-hunger in Osama's heart, for his father died when Osama was only ten years old (Robinson 2001, 50, 55).

THE DEATH OF OSAMA BIN LADEN'S FATHER: PSYCHOLOGICAL WOUND AND NARCISSISTIC INJURY

Though a multimillionaire, Mohammad bin Laden was poverty stricken when it came to paying the piper of parenthood. It was impossible for him to spend quality time with each of his 50 children, particularly his bright and perceptive son of the "lesser" Syrian wife. He espoused strict Wahhabist religious piety, but also worshipped making money. Osama was only 10 when his father disappeared from his life. Mohammad bin Laden was traveling home when his helicopter crashed in the desert. Observers reported that 10,000 men gathered for his funeral. Osama seemed deeply affected, as Robinson observed, and I quoted earlier. Family members recall him reeling emotionally and withdrawing.

Sigmund Freud described his reaction to his own father's death: "It was, I found, a portion of my own self-analysis, my reaction to my father's death—that is to say, to the most important event, the most poignant loss, of a man's life. Having discovered that this was so, I felt unable to obliterate the (memory) traces of the experience" ([1900] 1958, 14: xxvi).

Osama bin Laden's loss of his father also was poignant and seemed filled with ambivalence. Despite Osama's father's alleged religious devoutness and devotion to his children, a politically incorrect but ultimately more truthful view might be that it is impossible for any man to be an effective father and religious/ethical role model to 50 offspring. When his father died, Osama was probably left feeling sad, grieved, humiliated, alone, and probably narcissistically enraged at preconscious and unconscious levels. Paradoxically, many Arab and Muslim young people and adults perceive Osama as using his inherited wealth to fight injustice and American efforts to dominate Arab countries' lands and oil. There is truth to this. They also can identify with Osama's woundedness and his angry rebellion. It is also very possible that at an unconscious level, Osama felt ambivalence towards his father's wealth. I speculate that Osama's shame and ambivalence about the symbolism of his large inheritance led him to donate his money to rebellious *jihads.* He acted out against what he perceived as hypocritical Saudi father figures and "the West," yet also simultaneously enjoyed his followers' admiration for his altruism. Angry, frightened sheep find rebellious shepherds' leadership profound.

OSAMA'S SHAME AND HUMILIATION AS "SON OF THE SLAVE"

Another source of narcissistic wounds in Osama's childhood is found in the way he was treated by his half-siblings in the household. Osama's banished birth mother, Hamida, was spitefully referred to as "Al Abeda" (the slave). Osama was cruelly labeled "Iban Al Abeda" (son of the slave). This constant teasing and devaluation of Osama by his half siblings hurt him deeply and festered in his heart (Robinson 2001, 39).

After Osama's father died, Osama was sent to Tabuk to join his mother in their exile from the rest of the family. He tried to get reacquainted with her but, Robinson says:

> Some of the [bin Laden] family today explain that Osama came to resent both his father for removing him from his mother, and his mother for not attempting to bridge the gap with his father for his sake. The wounds healed but the scars remained. (Robinson 2001, 40)

A possibly important issue that Osama may never have registered in his conscious mind is an admiration for the strength and dignity that his mother Hamida (Alia) showed in her refusal to submit passively to Osama's father's control and chauvinism. It is doubtful if any of Osama's wives or daughters is regarded with dignity as coequal and valued confidants. Yet, I am sure he thinks of himself as a loving and devoted father. As we know, he does not send his sons or daughters to die with bombs strapped around them. That honor and privilege is reserved for others.

OSAMA'S EARLY PSYCHOLOGICAL LOSS OF A BEST FRIEND

During his preadolescent and early adolescent years of what must have been inner bitterness, Osama had one true best friend. This friendship with Abdul

Aziz Fahd began during the annual father-son desert camping trips with their fathers. They enjoyed periodic visits because their fathers were close, and they also spoke on the phone frequently. But when Mohammad bin Laden died in a helicopter crash when Osama was 10, the relationships changed. The bin Laden family remained respected by the Fahd family, but the closeness between the two families ceased (Robinson 2001, 59). What does it say when money, power, and male prerogatives determine the depth of intimate connection between two families of "friends" in a society? Shortly after Osama returned to Jeddah from Tabuk, he was delighted to learn that Prince Fahd was soon coming to Jeddah for a visit. His best friend Abdul Aziz would be with the prince. During Abdul's visit, Osama tried dozens of times to contact his friend by phone but was rebuffed. Osama was even turned away from the door of the house where Abdul was staying. Osama has never heard from or seen his friend again. This painful loss added another element to the acted-out hatred towards the "father-brother-land of Saudi Arabia" (Robinson 2001, 60). In 1994, Osama's Saudi citizenship was revoked because of his increasing threats against the Saudi leaders and America.

Osama's personal adolescent searches mirrored some of the turmoil of the Arab Middle East in the late 1970s. Some authors (Robinson, Bodansky, Dennis) describe Osama as going through typical adolescent rebellion. They say that he was a playboy, drinker, and womanizer in Beirut. Bergen (2006, 50) insists that Osama was always serious, devout, and not a drinker or womanizer. Bergen seems correct in his assessment, in my opinion.

Other than providing quality schools for his son, Mohammad bin Laden let money be his payment to the piper of parenthood. After his father died, Osama went to high school in Jeddah. He then studied management and economics at King Abdul Aziz University in Jeddah. His lifelong search for his father/himself had begun.

2

OSAMA'S PERPETUAL SEARCH FOR FATHER/BROTHER REPLACEMENT FIGURES: SOUL BROTHERS IN TERROR

Father, where is the way out?
When are we to have a settled home?
Oh, Father, do you not
See encircling danger?

—Osama bin Laden (Rohde 2002, 16)

Bergen points out that Osama bin Laden idealized his father. Osama said that his father was eager that one of his sons would fight against the enemies of Islam, and it is clear that Osama saw himself as that chosen son. Osama told a Pakistani journalist: "My father is very keen that one of his sons should fight against the enemies of Islam. So I am the one son who is acting according to the wishes of his father." Bergen continues, "Having lost his deeply religious father [but also very materialistic—author's comment] while he was still a child, bin Laden would, throughout his life, be influenced by religiously radical older men" (Bergen 2001, 55).

Psychoanalysts can find this observation to be important and compatible with the psychodynamic hypothesis that Osama has had a lifelong ambivalent and hungry search for father figures. This chapter introduces several of these key father/older brother surrogates of bin Laden. Many of them have similar childhood roots and soil of narcissistic issues, and many have dark epiphany experiences via conflict with authorities and prison experiences.

Osama's psychological search for father figures began at the school he attended during his childhood and adolescent years after his father's death (Coll 2005, 48). Al Thager ("the haven") Model School in the Saudi port city of Jeddah was founded in the early 1950s. The school got support from Faisal bin Abdul Aziz, who became the king of Saudi Arabia in 1964. King Aziz developed modern schools, roads, and hospitals, but he also tried to preserve the austere Saudi Islamic traditions. In 1971 or 1972, Osama joined an after-school Islamic study group at Al Thager led by a young, enthusiastic, charismatic Syrian physical education teacher. This Syrian father figure (Osama's mother is Syrian) was influenced by the ideas of the radical Egyptian Muslim Brotherhood (see life histories of Ayman al-Zawahiri, Sayyib Qutb, the Blind Sheikh Omar Abdel Rahman who inspired the 1993 World Trade Center bombing, etc.). The study club at Al Thager School adopted the styles and ideas of Islamic activists, such as letting their beards grow, shortening their trouser legs, and wearing shirts like the Prophet used to wear. Club members debated other students and advocated the restoration of pure Islamic law across the Arab world (Coll 2005, 50, 59). Osama's search for devoted radical Islamist father/brother figures and their ideas was well underway during his middle school and high school years.

In 1975 his psychotic nephew, Prince Faisal ibn Musaid, assassinated Saudi Arabia's King Faisal. Osama's Islamist professors/father-figures said the assassin had been driven insane by exposure to Western ways. Similarly, Osama's Islamist Saudi teachers taught that the terrible pain of the Lebanese in their 1975 war was a punishment from God for their sinful acceptance of modern Western materialism and excess. The fatherless Osama was deeply impressed by his conservative Islamist professors who taught that only return to strict Islamism could protect Muslims from the sins and materialism of the "Satanic West" (Bodansky 1999, 3).

THE ELOQUENT AND SPIRITUALLY CHARISMATIC AZZAM

During his college years, Osama began to show intense interest in Islamic studies. He was greatly influenced by several men. In his 20s, Osama met Sheikh Yussuf Abdallah Azzam in Pakistan. Azzam became Osama's mentor. Azzam had a large family and was a devoted father and devout Muslim. Osama was adopted like a son in Azzam's family. Azzam was a religious scholar who could mesmerize listeners with his reciting of the Koran and who conscientiously obtained a bonafide *fatwa* to support his book, *In Defense of Muslim Lands* (Bergen 2006, 26, 27). Together Osama and Azzam founded the Services Office in 1984. This institution dedicated itself to placing Arab volunteers either with relief organizations serving Afghan refugees flooding into Pakistan, or with the Arab factions fighting the Soviets on the front lines in Afghanistan (Bergen 2006, 24). Osama later joined the *jihad* against the Soviets and founded Al Qaeda.

Azzam was born in a village near Jenin, Palestine, in 1941. Sixteen years older than Osama, he graduated with a degree in theology from Damascus University in 1966. Azzam hated Israel, which he blamed for taking Palestinian land, and fought against Israel in the 1967 war. He got a master's degree and doctorate in Islamic jurisprudence at al-Azhar University in Cairo by 1973. Extremely charismatic, the eloquent Azzam established the worldwide network of *jihad* that definitively helped win the Afghan war against the Russian communists. Osama and Azzam believed fanatically in the need for *Khalifa,* the dream that Muslims around the world could be united under one devout Islamist ruler. They differed radically, however, about the killing of innocents and noncombatants—Osama was pro, and Azzam con. Azzam admired the charismatic Afghan patriot and brilliant military leader Shah Ahmad Massoud (Lion of the Northern Alliance of Afghanistan), but Osama (the Young Lion) apparently disliked Massoud though he had apparently never met him! Young, charismatic military leaders do not often share the limelight very well. Bergen (2006, 299) thinks that if Osama had met Massoud, it could have changed the course of history. I concur.

Often called Al Qaeda's second in command, Ayman al-Zawahiri was becoming an increasingly influential soul brother to Osama. Al-Zawahiri had been radicalized into the Egyptian Muslim Brotherhood via the Egyptian prison experience, and then gradually turned Osama against Azzam and toward Massoud's bitter rival and hard-line Islamist, Gulbuddin Hekmatyr. I would agree with Bergen (2006, 63) who points out the ideological (and, I think, destructive) symbiosis between Zawahiri and Osama.

Zawahiri and bin Laden have, in addition to a close collegial relationship reaching doppelganger-like proportions, continuing ambivalent rivalries and relationships with other radical Islamist leaders that have intense pseudohomosexual dynamics (Ovesey 1969). They thrive on a sense of power in front of passive admirers and converts. It is often difficult to tell who is influencing whom among terror cult leaders, and in what destructive direction that influence is moving at any one time. An additional and prime example of this point is the relationship between Osama bin Laden and Ayman al-Zawahiri and the now-deceased Jordanian Zarqawi who headed the infamous Al Qaeda in Iraq.

AYMAN AL-ZAWAHIRI: DOCTOR DOPPELGANGER OF DEATH AND OSAMA'S SOUL BROTHER

Ayman al-Zawahiri, the Egyptian physician turned radical Islamist, and Mullah Mohammad Omar (see Chapter 3), leader of Afghanistan's Taliban, became Osama's idealized surrogate brothers in rebellion and Afghan battles against the Soviets. They also served as symbolic replacements for Osama's Saudi half-brothers, who eventually disowned him over his terrorist commitments.

Dr. Ayman al-Zawahiri was born in Egypt in 1951, six years before Osama bin Laden's birth. He comes from an aristocratic, affluent Egyptian family. He grew up in an upper-class neighborhood in Cairo, Egypt, the son of a prominent physician and grandson of renowned scholars. An uncle says that Ayman as a boy was quiet, studious, deeply religious, and used to write poetry to his mother. He was educated as a pediatrician. In 1973, as a medical student, he joined an electrical engineer and an army officer in forming the Egyptian Islamic Group, which dedicated itself to the violent overthrow of the Egyptian state. He was arrested and imprisoned as a member of the Muslim Brotherhood's efforts to overthrow Gamal Abdel Nasser and later the assassination of Anwar Sadat. In prison he was severely tortured, and due to his charisma and fluent English, he became an international spokesman for the imprisoned Islamic activists. As early as 1983 he spoke about a worldwide Islamist front. I believe Zawahiri closely fits Eric Shaw's "Personal Pathway Model" to becoming a terrorist: (1) Early socialization by parents or their surrogates into values emphasizing radical social action but yet with a gap between the parents' personal behavior and espoused utopian politics; (2) Narcissistic injuries; (3) Escalatory events— often confrontation with police or the authorities; and (4) Personal connections with terrorist group members—often in prison or war (Shaw 1986, 365–66). Ayman al-Zawahiri, in addition to the harsh treatment by law enforcement authorities (tortured in prison), developed contacts and influence with other terrorists in prison. He was very close to Egyptian sheikh Omar Abdel Rahman, the so-called blind sheikh behind the 1993 bombing of the World Trade Tower and the assassination of Egyptian President Anwar Sadat in 1981. By the time he got out of prison, al-Zawahiri was in the top ranks of the Egyptian militants. He left Egypt in 1985 and made his way to Peshwar, Pakistan, where he worked as a surgeon treating the fighters who were waging holy war against the Soviets in Afghanistan. As he served as a medical officer in Afghanistan, where he was regarded as a hero, he met Osama bin Laden. If al-Zawahiri ever recited the Hippocratic oath, he either did not take it seriously or has abandoned it! Al-Zawahiri has grown very close to Osama (an older brother/father figure) over the years of their alliance in building what Bergen has called "Holy War Inc." Many experts feel that al-Zawahiri is the man who influenced Osama to morph from a donor of money to a warrior of violent *jihad*. He is a constant companion and mentor of bin Laden. In my opinion, al-Zawahiri has psychologically replaced and compensated for Osama's painful childhood loss of his best friend, Abdul Aziz Fahd, as well as his father and brothers (Robinson 2001, 210–12; Bergen 2001, 204–7). There is an intense psychological alter ego, even doppelganger quality, to Zawahiri and Osama's relationship. (Destructive male bonding?) Their twinship transference, when combined with Al Qaeda's groupthink, provides a powerful recruitment model and poster for their free publicity on Al Jazeera videos.

In 1998 Osama bin Laden and al-Zawahiri even merged their two terror groups, Al Qaeda and Egyptian Islamic Jihad, into The World Islamic Front for Jihad Against the Jews and the Crusaders (CNN October 4, 2006, 3). According to CNN, Zawahiri actually visited the United States twice for fund raising in the early 1990s, including a mosque in Santa Clara, California.

Sources in Egypt told CNN that Zawahiri was angry at the United States for abandoning his cause after the Soviets left Afghanistan, and when the United States pushed for extradition of a number of Egyptian Islamic Jihad members from Albania to stand trial in Egypt for terrorism. He promised retaliation, and in August 1998 suicide bombers destroyed the U.S. embassies in Kenya and Tanzania where 224 people died. After the United States attacked their camps with cruise missiles, during which they barely escaped, Zawahiri and bin Laden vowed retaliation. And, in October 2000, the USS *Cole* was attacked, and the 9/11 attacks occurred one year later. Clearly, Dr. al-Zawahiri has made his deadly terrorist commitments a higher priority than his Hippocratic oath. DR. Z and OBL, the doppelgangers-of-death twins continue to elude capture like ghostly Robin Hoods of terror.

In January 2006, an American unmanned Predator aircraft fired many Hellfire missiles into a house near the Afghanistan border in Pakistan, where al-Zawahiri was thought to be at a meeting. Ayman's son-in-law was reported killed along with top Al Qaeda leaders; Zawahiri narrowly missed death. Shortly after this event, Osama spoke out via an authentic audiotape that threatened further attacks on America. Was this perhaps in response to the close call that his older brother figure Zawahiri suffered? This is the first time that a bin Laden threat towards America was not quickly followed by an actual attack. The "father/older brother hunger" is a strong dynamic in Osama. It can help predict his behavior and account for an important domain of his appeal to Muslim youth as a figure with whom to identify.

C. SAYYIB QUTB AND OMAR ABDEL RAHMAN: RADICAL THEOLOGIAN/PHILOSOPHER, AND FIREBRAND PREACHER OF RADICAL ISLAMIST PASSIONS

Azzam was a friend of the famous *jihad* ideologue Sayyib Qutb (1906–1966; philosopher and hero of all the groups that eventually joined the Al Qaeda network) and the Egyptian sheikh Omar Abdel Rahman (who inspired the 1993 bombing of the World Trade Center). All three are heroes and mentors of Osama and leaders in the formation of an Internet network of holy warriors in the 1980s (Bergen 2001, 55).

Omar Abdel Rahman was born in Egypt in 1938. This 58-year-old radical firebrand cleric was blinded by diabetes when he was 10 months old (Meredith 2005, 444). As he studied for a doctorate at Cairo's University of al-Azhar, he was moved like so many others towards becoming a militant activist by the humiliating Arab defeat in the Six-Day War of 1967. He promoted the writings of Sayyib Qutb, and he traveled from mosque to mosque giving fiery sermons about *jihad* and martyrdom. He was imprisoned for eight months in 1970. This prison experience added a further element to the disability of his blindness as examples of features illustrating Shaw's "Personal Pathway Model" of terrorist formation. His status as a professor of theology at University of Asyut in 1973 added another credential to his charismatic spiritual mentoring for the network of underground revolutionary organizations like Gamma Islamiyya and Jamaat al-Jihad (Meredith 2005, 445).

The blind sheikh's fervor became exposed blatantly in his inspiration of the first effort to blow up the World Trade Center in New York in 1993. Now he is in an American prison and has been silenced via isolation when it was found that he was recording radical sermons over the telephone from prison for distribution to American mosques. His American lawyer was convicted of taking illegal messages to his colleagues from her visits with him at the prison. Pied piper terror cult music has many forms.

SAYYIB QUTB

When Qutb's work is finally fully translated, it will make 15 thick volumes in English. His ideas are articulate, sophisticated, and powerful. He had a traditional Muslim education and had memorized the *Koran* by age 10. He went to college in Cairo and did further studies in literature. He wrote novels, poems, and a book that is still well regarded, called *Literary Criticism: Its Principles and Methodology.* Qutb traveled to the United States in the 1940s and got a master's degree in education at Colorado State College of Education. Though admiring American scientific achievements, Qutb gradually grew disgusted with the drinking, sexual immorality, and materialism as he observed them on American college campuses and American society in general.

Sayyib Qutb was executed in 1966, but his writings in prison have led him to be called the Karl Marx of Islamist global *jihad.* Qutb wrote *Milestones* as well as his masterwork, *In the Shade of the Quran.* Qutb's work has inspired Al Qaeda, Egyptian Islamic Jihad, the Islamic Group (Egypt), and the Muslim Brotherhood (Egypt's fundamentalist movement in the 1950s and 1960s). Qutb is so important because his radical Muslim youth-inspiring prose comes not from an academic ivory tower, but from prison, where anti-Western hatreds so often find their spiritual headwaters.

PRISONS, THE HERMETIC AND TRANSCENDENCE: WHAT IS IT ABOUT PRISONS, CAVES, AND PASSIONATE CREATIVE VERBAL EXPRESSION?

Intense forms of spiritual power often emerge from preaching, writing, and letters written or spoken to followers in prison or from prison. The reader can be reminded of the apostle Paul and Silas (Acts 16:19–40); Martin Luther King Jr.'s powerful "Letter From Birmingham Jail," Nelson Mandela's *Long Walk to Freedom,* Alexander Solzhenitsyn's *The Gulag Archipelago,* and even Adolf Hitler's

Mein Kampf. In Chapter 6, we will see how Sheikh Rahman sent tapes from an East coast prison to inspire stark hatred of Israel and America in the Southern California mosque where Adam Gadahn and his mentors worshipped. What is it about prison that allows some people to be more courageous or to wax especially eloquent or creative? Perhaps it is the opportunity for solitude, as fear and loneliness are overcome? Is it that comradeship and bonding with fellow prisoners is more intense in prison? Could it be the cruelty and arbitrary power of prison guards?

UNIQUE INSIGHTS FROM A FORMER POW IN NORTH VIETNAM

In 1973 it was my privilege to work as a navy psychiatrist during operation recap-egress when navy pilots who had been POWs in North Vietnam prisons for many years were released and returned to America. During many hours of interviews with these men, I was profoundly impressed with their courage and strength of mind and character. One man I worked with had spent seven years of his captivity recalling every year of his life in a sort of self-analysis and composition of an auto-psychobiography. One of his prisonmates during his POW ordeal was James Stockdale, who after Vietnam became the president of the Naval War College and ran as Ross Perot's vice presidential candidate. Stockdale and Joseph Brennan wrote a survey of moral philosophy titled "Foundations of Moral Obligation." Joseph Brennan delivered this book's material as lectures that were based on Stockdale's experience as a POW from September 1965–February 1973. (Brennan 1994, xi).

During his navy-sponsored master's degree program at Stanford in 1961 (prior to his POW experience), Stockdale was deeply influenced by *The Enchiridion,* written by the Stoic philosopher Epictetus. He had committed some passages to memory, which were very helpful to him during his captivity. Stockdale offers some valuable observations and perspectives about the "closed-space" or prison experience germane to our question(s). He noticed that Americans, when incarcerated in a POW prison, were totally shocked at the torture and debasement, as if it shattered a popular myth of "human progress." Stockdale felt that he could move beyond the frustration, disappointment, treachery, and outrage by the application of the Stoic philosophy of Epictetus. He discovered that his inner self could be defeated only by the seeds of destruction that he allowed himself to carry. This philosophy served him well as a squadron commander in combat and leader of the underground in the POW prison. (Brennan 1994, xi).

THE HERMETIC

In Chapter 1, called "Prison and the Hermetic," Brennan (1994, 1) and Stockdale say:

The Egyptian leader Anwar Sadat said in his autobiography that there are only two places in this world where a man cannot escape from himself—a battlefield and the prison cell. Prison is one dire form of the closed-space experience, and its major effect is usually dehumanizing, depressing, degrading. It is like a disease that makes us twice-over body, that pulls us down from spirit to matter. So for most, indeed for all, prison has a negative effect, both moral and physical. But for some few, in addition to the initial depressing and degrading effect, prison can be a transforming and uplifting experience, a place of self-discovery, a locus of finding within themselves something that they did not know was there and that helps them transcend the dehumanization of captivity.

Hermetic—1. made airtight by fusion or sealing. 2. not affected by outer influence or power. 3. characteristic of occult science, esp. alchemy. 4. of or pertaining to Hermes Trismegistus [Egyptian priest/God Thoth of mystical, astrological and alchemical writings]. (Webster's College Dictionary 2001, 616)

Brennan and Stockdale focus in an insightful way on the second and third meanings of hermetic, above. These lesser-known meanings of hermetic belong to an ancient tradition that was closely related to the early history of science, philosophy, and religion. The hermetic culture began in ancient Egypt with the God Thoth and later the Greek Hermes. These roots involved connection with the notion of magical transformation that in the Middle Ages and early Renaissance involved the alchemists. The aim of the alchemist was to change a base metal by magical means into one of the precious metals, such as gold. Brennan and Stockdale describe how the radical magical change accomplished by the alchemists had its danger because it involved risky business and dangerous exposure to "hellfire." They say:

> Now if the material irradiated is not only outwardly ordinary but ordinary all the way through, nothing will happen. But if there is something a little unusual in it, you may witness or experience a phenomenon which some call *Steigerung*, that is to say, an upward movement, a metamorphosis, a transformation from a lower to a higher state. This is what can happen to a human under hermetic influences; a transformation of the soul from an inferior to a superior state, but in surroundings that are strictly sealed off, and in an environment that is dangerous. (Brennan 1994, 3)

Brennan and Stockdale press further into exploration of the unique spiritual and mystical powers described in the context of caves. The bedazzling nature of the Christian revelation of the Resurrection where Christ emerges from the stone cave of the sepulcher that Pontius Pilate had ordered sealed. They allude to the enormous power sealed in the prison of the atom until scientists released it in the 1930s for good or ill (Brennan 1994, 4–5).

These perceptive, imaginative, and creative warrior authors trace the cave theme deeper by references to stories of Plato, Socrates, and other philosophers and prophets. Brennan and Stockdale say:

Notice how often a cave comes into these stories. One tradition has it that Jesus was born in a stable ("and they laid him in a manger because there was no room for them in the inn"). It was not uncommon to use a cave as a stable; there the animals could be kept, and food and water brought in to provide for them. The Holy Koran tells us that it was in a cave, on the side of Mount Hera, three miles north of the holy city of Mecca, that the Prophet used to spend parts of the year in meditation. It was in that cave that he had the great vision, in which he felt everything that had impeded him fall away, and he heard a great voice crying, "Read!"

So we can imagine Socrates saying to his pupils, "Look, you see I am in prison and in a few moments I shall die. I await my death in this cave. And isn't it right that I should compare the soul's relation to the body to that of a captive held within a cave, a prisoner within a prison-house? I welcome death. It is the release of my immortal part." And the weeping jailor administers the poison to the old man. (Brennan 1994, 11)

Caves, prison cells, desert hideouts and other important "closed-space experiences" can be transformative locations for nonviolent leaders like Gandhi and Martin Luther King, or destructive terror cult leaders like Hitler or Osama bin Laden. Osama bin Laden loved and developed the caves in the Tora Bora mountains of Afghanistan. Bergen (2006) notes some key issues about this topic from his conversation with Abdel Bari Atwan, the editor of *Al Quds al Arabi* newspaper, who said:

> I was told [by bin Laden] he chose to meet me in the cave because he loves it; because this cave in particular in Tora Bora, he used to stay during the jihad against the Soviet Union. And he told me he fought a lot of battles in Tora Bora and they managed to win one of the battles in that place, so it was very dear to him. The other thing he loves is the mountain, as he told me. He said, "I really feel secure in the mountains. I really enjoy my life when I am here. I feel secure in this place." (171)

Terrorism expert Eric Shaw (1986), who I mentioned earlier in conjunction with Ayman al-Zawahiri, describes what he calls the "Personal Pathway Model" of terrorist formation to explain the way terrorists are born in a social psychological sense. One of the four ways Shaw found that terrorists solidify their identity is through the group cohesion and personal connection instilled in them through shared experiences of harsh treatment they receive from security forces and prison experiences. Shaw (1986, 2) also mentions narcissistic injuries that I discuss extensively in terms of Osama bin Laden's childhood shame, humiliation, and ambivalent idealization of his father who then died when Osama was 10. Shaw (1986, 3) also found that a telling contradiction in future terrorists' experiences occurs when they realize that there are glaring inconsistencies between their parents and/or families of origins' political philosophies and beliefs, and their actual impotence in terms of social or moral action.

Shaw (1986, 4) also observed that young nascent terrorists are frustrated about failure to achieve a traditional professional or vocational place in society, even though they have had very adequate educations. Just as prison can provide a personal connection, spiritual inspiration, and group identity for a future terrorist, so Osama and al-Zawahiri implement a comparable but calculated psycho-inspirational charismatic mystical indoctrination and group connection in their training camps.

In her timely article, "Islamic Radicalization Feared in Europe's Jails," Jennifer Carlile quotes from the work of Michael Radu, who is a terrorism analyst at the Foreign Policy Research Institute. Radu states, : "Every (terrorist) attack has converts, and most of them have criminal records and were converted within prisons" (Carlile 2006, 1).

Radu noted that the British "Shoe Bomber" Richard Reid and Jose Emilio Suarez Trashorras, the Spaniard who supplied the explosives used in the 2004 Madrid bombings, had converted while incarcerated. Carlile's report goes on to note that Trashorras and Jamal Ahmidan (a nonobservant Muslim), were both brainwashed into radical Islam in prison and participated with an Al Qaeda Moroccan group that made use of drug money to fund terrorist activities. These two *prison* converts to radical Islam took lead roles in the deadly Madrid train bombings. It can be noted that Muslims account for 50 percent of France's prison population and some jails on the outskirts of Paris hitting 80 percent. As opposed to France, where Muslims tend to live in poor ghetto areas, American Muslims tend to be middle class, educated, and not involved in crime. Western Europe does have a situation that needs to be dealt with in terms of the "closed-space experiences" of Stockdale and Brennan, and when the Paris suburban prison converts mushroom exponentially. American prison authorities and our politicians cannot afford to be complacent. Black Muslim groups have long gained converts among incarcerated black American young men. Radical Islamist Imams could quite easily seek appointments as chaplains in American prisons and spread their gospel of hatred of America among angry prisoners. These young rebels in search of a cause are already bitter at law enforcement and authority.

QUTB'S PRISON CELL PONTIFICATIONS

Sayyib Qutb's ideas about America, the West, and "modernity" are echoed in Osama's writings in 2002 (Lawrence 2005, 160–85). Qutb felt that mankind's intelligence and moral fabric was degenerating. He saw the richest nations as the unhappiest, and although he respected science and economic prosperity, he thought that Western people were turning in their unhappiness to drugs, existentialism, and empty sexual pleasures. The cause for man's unhappiness, he wrote, was a split between our true nature, as found in the *Koran,* and modern life (Berman 2003, 4).

Qutb plays intellectual and spiritual music that tunes in to the malignant melodies of Osama's soul. Zawahiri and Osama bin Laden are like Qutb's spiritual grandchildren via their voracious reading of his books. Qutb's depth of thought and idealism appeals to youth in all societies because of its iconoclastic truth. (There is a profound conservatism here, a nostalgia for an earlier, simpler time, that resonates in Western philosophy from Rousseau to Thoreau, and many twentieth-century poets, songwriters, and others who reject the materialism of modern life and yearn for a preindustrial Eden of some kind. Osama exploits this corollary of youthful idealism in his pied piper music of terror cult recruitment.) As Qutb's writing grew angrier, his words have been used to encourage martyrdom and violence. Violence and terror have become primary solutions for radical Islamists. The violence proposed towards Christians, Jews, and infidels by Osama and Zarqawi (particularly toward Shiites) seems eerily similar to the fervor of the Crusades, the Inquisition, and Hitler's global utopian, antisemitic, and genocidal plans. Some American scholars are finally realizing the importance of studying, understanding, and where possible effectively challenging and refuting Qutb and the raft of other theologians of contemporary radical Islamism. Here is an example of Sayyib Qutb's erudition and sweeping, haunting philosophical pontification.

> We are indeed at the crossroads. We may join the march at the tail of the Western caravan, which calls itself democracy; if we do so we shall eventually join up with the Eastern caravan, which is known to the West as communism. Or we may return to Islam and make it fully effective in the field of our own life, spiritual, intellectual, social and economic. We may draw our strength from it, and we may promote its growth through development and legislation within the limits of its universal and comprehensive theory of life, and we may fulfill its demand on life and property.
>
> And certainly if we do not do this today, we shall not do it tomorrow. The world is broken by two consecutive wars, disturbed in faith and shaken in conscience, perplexed among varying ideologies and philosophies. It is today more than ever in need of us to offer to it our faith and our social system, our practical and spiritual theory of life. (Qutb 1953, 318–19)

This author wants to share a utopian, perhaps audacious association of my own here. I believe that Allah, God, Yahweh, would value and find joy in serious and compassionate religious and secular scholars coming together in a tradition like a Quaker congregational meeting (where clear guidelines for respectful discussion and group decision-making are maintained) or a Jewish Yeshiva.

ye·shi·va or **ye·shi·vah**
> An institute of learning where students study sacred texts, primarily the Talmud.
> An elementary or secondary school with a curriculum that includes religion and culture as well as general education. (American Heritage Dictionary)

It is fascinating to read Internet material about Yeshiva Chofetz Chaim, Rabbinical Seminary of America (RSA). It has a branch in the Sanhedria Murchevet section of Jerusalem. This yeshiva is named in the memory of Rabbi Yisroel Meir Kagan, known as the Chofetz Chaim. This pen name I find very psychologically significant because it means "Seeker/Desire [of] Life" in Hebrew, and his book was about avoiding slander. The vast majority of radical Islamist anti-American propaganda is slanderous and filled with distortions. Rarely or never do media in Arab or Muslim countries confront the ungodly violence perpetrated by radical Muslim terrorists. Yet, they protest loudly if civilian deaths occur during American or Israeli attacks where civilians are used as shields. The truth suffers when integrity-deficient media is used for religious/political causes.

Yeshiva Chofetz Chaim (RSA) has four unique and vitally important characteristics:

1. An emphasis on unfolding the latent processes of reasoning within the steps of the Talmudic *sugya* ("section") being studied. A careful, prayerful [my word], rigorous study process and dialectic occurs from the initial Talmudic thinking to the final contemporarily relevant understandings.

2. The approach to ethical and biblical texts and commentaries emphasize a rigor about how contemporary interpretations are reached through processes respectful of the original sage.

3. The study of ethics (Mussar) by attending and reviewing semiweekly lectures and daily individual study occurs over many years and with an expectation that the clergymen will personally improve in character traits by increasing self-awareness and self-control. It is most important to become a mensch ("a good person") in the process.

4. The graduate goes on to teach the ideals of Judaism.

These four points remind me of the lengthy educational and maturational process of becoming a psychoanalyst. Not that we psychoanalysts should be put up on pedestals, but we do have the opportunity in our personal analyses to face our inner demons and prejudices. A cleric or judge in a Sharia setting or Islamist court has no opportunity to face and resolve his inner hang-ups and biases that might actually make Allah sad about such questionable "justice" rendered.

Rabbinical students at Yeshiva Chofetz Chaim typically spend a decade or more in their studies. My imagined ecumenical world gathering of sincere Islamic, Jewish, and Christian scholar-statesman-tribal leaders might spend two decades reaching enlightened compromises between Sharia law, the Torah, and Biblical concepts. They could have genuine discussion of "social justice" towards an ecumenical resolution so religious freedom could exist side by side with political structures, to insure the best possible resolution of the myriad of intensely conflicting social, social-psychological, cultural, economic, and religious interests (see the discussion of Swogger's work later in this chapter).

THE WISDOM OF SOLOMON IS REQUIRED TO CUT CONFLICTED RELIGIOUS BABIES IN HALF

[T]wo young prostitutes came to the king [Solomon] to have an argument settled.

"Sir," one of them began, "we live in the same house, just the two of us, and recently I had a baby. When it was three days old, this woman's baby was born too. But her baby died during the night when she rolled over on it in her sleep and smothered it. Then she got up in the night and took my son from beside me while I was asleep, and laid her dead child in my arms and took mine to sleep beside her. And in the morning when I tried to feed my baby it was dead! But when it became light outside, I saw that it wasn't my son at all."

Then the other woman interrupted, "It certainly was her son, and the living child is mine."

"No," the first woman said, "the dead one is yours and the living one is mine." And so they argued back and forth before the king.

Then the king said, "Let's get the facts straight: both of you claim the living child, and each says that the dead child belongs to the other. All right, bring me a sword." So a sword was brought to the king. Then he said, "Divide the living child in two and give half to each of these women!"

Then the woman who really was the mother of the child, and who loved him very much cried out, "Oh, no, sir! Give her the child—don't kill him!" But the other woman said, "All right it will be neither yours nor mine; divide it between us!"

Then the king said, "Give the baby to the woman who wants him to live, for she is the mother!"

Word of Solomon's decision spread quickly throughout the entire nation, and all the people were awed as they realized the great wisdom that God had given him. (1 Kings 4:16–28)

If my imagined ecumenical Yeshivah would ever work out, it would take massive efforts in the psychopolitical arena that John Adams called, "the passion for distinction," along with related issues having to do with the irrational domains of human nature. Volkan (2004, 15) reminds us that at Anwar Sadat's historic 1977 visit to Israel, Sadat declared to the Israeli Parliament that seventy percent of the problems between Arabs and Israelis were psychological!

This treacherous but absolutely crucial arena of healthy political and religious compromise could be aided by insights about normal and pathological narcissism. The working through of political and religious compromises takes insight and more importantly vigorous debate, discussion, and respectful listening to persons with very different views. Most otherwise intelligent and educated people really only rarely listen in depth. This process may find some parallels with effectively conducted marital and family therapy. If conducted well, these two difficult forms of therapy ultimately have a chance of succeeding if the health and best development of the children are held as the goal and best criterion for success. Similarly, vigorous debate, the democratic dialectic of free discussion prior to voting, and authentic respectful listening can result in successful political problem solving. Glen Swogger Jr. creatively applies psychoanalysis and individual and group psychodynamics to examine this issue in his seminal paper, "The Psychodynamic Assumptions of the U.S. Constitution."

Swogger for instance, reminds us that John Adams, like many of the sagacious seventeenth- and eighteenth-century thinkers he studied, thought that the dominant irrational, unconscious passion motivating behavior was pride—also called vanity, desired fame, glory, and superiority (Swogger 2001, 367). Adams was intensely introspective and struggled ambivalently his entire life with his own ambitions and desire for public recognition. Adams concluded that even virtuous and talented persons who sought political power were simultaneously seeking acclaim, recognition, and honors. They were not above avarice, craftiness, cunning and intrigue. Adams studied history in a search for government structures and policies that might help put checks and balances on human nature's ordinary illusions of self-interest and possibly even human nature's more irrational domains (Swogger 2001, 368).

Swogger's applied psychoanalysis of the irrational and unconscious forces to be reckoned with in the political domain can lead us further into the related and similarly consequential domain of religion. If Islamic, Jewish, and Christian leaders really want to pursue peaceful solutions to contemporary hostilities between their three great religions, they will need to seriously explore the introspective domains of narcissism that John Adams called "the passion for distinction." Swogger describes Adams's idea that a person's desire for the esteem of others was as basic a drive as hunger; and Swogger notes that John Adams concluded that intense religious introspection can be applied to political behavior and ambitions. Religious scrutiny leads to a search for the motives behind political behavior, and Adams concluded that laudable acts, self-sacrifice, and even apparent humility itself were really all related to spurious roots in human vanity (Swogger 2001, 367). This seems too harsh, and certainly many of us would believe that virtuous efforts of political behavior deserve public recognition, approval, and recognition for altruistic public servants. In this sense, effective political behavior can be seen as what Kohut called a higher transformation of narcissism.

Swogger appropriately links this with the psychoanalytic concept of the *ego ideal*. Many contemporary religious leaders of all vintages cavort around in their own self-absorption, ambitions, and lust for recognition and power. They often seem to have no empathic contact with the genuine economic, educational, and spiritual needs of their people.

Any effective analysis of radical Islamist terrorists or Christian, Jewish, or other religious fundamentalist advocates of terror in the name of God must grapple with those taboo topics, religion and politics. The old adage about even the best of friends and most loving of family members can be seriously alienated during discussions of religion, and/or politics, is true. It is often said that religion is "such a personal thing." It is also, like politics and politicians, filled with issues of normal and pathological narcissism. Fundamentalists Pat Robertson, Rabbi Kahane, Sheikh Abdel Rahman, or Hassan Nassrallah, when they preach hate, murder, assassination, and genocide to their audiences, can be swept up in their own personal narcissistic issues as well as exploiting and manipulating the narcissism of their groups or congregations.

Just as charismatic politicians can stir up misguided group fears and rage through self-aggrandizing rhetoric, so can charismatic religious leaders, hovering on the fine line between religious devotion and political polemics, stir up blind hate and slanderous accusations of other groups. George W. Bush's macho slogans "Bring it on," "Osama dead or alive," or "Cut and run" describing those seeking new Iraq solutions, are as ignorant of key narcissistic domains as are the president of Iran's insults to Bush's religion or calls for Jews to be exterminated, when he probably has not spent serious respectful time listening to a Jew besides Mike Wallace.

PSYCHOANALYSIS, RADICAL ISLAM, AND POLITICS: A HYPOTHETICAL BOMBLESS, BULLETLESS CONFRONTATION

If only Arab and Western "leaders" had been able to engage a future powerfully influential scholar and philosopher like Sayyib Qutb in dialogue about such issues in the 1960s; if only Qutb had made authentic friends among faculty colleagues in America when he studied and wrote here; if only he had experienced genuine affection, friendship, and spiritual connection with good American listeners—perhaps he could have seen that communism, fascism, and radical Islamism are false utopias. Utopias and totalitarianisms never satisfy human beings. The messy, bickering, often petty but wonderful freedom to make mistakes and learn from them in American democracy is worthy of exploration. Democracy is the best social-political road for fallible but sincere human beings searching for social justice. I would have loved to engage the Qutb brothers, and especially Sayyib, in a long discussion of his books and my favorite applied psychoanalytic article about politics, Swogger's "The Psychodynamic Assumptions of the U.S. Constitution" (2001).

An in-depth study of Swogger's profoundly cogent paper might help correct Qutb's and other radical Islamists' tragic misunderstanding of our core American political values, attitudes about religious freedom, and social justice. The utopian monoliths of fundamentalist political thinking, like Nazism, Communism, fascism, and Islamofascism, all fail to fully take into account mankind's irrational, narcissistic, and self-serving emotional drives. The enforced and coerced passive submission to the merged religious-political authority of Sharia law and radical Islam is as defective as the totalitarian rigidity and ineffectiveness of fascism or communism. This is particularly true in day-to-day life in a large literate society with diverse levels of education, opinions, perceptions, ambitions, and religious convictions or lack of any of the above. The irrational core of human nature and human groups always trumps any one person's theories about how political, economic, civic, and religious life should be conducted. The messy evolving Western democracies offer some hope for order in an increasingly over-populated world that has seen the terrors and failures of the extremes of anarchy and totalitarian systems.

Swogger elegantly summarizes his important paper as follows:

> The designers of the U.S. Constitution were acutely aware of irrational and self-serving emotions driving individuals and groups and their impact on the function and viability of democratic government. They designed government with explicit reference to how these structures might contain individual ambition and the drive for power; group conflict, and the conflicts of various social, religious and economic interests; the needs of the groups to define boundaries and enemies; the tendency of large groups to irrationality, impulsiveness and grandiosity; and the tendency of dominant groups to tyrannize and scapegoat minorities. The understanding of human behavior and motivation by the designers of the Constitution arose from a rich tradition of scrutiny and theorizing about human behavior by theologians, moral philosophers, poets, satirists and political theorists of the 17th and 18th centuries. (Swogger 2001, 353–54)

The value of Swogger's paper lies in his recognition and description of how the theories propounded and implemented by our American group of founding fathers are congruent with modern psychoanalytic perspectives on narcissism, leadership, group dynamics, and the indispensable role of transitional space in cultural/political life. Swogger summarizes key points made by Madison, Hamilton, Adams and others in *The Federalist Papers* and other writings of the period.

It is not because of some imperialistic, elitist, or inherent superiority that American or "Western" democracies are a better form of government. (Despite the fact that some of the characteristics of "the West" and particularly America are rather obnoxiously materialistic, narcissistic, and arrogant.) Thanks to our founding fathers' attention to human nature's profound irrationality, pettiness, and group pathologies, our system of government at least recognizes the elephant in the living room. Human nature's vast domains of irrationality.

Muslim countries and communities fuse and merge politics and religion. Western countries must not fear strong intellectual confrontation of this crucial political issue. One must remain strongly respectful of the Muslim religion. But we must not become fearful that rigorous confrontation with the massive problems that occur when politics and religion are fused and confused is a sign of intolerance or disrespect.

Emerging Muslim countries can hopefully find their own founding fathers and especially mothers, to implement healthy political processes that deal honestly and fairly with human irrationality and related emotional passions. The working out of these paradoxes of human nature is crucial. Survivable and possibly peaceful group life cannot occur via fundamentalist mentality. No one person's or group's theological or political interpretation can dominate or dictate the laws that have hope of sustaining a relatively peaceful society with a minimum of violence. The reason for this is that unless the majority of citizens embraces and helps sustain the society or large group's laws, only brute force can force acquiescence. Endless insurgent and underground resistance usually accompany such forced acquiescence to the totalitarian rulers. The murder, assassination, torture, and suppressive genocide that is required to maintain power and control by such rulers, though sometimes appearing peaceful on the surface, is ultimately corrosive of the spiritual and ethical fabric of the group. Iraq under Saddam Hussein was a prime example of this situation. Postwar Iraq is drained by a massive struggle to find its political identity and soul. Postwar Iraq is the epitome of a large group of "in-betweeners" (see Chapter 3), in social, political, and spiritual transition.

WILL ISLAMIST YOUTH OR THEIR LEADERS SEE BEYOND THE FOG OF HATE AND LISTEN TO SOLUTIONS AMERICA'S FOUNDING FATHERS STRUGGLED TO FIND?

In the first section of his treatise, Swogger (2001, 353) discusses how James Madison thought a well-constructed government might "control the violence of factions." Madison defined *faction* as a group of citizens who are united by an idea or impulse that is against the rights of other citizens or the whole community.

"Modern" Iraq and so many Arab and Muslim countries and communities are cauldrons of hate-factions in overt or covert conflict. Ultimately their irrational humanity is no different from our own. I doubt their revolutions and civil wars will be less bloody, but I hope so. The merits and advantages of a democratic system of government begin to be slowly apparent when it is explored in terms of the ways it tries to deal with the irrationality, potential pathological narcissism, and grandiosity of individuals and groups. Relevant to Middle East and Muslim countries is how religious diversity can be dealt with politically without a government resorting to violent suppression, assassination, torture, or insurgency.

Swogger goes on in his paper to describe Madison's valuable thinking. Madison had located *three crucial paradoxes,* entwined with factions, that democracy offers clumsy and vexing, but potentially effective, ways of dealing with:

1. For liberty and democracy, factions are the greatest danger, but also its essential element. Our human reason comes to a diversity of conclusions about religion, law or behavior. When we participate fully in the democratic process we experience not only rational and civic-mindedness, but all the passions of the psyche. Property

(economic, intellectual, spiritual, etc.) in all its meanings becomes a fundamental interest.

2. Those characteristics that lead people to be different and to form different, conflicting factions reflect abilities and achievements of great value.

3. Most profoundly paradoxical is that individuals and groups participating in the democratic process, biased as they are by their own interests, must make impartial judgments for the common good and if peaceful intercourse is to prevail (Swogger 2001, 354–55).

Swogger traces Madison's thinking into a crucial domain of democracy. Madison clearly thought that no individual can be the judge in his own cause because his self interest inherently biases his judgment. Similarly, groups can't effectively be judges and parties at the same time. (Swogger, 355).

Swogger (2001, 356) notes that Madison would *not* rely solely on higher values or a "moral elite" as a solution to this intense problem with conflict of interest. There will not always be wise or enlightened leaders with enough wisdom, foresight and maturity to protect the rights of an individual or the good of the whole.

In my opinion, one of the key dilemmas in Muslim countries is that if Sharia law and radical Islamism prevail, then political rigidity will also prevail towards non-Muslim interest groups and moderate Muslim interest groups. All but Islamist "true believers" will face social injustice, persecution, or worse. If the mysteries of God and the spiritual domain are the source of the wisdom of an Islamist Imam's judgments about civil matters via Sharia law, it is unfair to a sincere nonbeliever who is respectful of his neighbors' rights but not accepting of an Islamic court about civil matters.

There are no more dramatic examples of sincere, "enlightened statesman" or philosophers than some of the current Sunni, Kurd, and Shiite leaders of Iraq, or Sayyib Qutb in the 1960s. (However, there have NEVER been enough women to fully participate in the process of forming an Iraqi democracy!)

Many years ago, at a combined meeting of the American Psychiatric Association and the Canadian Psychiatric Association, I had the privilege of hearing Senator Eugene McCarthy discuss the American presidency. To my best recollection, he said that any one person who thinks they can be a U.S. president needs the attention of every one of you psychiatrists in this room. He advocated that three candidates should run as a triumvirate for the presidency. One would best be an expert in diplomacy and international affairs; one an expert in military and economic affairs; and one an expert in domestic/political issues. With no abstentions allowed, this would foster clear and crisp decisions. Two of the three running for president should always be women. When asked why, McCarthy said, "There would be fewer wars."

The political issues around social justice, however, stay stuck in many Mid-East countries because of passionate religious and tribal *interests*. These religious and tribal issues are often perpetuated and dominated by insecure, pathologically narcissistic, and unempathic men who are more concerned about their own power than about the well-being of their people. It would be helpful if many more intelligent and capable Iraqi women were elected and active as lawmakers. And, in the midst of such profound conundrums created by Iraq's abrupt confrontation with long-festering large-group irrationality, impulsiveness, and grandiosity, the daily political reality highlights the profound but painful truth that Swogger's summary of Madison reveals:

> Madison believed that ambition and self-love, as well as the passions engendered out of membership in a faction, adherence to a religious sect, or other intense belief system, will obscure in many instances a thoughtful, reflective, long-term consideration of social goods and government policy. The interests that lead to factions are not "bad." They reflect our vital relationship to community, livelihood, and belief. Democracies are formed just so interests may be represented. But democratic government poses the eternal problem of transmuting individual and group interests into goals and policies for the larger society. (Swogger 2001, 356)

The explosions of destruction and nightmare rivers of innocent blood in Iraq today have reached truly psychotic levels of group behavior stemming from intense conflicts of political interest. There may be hope that president al-Mahliki of Iraq and his successors and colleagues can contact in a mystical way the creative, questing, pragmatic spirit of Madison and find Iraqi counterparts to America's founding fathers. He need not be Bush's or America's "man," but perhaps he can be receptive to the unique, imperfect, but profound wisdom of Madison, Jefferson, Adams, Hamilton, and Franklin. They were acutely aware of the vast domains of human irrationality and the need to find creative ways not to be in *denial* about this. Iraq, as President George W. Bush frequently says, has lots of work to do. And the work of governing in Iraq requires effort in many domains beyond military and economic activity. When basic safety is in question, it is difficult for people to assert themselves politically. Like the old saying goes, "When you are up to your ass in alligators, it is difficult to drain the swamp." However, there is an inherent value and promotion of dignity and ego-strength when citizens find ways to assert themselves in political life and not when they are just left alone. The American founding fathers' ideas and concept of "separation of church and state" do not have to be glibly declared heresies of Western infidels. It is possible for Iraqi leaders to embrace the helpful and useful ideas that democracy offers.

NORMAL NARCISSISM VERSUS DANGEROUS NARCISSISM IMPINGING ON POLITICS AND GOVERNMENT: A LIFE AND DEATH ISSUE

Swogger describes John Adams's notion of "the passion for distinction...the desire to be observed, considered, esteemed, praised, beloved, and admired by his fellows," and concludes, "Adams saw the passion for distinction as both natural, acceptable and useful, and that at the same time potentially pathological and destructive" (Swogger 2001, 367–68).

Swogger points out that representatives of the people in a popularly elected assembly seem too ready in a grandiose way to fancy that they ARE the people themselves (2001, 360). Most political and spiritual leaders have narcissistic character traits, but so many radical Islamist leaders and theoreticians have pathological levels of narcissism and defensive narcissistic rage.

Too often in Iraq today, the impatience with government leads to kidnapping, torture, and assassination. There is a crying need in Iraq for what Swogger refers to as "Constitutional Space." Winnicott wrote about Tansitional Space in a therapy relationship. It is the safe arena in which a child or an adult patient can temporaly feel that they are freely playing without ultimate consequences. At the same time the patient is exploring ideas, metaphors, and behaviors that have great implications for the world of interpersonal relationships and social institutions (Swogger 2001, 374). There is precious little of such transitional space in present-day Iraq.

If only Iraqi police, American forces, and the coalition can mobilize political patience so the fledgling Iraqi political arena can be helped to have some "constitutional space" referred to by Swogger. Given such a space, the men and women in the Iraqi congress can hopefully become quick studies on their front lines of life and death of Mideast politics. Democracy's spirit is respectful of all religious faiths and interest groups that desire peace. The rigid religious militias and death squads of revenge and malignant group narcissism bring only future and endless cycles of revenge that brings tears to God's eyes.

BACK TO OSAMA BIN LADEN'S PROTOTYPICAL AND SAD JOURNEY

In 1989 bin Laden returned to Saudi Arabia, his homeland, after serving as a hero of great renown in the successful *jihad* and defeat of the Soviet Union in Afghanistan. It appeared that Osama would settle down, but on August 2, 1990, Iraq invaded Kuwait. Osama presented a detailed plan for self-defense of the Saudi kingdom, bolstered by battle-hardened Saudis who had fought in Afghanistan. Bin Laden offered to recruit the "Afghans" and said his family construction company could quickly build fortifications. He warned that inviting or permitting infidel Western forces into the sacred lands of the kingdom would be against the teachings of Islam and would offend the sensibilities of all Muslims.

Osama was not alone in these concerns among the Saudi leadership, but his offer was ignored despite his degree of popularity at the time. When he grew more harshly critical and insistent, the Saudi leadership threatened his extended family. In 1991, fearing reprisals for his outspoken anti-American and anti-Saudi pronouncements, bin Laden bitterly left for exile in the land of a more friendly father-figure: Turabi of the Sudan. Turabi became Osama's mentor/father-figure and Islamist colleague (Bodansky 1999, 29–32).

TURABI OF SUDAN: A POLITICALLY SHIFTY FATHER FIGURE

Another outspoken Muslim and father figure to Osama bin Laden is Hassan Abdullah al-Turabi, born in 1932 in Kassala, eastern Sudan. Turabi received a secular education in English schools in Sudan. He got a law degree at Gordon University in Khartoum in 1955. His secular education and radical Islamism get reflected in his political vacillations about the remarkable "Moderate Martyr" Mahmoud Mohamed Taha (Packer 2006, 61–69). Turabi was a clandestine member of the Egyptian Muslim Brotherhood even as he earned a master's degree in law as a scholarship student at the University of London in 1957. He completed his doctorate at the Sorbonne in 1964. Turabi became the spiritual leader of the National Islamic Front (NIF). He became Sudan's spiritual leader under General Omar al-Bashin after a coup in June 1989.

Packer (2006, 65) describes Turabi's devious political plotting and chameleon-like political posturing. We will discuss Turabi again later in reference to his likely role in the execution of the hopeful, moderate theologian of liberal Islam, Mahmoud Mohammad Taha. Turabi's political plotting and self-serving behaviors certainly illustrate John Adams's and other American founding fathers' concerns about pathological narcissism run amuck in politicians who lose touch with the real needs of their people.

SOME APPLIED PSYCHOANALYTIC THEORIZING ABOUT OSAMA BIN LADEN'S PSYCHE

Osama seemed perpetually (unconsciously) caught between his increasingly radical Islamist beliefs and the dazzling financial success from his dead father's affiliation with the materialistic Saudi leaders and their American "friends." Today it seems that Osama seeks both the destruction of the father figures of the Saudi regime that disowned him and the destruction of the Saudis' American "friends." On a conscious level, he idealized his father; but on an unconscious level, he held tremendous ambivalence even toward his admired mentor Azzam.

A psychoanalytic theory here would be that unconscious, unresolved grief, disappointment, and shame over his dead father's wealth (unconsciously equated with Western materialism) seem to have focused and magnified Osama's identity as a self-appointed, anti-Western, radical Muslim warrior chieftain. Osama's relentless grief-laden search led him to find other radical, admired, and admiring father figures. His relationships with Azzam of Afghanistan and Turabi of Sudan filled the bill. Bodansky (1999, 19–20, 30–35) further documents in great depth and detail the mutual admiration reverberating between Osama and these men.

OSAMA THE WOULD-BE SAUDI RETURNING WAR HERO, AND A KEY PLAYER IN AN AFGHAN VERSION OF *TOTEM AND TABOO*

Osama truly was a heroic, fearless military leader in Afghanistan's successful war against the Soviet Union. For bin Laden, the Afghanistan war was a profoundly spiritual experience (Bergen 2001, 61). This enabled him to be both an admired warrior son of radical terrorist leaders and a legendary hero/older brother/mentor for millions of angry young Muslims. We can see how money has never been able to compensate for Osama's grief and ambivalence for a father who was not around when the adolescent Osama most needed his guidance. Fathers of adolescent sons often feel superfluous or devalued by their sons. But beneath this surface of rebellion in the service of fledgling independence and identity searching is a desperate need for a father with moral strength and dignity. Malignant figures like bin Laden seem to be unconsciously preoccupied with ambivalent longing for and hatred of the father who did not stand up to them and for them. This leads them to try to be the ultimate father/themselves unto themselves. This remarkable inner tautology by Malignant Pied Pipers of terror cults requires massive unconscious denial (Olsson 2005, 144).

Rohan Gunaratna, in *Inside Al Qaeda: Global Network of Terror,* gives a good example of Osama's severely ambivalent conflicts with even his mentor/father figure Yussuf Abdallah Azzam. Azzam felt that noncombatant women and children should not be killed in the *jihad.* In his strict Wahhabi fundamentalism, Osama believed that all infidels should die—even women and children. Gunaratna raises the serious question as to whether Osama held symbolic patricidal urges, when he probably even passively acquiesced to Azzam's assassination (Gunaratna 2002, 32–33). The furiosity of battles in Afghanistan in the late 1980s and early 1990s was not only with the Soviets and Afghan communists, but prevailed in a *Totem and Taboo* emotional atmosphere among rival Arab, Afghan, and Islamist military leaders. The intensity of these brutal power struggles among these leaders illustrates Freud's allegory about primal tribal battles between fathers and sons found in his essay *Totem and Taboo* (Bergen 2006, 92–93).

Azzam thought that the remarkably talented Ahmad Shah Massoud of the Northern Alliance was the hope for Afghanistan's future. Abdullah Azzam was assassinated on November 24, 1989. Osama bin Laden had drifted away from Azzam and was apparently not in Pakistan at the time of the assassination. But it is likely that the severely radical Egyptian jihadists like Zawahiri, who had influenced Osama to split from Azzam, colluded with the Machiavellian Afghan warlord Gulbuddin Hekmatyar to accomplish Azzam's assassination. With Azzam dead, Massoud lost his respected Arab advocate, and the Egyptian jihadists could go on with their ever more radical Al Qaeda terror projects (Bergen 2006, 93).

OSAMA'S POETRY: A GLIMPSE INTO THE PSYCHE OF A MALIGNANT PIED PIPER[1]

Poems often say volumes about the unconscious mind and emotions of the poet. Osama's literary gifts and the charismatic projection of his poet-prophet video image is part of his powerful appeal in the Muslim world (Lawrence 2005, xvii).

On April 7, 2002, the *New York Times* published a poem, "The Travail of a Child Who Has Left the Land of the Holy Shrines," coauthored by Osama bin Laden and the poet Dr. Abd-ar-Rahman al-Ashmawi. Half of the 42 verses were written by bin Laden. Eighteen of Osama's verses mention father, son, brother, child, or family. One line mentions mother. Let's examine some selected verses from Osama's poetry because of their reflection of bin Laden's emotional search for his father/himself.

> Father, where is the way out?
> > when are we to have a settled home?
> Oh, Father, do you not
> > See encircling danger?
> Long have you made me travel, father,
> > Through deserts and through settled lands.

Osama continues later in the poem:

> As, marked by manliness and pride,
> > Does our commander, Mullah Omar. [Leader of the Taliban and clearly a father/brother figure; he also married one of Osama's daughters! Add the spice of symbolic incest?]
> Why, father, have they sent
> > these missiles thick as rain,
> Showing mercy neither to a child
> > Nor to a man shattered by old age?
> Father, what has happened?
> > so we are pursued by perils?

It is a world of criminality, my son
>   Where children are, like cattle, slaughtered.
Zion is murdering my brothers,
>   And the Arabs hold a congress!

Bin Laden's poetry can be seen as free associations similar to those psychoanalysts hear from the couch. In other lines of this poignant poem, bin Laden reveals his emotional search for a psychological home and father/ brother figures in Sudan and Afghanistan:

A decade has passed, whose years were spent
>   In homelessness and wanderings.
I have migrated westward
>   To a land where flows the Nile. [Clear reference to father surrogate Turabi of
Sudan.]
Of Khartoum I love the character,
>   But I was not permitted to reside.
So then I traveled eastward
>   Where there are men of radiant brows.
Kabul holds its head up high [idealized fighting brothers and fathers in Afghanistan]
>   Despite the hardship and the danger.
Kabul, with a shining face,
>   Offers all-comers shelter and help. (Osama bin Laden, quoted in Rohde 2002, 16)

Often, when captured by the poetic muse, the poet reveals his or her inner feelings about the core of self. Poetry of this sort provides access to the more unconscious levels of the poet's psyche. Osama's poetry reveals a lot about his inner pain, loneliness, narcissistic injury, and psychologically nomadic-search for his father/himself. Beneath the surface of his bold threats towards America lies his ambivalent personality's core that is the source of his narcissistic rage.

DEADLY LITTLE BROTHER ZARQAWI'S DEATH STIRS GRIEF WORDS

Even though Osama chastised Zarqawi for his especially brutal attacks on fellow Muslims in Jordan, Osama used grief-flavored words in his public comments about the fallen Al Qaeda leader in Iraq—very much as if a younger brother had died. It would appear that their relationship was actually paved with intense ambivalence and suspicion.

Abu Musab al-Zarqawi (1966–2006; real name Ahmed Fadeel al-Nazal al-Khalayleh), was born in Zarqa, a town near Amman, Jordan. Before he was killed in an air strike in Baquba, Iraq on June 7, 2006, Zarqawi was regarded as the most fearsome and brutal Al Qaeda terror cult leader, and who had been known for his beheading of hostages (Nicholas Berg), suicide bombings, and the killing of soldiers, police officers, and particularly civilians. Zarqawi's second wife Isra and their 18-month-old son Abdul Rahman Zarqawi died in the air strike that killed Zarqawi. Isra was 14 when they married and 16 when she died.

Zarqawi grew up in poverty and squalor and was a street thug who dropped out of school at 17. He was apparently jailed for drug possession and sexual assault in the 1980s (Wikipedia). In 1989 Zarqawi traveled to Afghanistan to join the insurgency against the Soviets, but they were leaving by the time he arrived. He met and befriended Osama bin Laden. He worked as a reporter for an Islamist newsletter and started the al-Tawhid paramilitary group after traveling to Europe. Al-Tawhid was dedicated to installing an Islamic regime in Jordan.

As is typical of so many terrorists' life trajectories, Zarqawi spent five years in a Jordanian prison after his arrest in 1992 for possessing explosives. He supposedly memorized the Koran in prison and he became a feared leader among inmates and tried to draft his cellmates into the radical cause. One prisonmate told *Time* magazine that he was very concrete in his thinking, and you were either with him or against him. Other inmates said that he lacked charisma or intelligence. In prison he did meet the articulate Jordanian journalist Fouad Hussein, who in 2005 published a book about Zarqawi and Al Qaeda's strategy.

FOUAD HUSSEIN: ZARQAWI'S DOPPELGANGER

Wright (2006) thinks that Fouad Hussein's book, *Al-Zarqawi: The Second Generation of Al Qaeda,* is the most definitive and chilling outline of Al Qaeda's master plan. Hussein claims that dragging Iran into conflict with the United States is important for Al Qaeda's future strategy. The 20-year plan began with what Hussein calls "The Awakening" in 2003, when American troops entered Baghdad and the Islamic nation began coming out of a long hibernation. The second "Eye-Opening" stage will last through 2006, as Iraq becomes the massive recruiting ground for anti-Western *jihadis*. The third stage, "Arising and Standing Up," will last from 2007 until 2010. Al Qaeda will focus on Syria and Turkey, but it will directly confront Israel. The fourth stage, "The Creeping Loss of Regimes," will last until 2013. The demise of Arab governments and U.S. power will occur through attacks on the petroleum industry. The fifth stage of Al Qaeda's plan will last until 2016, as Israel weakens, Europe falls into disunity, and China will be an economic ally. The sixth phase is described as "total confrontation," during which the caliphate's Islamic Army will instigate a fight between the "believers" and the "nonbelievers." Hussein promises definitive victory after the world experiences the real meaning of terrorism (Wright 2006, 57–58). The groupthink of jihadists occurring in Jordanian, Egyptian, or U.S. prisons is just as frightening as the groupthink of Zarqawi and bin Laden in Pakistan's mountain caves. Though Zarqawi's sword has been silenced, the pens of men like Hussein sound remarkably similar to the Bible's book of Revelations and its portended battle of Armageddon that fundamentalist Christians predict.

After his release from prison in 1999, Zarqawi was involved in an attempt to blow up the Radisson SAS Hotel in Amman, Jordan. He fled to Afghanistan, where he established Harat, a militant training camp near the Iranian border. Zarqawi was allegedly wounded in a U.S. bombardment in Afghanistan after 9/11 as he fought with Al Qaeda and Taliban forces.

Mary Ann Weaver, an Israeli intelligence official, noted in an *Atlantic Monthly* article that Osama bin Laden disliked and distrusted Zarqawi from the very beginning of their relationship. Osama did not like Zarqawi's swagger or his tattoos. His tattoos were regarded as un-Islamic. In addition to Zarqawi's aggressive ambition and overbearing style, Osama disliked Zarqawi's hatred of Shiites. Weaver points out that Osama's mother is a Shiite. Zarqawi refused for years to take an oath of allegiance to Osama bin Laden. Finally after many months of tense negotiations, Zarqawi took the oath in 2004 (Wikipedia).

In my opinion, Zarqawi showed many patterns of a narcissistic personality disorder with elements of severely malignant narcissism (see Osama's psychiatric diagnosis discussion in Chapter 7), but I think Zarqawi had the additional element of psychopathic personality disorder.

ABU MOHAMMAD AL-MAQDISI: ZARQAWI'S IDEOLOGICAL DOPPELGANGER

Maqdisi is a Palestinian sheikh who Zarqawi met in Pakistan in the early 1990s. Maqdisi had long been a notable ideologue in the radical Islamist movement. Wright (2006) describes him as sharp-tempered and his Puritanism shone through in his book, *The Evident Sacrileges of the Saudi State.* Maqdisi declared a *fatwa* excommunicating the Saudi royal family that is encouraging *jihadis* to murder the Saudi royal family. According to Wright (2006, 52), the book influenced the men who bombed a Saudi National Guard training center in Riyadh in 1995, and those who attacked American troops in Khobar in 1996.

The doppelganger-like bond between Maqdisi and Zarqawi has been described as an alliance of the "man of thought and the man of [brute] action" (Wright 2006, 52). Suicide bombings became Zarqawi's trademark, but Maqdisi condemned them, along with Zarqawi's beheadings and assassinations, as un-Islamic. From prison, Maqdisi chastised Zarqawi with unusual words: "There is no point in vengeful acts that terrify people, provoke the entire world against mujahideen, and prompt the world to fight them" (Wright 2006, 52–53). I believe that Zarqawi's pure personal meanness and self-absorption led his colleagues to betray him. Again we see groupthink, doppelganger pairings, and prison bonding and recruitment as the many wombs for terrorists' social-psychological birth.

HOMES AWAY FROM HOME

In the terrorist training camps of Afghanistan, bin Laden both found and became his own lost family: father, brother, and mother. Osama bin Laden's psychological father-hunger may have been relentlessly and destructively acted out with an uncanny resonance with thousands of father-hungry young Muslims around the world. Has bin Laden's denial of his own grief, loss, and fear of being alone become part of the destructive illusions and delusions he offers his young terror cult followers? Does he cloak these illusions in the radical Koranic interpretations offered by his mentors? Muslim clerics who resonate with bin Laden's radical Islamist theology of hatred teach in Madrassahs all over the Muslim world. They seem to act as lieutenants to recruit and indoctrinate followers for Al Qaeda and its warrior prophet bin Laden. Osama and his colleagues from Al Qaeda have even seduced American youths such as John Walker Lindh, Adam Gadhan, Jose Padilla, and the British misfit Richard Reid with their deadly music (see Chapter 4). Osama bin Laden and clones seem to have become the ultimate Malignant Pied Pipers, and their music goes on and on.

PAYING THE PIPER

Osama bin Laden's Al Qaeda terror cult network manifests remarkably similar dynamics to the Malignant Pied Piper patterns found in the destructive cult groups of Jim Jones (Jonestown, Guyana), David Koresh (Waco, Texas), and others. But Osama's terror cult operates on an infinitely wider scale. In this cult model, charismatic leaders with sadly distorted personalities lead idealistic, father-hungry, or disillusioned young people away from their home villages (Olsson 2005). But it is not only the children who are seduced—it is entire villages.

The price all competent and loving parents pay the piper of parenthood is quality time. This means significant chunks of time devoted not to what the child can do to promote the self-esteem, evidence of prowess, reputation, or psychological well-being of the parent; but towards what the parent can try to do to help the development of solid identity, self-esteem, realistic self-confidence, and solid moral development of the child. This investment of parental time is especially important during a particularly intelligent and perceptive child's adolescent identity crisis.

"SWEET REVENGE"

When his father died, Osama was grief-stricken but profoundly ambivalent and very likely left feeling bitter, humiliated, alone, and eventually narcissistically enraged at an unconscious level. The Rev. Jim Jones got his piper-payback of fantasized powerful revenge in the form of 913 loyal Kool-aid drinkers at Jonestown in 1978 (see Olsson 2005, Chapter 2). David Koresh played the ultimate strong father as he led 85 Davidian sheep to a fiery death in Waco, Texas (Olsson 2005, Chapter 3). Osama bin Laden got thousands of lives as piper-payback on 9/11 alone. Osama's radical Islamist pied piper music has led many young Muslims away from moderate Muslim villages where parents could never pay the piper enough.

NOTE

1. Portions of this analysis of Osama's poetry first appeared in *Malignant Pied Pipers of Our Time* (Olsson 2005, 145–46).

OSAMA BIN LADEN'S DARK EPIPHANY AS PROTOTYPE OF ISLAMIST LEADERS' PATHOLOGICAL NARCISSISM

> *You cannot defeat heretics with this book* [Koran] *alone, you have to show them the fist!*
>
> —Osama bin Laden (Bodansky 1998, 387–38)

The early childhood disappointments, shame, and empathic parental failures of future destructive cult leaders are further magnified and compounded by "dark epiphany" experiences in late adolescence or young adulthood (Olsson 2005, 18, 38–39). This is true for Osama bin Laden. Let us backtrack a little to focus on one of Osama's dark epiphanies.

Osama returned to Saudi Arabia in 1989 as a hero of the war against the Soviet Union in Afghanistan, but events of the next two years left him feeling rejected and threatened by the Saudi leadership, who ignored his offers to help defend the country when Iraq invaded Kuwait. This rejection slowly smoldered into a "dark epiphany" of molten rage and vengeance toward the betraying Saudi father figures and their American "infidel friends." There undoubtedly were echoes and reminders of Osama's early loss of his father and the ambivalent feelings surrounding his memory. Would the Saudi rulers have treated Osama that way if his father had still been alive? Would Osama's father have opposed how far his "favored" son has taken his Wahhabism?

In Afghanistan after the Soviets left, America and our Saudi "friends" did not *pay the piper.* Why did we abandon a crumbled Afghanistan and allow a Robin Hood–like figure called bin Laden to emerge? We certainly missed an opportunity to try to befriend the "young lion" bin Laden. The establishment of authentic friendships seems difficult for the formal diplomacy of American diplomats, and perhaps some unique special forces soldiers come closer to these friendships in their work in Afghanistan (Rubin 2006, 59–63). It would have been difficult, but worth the effort to have tried. Bin Laden commanded the respect of many young Arab men because of his bravery and effectiveness in defeating the Soviets in Afghanistan. There are many future bin Ladens born daily around the world. In the past, we have done little to prevent their psychological births. Some authors think we have other options in countries caught in the transition between war, occupation, and economic collapse and the subsequent search for peace, recovery, and stability.

What are some of the psychosocial factors that render otherwise normal human beings vulnerable to recruitment by a terror cult?

THE VULNERABLE IN-BETWEENERS

This author (Olsson 2005, 113) has cited and applied to terror cults Margaret Singer's cogent idea about the "in-betweener," or life-transition experience(s) of an individual and his or her vulnerability to seduction by an exploitive cult. Singer (1995, 21) wrote:

> Vulnerable individuals are lonely, in a transition between high school and college, between college and a job or graduate school, traveling away from home, arriving in a new location, recently jilted or divorced, fresh from losing a job, feeling overwhelmed about how things are going, or not knowing what to do next in life. Unsettling personal occurrences are commonplace. The college of her choice rejects a high school senior. A man's mother dies...At such times, we are all open to persuasion, more suggestible, more willing to take something offered us without thinking there may be strings attached.

Some exploitive cults have training manuals and training programs for their cult recruiters. Such training manuals saturated with Islamist religious dogma were found in Al Qaeda training camps in Afghanistan and on the Internet.

Al Qaeda training camps and some Madrassah schools provide ideal climates to satisfy Singer's Six Conditions (1995, 64–69) to put thought-reform ("brainwashing") processes into place:

1. Keep the person unaware that there is an agenda to control or change the person. [The terrorist training camps use peer-modeling, peer pressure, and the military; the weapons and explosives training that is provided is exciting to young men. The radical Islamist theology of *jihad* is presented as normal extensions of the recruits' earlier Koranic study and Muslim beliefs learned in their childhoods.]

2. Control time and the physical environment (contacts, information). [This is easily accomplished in Al Qaeda mountain camps.]

3. Create a sense of powerlessness, fear, and dependency. [The charismatic leaders hold forth a fantasy of shared grandiose power and merger with their visions of victorious *Jihad.* Most adolescents love to feel a part of a noble and idealistic cause.]

4. Suppress old behavior and attitudes. [Islamists manipulate systems of rewards and punishments that are their own versions of interpretation of the Koran. There are no debates or discussions.]

5. Instill new behavior and attitudes. [Manipulate by implying rich rewards for being a part of the new terrorist identity and ideology.]

6. Put forth a closed system of logic. [Us versus Them, In-group versus Out-group, True believers versus Infidels.]

Robert Lifton has identified eight psychological themes that are central to totalistic environments. Terror cult recruiters use these themes in promoting radical behavioral and attitudinal changes in Muslim youth as they convoy them toward terrorism and martyrdom. The parallels to Singer's six conditions are self-evident.

1. Milieu Control. Gossip or expressed doubts are negatively sanctioned and the Muslim recruit is impressed by the rigorous physical and technical explosives and weapons training.

2. Loading the Language. The leaders insist on the jargon of radical Islamist theology and the "groupspeak" and "groupthink" of *Jihad.*

3. Demand for Purity. The us-versus-them orientation in the camps is promoted by an all-or-nothing, "our way or the highway" belief system.

4. Cult of Confession. This is not necessary in Al Qaeda camps because the recruit has no doubts about the evil nature of Jews, Christians, and infidels. He has been exposed to these ideas from the youngest of his childhood school experiences.

5. Mystical Manipulation. A sense of the "higher purpose" of Allah is conveyed as if Osama et al. deem themselves to be Allah's spokespersons. Lifton (1989, 423) says,

> The individual then responds to the manipulations through developing what I shall call the *psychology of the pawn.* Feeling himself unable to escape from forces more powerful than himself, he subordinates everything to adapting himself to them.

6. Doctrine Over Person. The all-encompassing doctrines of the vibrant theology and ideology of radical violent *jihad* are center stage. Individuality and personal freedom are regarded as evil doctrines of the Americans, Jews, and Westerners.

7. Sacred Science. Intellectual and scientific creativity is focused on weapons training, explosives handling, chemical and biological weapons, and computer proficiency for the terror cult's purposes.

8. Dispensing of Existence. The elite, special, and Allah-blessed status of *jihadis* as a superior group with rewards for them personally in paradise, and for their family after they are martyred, is a constant teaching by Islamist gurus.

"IN-BETWEENER" COUNTRIES, COMMUNITIES, AND THEIR YOUTHS

Like "in-betweener" individuals, countries and communities sometimes can become "in-betweeners." They are vulnerable on a larger scale to terror cult recruitment efforts. This is particularly true for late adolescent and disaffected young adult populations. In countries or population groups in transition, such as Afghanistan after the Soviet occupation, Iraq after the defeat of Saddam, among immigrant Muslim youth rioting in France, or in politically unsettled Lebanon after the departure of Syrian armed forces, there are extended periods of vulnerability to the recruitment efforts of terror cults like Al Qaeda. Between their heroic service during the defeat of the Soviets in Afghanistan and their new battles picked with America and the "West," Osama and Zawahiri fit the "in-betweener" pattern we have previously discussed in terms of terror cult recruitment and identity formation. Zarqawi's replacement terror cult leaders in Iraq and the rocket-spewing militant components of Hezbollah and Hamas also are exploiting "in-betweener" populations in southern Lebanon and Gaza.

In her important book, *Terror in the Name of God: Why Religious Militants Kill,* Jessica Stern describes in detail the Madrassah schools in Pakistan. She offers a poignant interview with Syed Qurban, a traditional doctor of herbal medicine and father of seven sons, all of whom were trained as *mujahideen*fighters in Afghanistan. One son died a martyr in the *jihad.* He had been educated through eight grades, learning the *Koran* by heart in a Madrassah. Stern (2003, 220–21) writes:

> Hussain tells me he is happy to have donated a son to the cause of *jihad:* "Whoever gives his life in the way of Allah lives forever and earns a place in heaven for seventy members of his family, to be selected by the martyr. Everyone treats me with more respect now that I have a martyred son. And when there is a martyr in the village, it encourages more children to join the *jihad.* It raises the spirit of the entire village."

Osama's Al Qaeda cult is similar to Rev. Jim Jones's Peoples Temple and David Koresh's Waco Branch Davidians. They all are built on the intricate interweaving of pied piper theology and the "just cause" for the group as posited by the self-appointed malignant messiah. Radical Islamic terror groups like bin Laden's Al Qaeda use and twist Muslim teachings and scripture to suit their own ends in recruiting and indoctrinating recruits. Madrassah schools are like prep schools for *jihad.* These recruits to terror cults come to understand death by martyrdom as a desirable end that brings respect to the martyr's family.

Are there other alternatives to offer such vulnerable populations? Let us examine some less flashy but ultimately more substantial options and possibilities. Certainly a very basic measure would be the use of American foreign aid to sponsor and fund Pakistani schools that are excellent but secular. The president of Pakistan has spoken out in strong support for these programs, but our American media seems to only cover our American pressure for military strikes against Al Qaeda. The quiet, slow-but-certain wheel of educational progress is a more powerful force against radical Islamic terrorist recruiters than hundreds of tanks and smart bombs given to the Pakistani military.

UNOFFICIAL DIPLOMACY

Volkan (2004, 265n4; 1997, 202–24) describes his concept of "Track II or Unofficial Diplomacy." (A detailed discussion of Track II Diplomacy is in Chapter 9.) In this model, nondiplomats from different countries meet for discussions, mutual projects, and efforts to understand each other. This potentially therapeutic intergroup process over time (often many years) has the potential to build friendships and prevent violent conflict—a true preventative medicine and infinitely more valuable than the notion of preemptive war or Abu Ghraib projects.

Creative forms of unofficial diplomacy could involve exchange students and pen-pal relationships between professional colleagues (nondiplomats). American foreign policy does have life or death consequences for us. Can America continue to give billions to repressive dictators in Arab countries with no benefits to the ordinary people? Creative diplomacy, unofficial diplomacy, and empathic foreign aid take creativity, sacrifice, and an exponentially expanded spirit like the early days of the American Peace Corps. And, they offer hope.

BIN LADEN'S FAST AND LOYAL FRIEND AMONG THE TALIBAN

Ahmed Rashid, in his brilliant book *Taliban* (2001, 23–25), says that Mullah Omar is surrounded by extreme secrecy, but does provide some information about Osama's pious, powerful, and loyal brother figure. Rashid documents Mullah Omar's elemental but impressive political leadership skills and effective grasp of stark and powerful, politically applied religious symbolism. Located in Kandahar is the tomb of Ahmad Shah Durrani, the founder of the Durrani dynasty. Next to the tomb is the holy shrine of the Cloak of the Prophet Mohammad. Rashid describes how Mullah Omar, in order to legitimize his role as Afghanistan's leader in 1996, took out the cloak in front of a large crowd of Taliban who named him Amir-ul Momineen, which means "Leader of the Faithful" (Rashid 2001, 20).

Mullah Mohammad Omar was born around 1959 in Nodeh, a village near Kandahar. His family were poor landless peasants of the Hotak tribe of the Ghilzai branch of Pashtuns. Like Osama and many of Osama's colleagues in terror, Omar's father died while he was a young man, which left him to fend for his mother and extended family. Omar's Madrassah studies were interrupted by the war with the Soviets. He had achieved status as a village mullah at a young age. He has three wives, who live in his home village, and five children (Rashid 2001, 23–24).

Mullah Omar is described as tall and well-built, with a long black beard, and he wears a black turban. Despite having a dry and sarcastic wit, he is shy and retiring, though brilliant in his capacity to assess and lead people (Rashid 2001, 24). In light of my formulations about pseudohomosexual issues, rigid sexual attitudes, and unconscious gynephobia among Christian, Jewish, and Muslim radical fundamentalist men, it is interesting that under Mullah Omar's intense leadership, the Taliban clamped down on homosexuality. (Reaction formation? Denial?) Rashid observed that Kandahar's Pashtuns were notorious for the rape of young boys by warlords and, in addition to the drug trade, was a key motive for Mullah Omar's mobilization of the Taliban. The punishments for homosexuality were bizarre, and were the source of endless debates and ruminations by Taliban scholars. Singing, dancing, and television were banned because they prevented the proper study and implementation of Islam (Rashid 2001, 115).

Like other colleagues of Osama bin Laden, Mullah Omar has a deformity (loss of an eye). Omar fought with commander Nek Mohammad of Khalis's Hizb-e-Islami against the Najibullah regime between 1989 and 1992. Omar was wounded four times, once in the right eye, which became permanently damaged (Rashid 2001, 24). Omar has profoundly strong religious convictions and charisma and, like his soul brother Osama, has no hesitancy to defy authority and act as a powerful father figure.

MULLAH OMAR DEFIES AND INSULTS SAUDI PRINCES AND THE AMERICAN PRESIDENT IN DEFENSE OF HIS FRIEND OSAMA BIN LADEN

After the 1998 U.S. embassy bombings in Africa, the United States increased pressure on Saudi Arabia to extradite Osama bin Laden from Afghanistan to the United States. Prince Turki went to Afghanistan to persuade the Taliban to hand over bin Laden. Mullah Omar refused and in essence called the Saudis a pawn of the United States. The angry Saudi government suspended diplomatic relations with and cut off aid to the Taliban (Rashid 2001, 138–39).

After the August 1998 U.S. cruise missile attack on Osama's Afghan training camp, the Taliban was enraged and organized anti-U.S. and UN demonstrations. Mullah Omar verbally attacked and insulted President Clinton, saying,

If the attack on Afghanistan is Clinton's personal decision, then he has done it to divert the world and the American peoples' attention from that shameful White

House affair [Monica Lewinsky] that has proved Clinton is a liar and a man devoid of decency and honor. (quoted in Rashid 2001, 75)

Omar further accused the United States of being the biggest terrorist in the world. He said that Osama was the guest of the Taliban and the Afghan people and that Osama would never be handed over to the United States. Such bold, bombastic, iconoclastic, and defiant statements to the "Western" father/authority figures really appeals to the adolescent rebellion simmering in the disaffected psyches of many adolescents in search of a cause.

Volkan (2004, 156) observes that the very name of the Taliban movement means "students," and that in the post-Soviet power vacuum, the Haggania Madrassah promoted jihadist ideology and taught hatred of infidels and hero worship of Osama bin Laden. Volkan resonates with and extends our theme of Osama's narcissistically tinged search for a father figure, saying:

> It seems to me that in Afghanistan there was a particularly "good fit" between a hurt and victimized country and a man whose extreme hate may be a reflection of personal pain and sense of victimization. Bin Laden first became interested in Afghanistan through his spiritual mentor, Azzam—who, impressed by the devotion and heroism of the *mujahideen,* had moved his family to Pakistan just one year after the Soviet invasion. Already a father figure to bin Laden, Azzam founded the Mujahideen Services House in Peshawar, Pakistan, and supplied help to the Afghan opposition cause, including volunteers to fight. (Volkan 2004, 156–57)

And Osama bin Laden's millions of dollars helped the cause.

Volkan traces the powerful connections between a hurt and victimized country and the spiritual warrior-leader who himself feels personally victimized. A large group or country thus claims a leader to focus its collective hate, revenge, and hoped-for triumph.

Volkan (2004, 157) also asks a fascinating and important question:

> But how does a pathologically vengeful individual such as Osama bin Laden [or Mullah Omar] persuade other individuals to die intentionally for his politico-religious cause?

In essence, Volkan's answer is that through charismatically applied and religiously saturated indoctrination, education, and social approval, a person's large-group identity/group-self is made to supercede his individual identity. Volkan (2004, 159) concludes,

> Thus, future suicide bombers feel normal, and often experience an enhanced self-esteem. They become, in a sense, a spokesperson for the traumatized community and assume that they, at least temporarily, can reverse the shared sense of victimization and helplessness by expressing the community's rage.

HOW TERRORISTS USE TELEVISION TO AID THEIR CELEBRITY STATUS AND APPEAL TO RECRUITS

Cults and terrorism as a means of social rebellion and control have existed since antiquity. In a confounding and paradoxical way, modern media coverage provides a perfect magnified psychodrama stage for the terrorist's ghastly reality drama. If terrorists had to buy television time to cover their events, they would have to pay millions of dollars for what they get for free. The media provides both publicity for the terror event and grandiose narcissistic affirmation of the terror cult and its leader. These issues are clearly in evidence when one studies Osama's low-key, mystical, yet subtly hubristic videotape performances. The terror cult leader becomes an exciting, flamboyant, and darkly charismatic modern television celebrity.

Freud described the leader of a horde or mob as an idealized, mythical hero who symbolizes the original idealization of the Oedipal father. He reflected upon the archaic, powerful sense of closeness in crowds, and concluded that this results from their collective projection of their ego ideals onto the leader. This group regression results in diminished maturity of conscience and collective intelligence. Freud felt that the mobilized group processes of primitive idealization, introjection, and identification were analogous to the uncanny powers of the hypnotist. Freud's comments, I believe, can be directly applied to understanding what Osama, Zarqawi, and al-Zawahiri are trying to mobilize with their video-sermonizing performances. Freud said:

> Even today the members of a group stand in need of the illusion that they are equally and justly loved by their leader; but the leader himself need love no one else, he may be of masterful nature, absolutely narcissistic, self-confident and independent. (Freud [1921] 1958, 8:123)

Freud's concepts can be used to interpret the coaxing, soothing qualities of Osama's hypnotic television efforts, which are modeled on maternal imagery (his mother/himself), and the threatening aspects of his message, derived from a stern father image. Freud comments further as to the paternal imagery, saying:

> The hypnotist awakens in the subject a portion of his archaic heritage which had also made him compliant towards his parents and which had experienced an individual re-animation in his relation to his father; what is thus awakened is the idea of a paramount and dangerous personality, towards whom only a passive masochistic attitude is possible, to whom one's will has been surrendered,—while to be alone with him, "to look him in the face," appears a hazardous experience. It is only in some way as this that we can picture the relationship of the individual member of the primal horde to the primal father. (Freud [1921] 1958, 8:127)

Fortunately, America has not taken a passive masochistic stance toward Osama and Al Qaeda. It is not hard to imagine how exponentially terrifying and uncanny Osama's televised threats would be, if further successful attacks like 9/11 occur. Many people who saw the World Trade towers hit by airliners said, "It was surreal!" or "It looked like a Hollywood movie." In fact, good movie-makers or horror fiction writers exploit the same experience of "the uncanny" that a terrorist does (Freud [1919] 1958, 17:219–52).

Every horror movie screenwriter should read this lesser-known paper by Freud—Stephen King breathes these concepts in his work. The intuitive and/or calculated impact of the terrorist act counts on our tendency to regress to magical, black-and-white, superstitious, or primitive thinking under stress or shock (Freud [1919] 1958, 17:240). Our shocked nervous systems and minds become more fragile and vulnerable. Osama bin Laden had issued threats and warnings months before his terror cult's actions. This gave a magical, grandiose, prophetic quality to the 9/11 events, as if Osama had studied Freud's paper on "The Uncanny."

4 ──

HOW OSAMA AND COMPANY BECOME HEROES TO MUSLIM YOUTH VIA MANIPULATION OF THE WOUNDED GROUP-SELF

I am telling you, and God is my witness, whether America escalates or de-escalates this conflict, we will reply to it in kind, God willing. God is my witness; the youth of Islam are preparing things that will fill your hearts with tears.

—Osama bin Laden, October 6, 2002, via Al Jazeera satellite TV
(Gunaratna 2002, xxvii)

Every young child seems to experience two basic forms of self-love during his or her first three years. At times there is a sense of grandiose-exhibitionistic self-delight; and at other moments, an admiration and resonance with the idealized image of the parent or their surrogate childhood hero (Kohut 1971, 64–67).

The smooth, steady, and healthy integration of the self is facilitated by responsive, empathic, and confidently affirming participation by parents or their surrogates. Empathic parenting helps modify the child's early grandiose fantasies of undue power, ambition, and significance in interaction with the strength of parental heroes. This socialization process provides realizable goals, values, and guiding principles for the young individual. These early, crucial, and transitional self-other experiences with parents or role models provide models in the young mind for self-love, self-esteem, and confidant, responsible actions.

THE GROUP-SELF, AN IMPORTANT DOMAIN OF PAIN AND POWER

A group can become greater or lesser than the sum of its members. There is a parallel process by which an individual's sense of himself as an individual and himself as part of a group is formed (Kohut 1978, 837–38). In essence, inner representations of our self and our self-in-a-group are parallel and conjoined during very early developmental and maturational process experiences.

Volkan (1988, 27–34) has observed that children often experience angry or destructive feelings as dangerous or alien. These dangerous impulses are often displaced onto the external world of "others." This externalizing process is the way we all form a concept of "the enemy," really a projected part of our own feelings. As our sense of self and self-in-a-group is forming, there are other influences besides our parents. These have been called "extensions of the self" (Wintrob 1978, 103), extensions of the group-self experience or "cultural amplifiers" (Volkan 1988, 31). These self-extensions include the national geography or terrain, as well as symbols and monuments such as the flag, churches, mosques, or synagogues. They also often include charismatic political figures from outside the family. Fiery and grandiose hate speeches can stir the rebellion or idealism of youth, whether they are delivered by Nasrallah in Beirut, or Hitler to the throngs of his Nazi youth movement.

The cohesive self formed in preadolescent years is vital for subsequent secure identity formation in one's cultural or community group. In times of societal stress, deprivation, persecution, or crisis, charismatic leaders like Osama bin Laden serve as messianic extensions of the group-self or identity formation. It is at this location that youths are vulnerable to Islamist Malignant Pied Pipers.

IMAGES OF PALESTINE AS "SHARED TRAUMA" FOR ARABS AND MUSLIMS

Most psychologists agree with Erik Erikson, who thought that individual identity is consolidated with enthusiastic intensity in the adolescent years (Erikson 1950, 261–62). Charismatic/messianic culture heroes and antiheroes have a particularly important impact on self and identity formation in young people in countries where parents and families are forced into humiliating refugee camps or other painful group exiles. In his 1986 book, *After the Last Sky: Palestinian Lives,* Edward Said presented poignant examples of families in these dilemmas. Said described the humiliation of the refugee experience in this brief vignette:

> When A. Z.'s father was dying, he called his children, one of whom is married to my sister, into his room for a last family gathering. A frail, very old man from Haifa, he had spent his last 34 years in Beirut in a state of agitated disbelief at the loss of his house and property. Now he murmured to his children the final faltering words of a penniless, helpless patriarch. "Hold on to the keys and the deed," he told them,

pointing to a battered suitcase near his bed, a repository of the family estate salvaged from Palestine when Haifa's Arabs were expelled. These intimate mementos of a past irrevocably lost circulate among us, like the genealogies and fables of a wandering singer of tales. Photographs, dresses, objects severed from their original locale, the rituals of speech and custom: much reproduced, enlarged, thematized, embroidered, and passed around, they are strands in the web of affiliation we Palestinians use to tie ourselves to our identity and to each other. (Said 1986, 14)

Collective empathy in a community group via "chosen traumas" has powerful consequences over several generations.

Enter a Hamas recruiter with a bomb vest.

Volkan (2004, 48–51) describes in detail the role of a "chosen trauma" in the mental life of large groups of people. (Chosen trauma means "the collective mental representation of an event that has caused a large group to face drastic common losses, to feel helpless and victimized by another group, and to share a humiliating injury.")

Volkan points out that such chosen traumas have the associated characteristic of transgenerational transmission. This unconscious process moves beyond sympathy into the actual deposits of injured self-images into the next generation(s). The result is specific task assignments that hope to reverse shame and humiliation, turn passive victimhood into active assertion of power, and mourn the original painful losses. Osama's transgenerational task vis-à-vis his father is saturated with ambivalence. The vast wealth of his father aligned his image with the Saudi ruler friends of the West. Yet Osama's father's piety led Osama to identify with the teachings of radical Islamist clerics after his father's death.

Let us recall that bin Laden's hero-mentor, Azzam, was born in a small village near Jenin, Palestine, in 1941 (Bergen 2001, 55). The hatred of Israelis and radical belief in *jihad* simmered in Azzam and his colleague at al-Azhar University in Cairo, sheikh Omar Abdel Rahman. These mentors and their hero worshippers, Ayman al-Zawahiri (older brother-figure) and bin Laden, make clear the symbolic emotional connection for bin Laden between Egyptian *jihad,* the Palestinian cause, and his search for a radical Islamist "father" to please. The radical Islamist jihadists want to bury us, our allies and our friends in revenge for such symbolic reasons of "chosen traumas."

Osama's childhood losses and the generic Palestinian pain situation described by Said (1986, 38) have profoundly important transgenerational impact on both Osama and Arab and Muslim youth. Zawahiri and Osama found intense bonds of friendship. They both had subtle but important disappointment in and rebellion toward their aristocratic or wealthy families of origin. They formed a new family of Al Qaeda.

Nasser al-Bahri, a key lieutenant and cult follower of Osama bin Laden, has described how he, like Osama, had fallen under the influence of radical Saudi clerics. Al-Bahri responded personally when he heard bin Laden describe his country as an agent of the Americans and pledged to drive America from the Arabian Peninsula. In bin Laden, al-Bahri said, he had found "A new spiritual father" (Mahler 2006, 5).

THE PROFOUND DANGERS OF GROUPTHINK

In the global radical Islamist *jihad* brain trust (Osama bin Laden, Azzam, Zawahiri, Turabi, Rahman, Qutb, etc.), we can see elements of groupthink. Janis and Mann (1972) explain the Bay of Pigs mistake by John F. Kennedy and his entourage according to the "groupthink hypothesis." Janis wrote, "Members of any small cohesive group tend to maintain esprit de corps by unconsciously developing a number of shared illusions and related norms that interfere with critical thinking and reality testing."

The major symptoms of groupthink Janis cited are:

1. A shared illusion of invulnerability, which leads to excessive risks.
2. A shared illusion of unanimity, based on the reluctance of individuals to voice their doubts and the assumption that silence implied consent.
3. The related tendency of group members to self-censor their own misgivings and, in some cases, to discourage others from sharing their concerns with the leader.
4. A tendency for the leader to handle the group's meetings in a way that discouraged discussions of the drawbacks of the emerging plan (Janis and Mann 1972, 35–36).

My hunch is that such groupthink occurred at the many Turabi–bin Laden–Zawahiri planning meetings of Turabi's Islamic Charter Front during 1991–93 (Bodansky 1999, 32–33). Pervasive groupthink occurred as the worldwide *jihad* plans unfolded. Azzam tried to break through the Al Qaeda group *jihad* death-think. Gunaratna (2002, 30–32) says that when Osama's formerly beloved mentor Azzam opposed the slaying of women, children, and noncombatants in the *jihad* terror plans, Osama turned on his father figure Azzam, and probably colluded in his assassination.

Our U.S. president, our government, and the president's entourage/advisors are not immune from groupthink. The George W. Bush administration's philosophy of preemptive war is by no means beyond the dangers of groupthink. It is likely that Vice President Cheney is the leader of distorted groupthink in the current Bush administration. Cheney, Donald Rumsfeld, and Paul Wolfowitz erroneously believed in the faulty intelligence of Ahmed Chalabi and other biased expatriates who supposedly thought coalition troops would be greeted with open arms in Baghdad. At an unconscious level, they as individuals and a small "neocon" group seem to have been caught up in an experience of groupthink. In a sense, the very notion of "preemptive war" requires far more accuracy of intelligence than is humanly possible. The unintelligent intelligence of Bush, Cheney, Condoleezza Rice, Rumsfeld, and Wolfowitz's neocons has now been proven wrong. Many sound expert opinions about vital preparations for the "war after the war" in Iraq were ignored; as were painful lessons from the history of warfare from as far back as Sun Tzu and Thucydides. All very possibly because of the power of "neocon" groupthink and flagrant ignorance about history.

PSYCHOLOGY OF THE GROUP-SELF AND AL QAEDA RECRUITMENT

Al Qaeda finds foot soldier recruits in Muslim communities where parents are humiliated, devastated, and even killed in plain view of their children. Poverty-stricken refugee Muslim communities and even poverty-stricken ghettos of large American cities become spawning grounds for future terrorists. The narcissistic injury to the parent and their surrogates results in wounds to a child's inner hero. This, of course, does not always lead to a career as a terrorist, but vulnerable youths turn outward towards "the extended self" for heroes. Enter the enchanting music and mystical charisma of a rebel hero like Osama bin Laden. He spuriously offers to lead the injured individual and group-self out of psychological exile by turning passive pain into bold actions. As we discussed in the introduction, charismatic radical Islamist terror cult recruiters also exploit the normal tendency of adolescents to rebel against or assert autonomy from their parents and seek noble, exciting, and idealistic causes.

Bin Laden himself is currently an ambivalently disowned outcast from his country and his large family of Saudi millionaires. I hypothesize that he has tried to heal his own disappointments, narcissistic injury, and rage by becoming the self-appointed savior, martyr, and older brother/father/messiah for his followers and admirers. He has been largely successful, as is evidenced by the cheering Arab and Muslim crowds in many places in the world in response to 9/11.

Osama bin Laden's role as a terrorist leader allows him to act out his unconscious inner narcissistic rage at his father, mother, siblings, rejecting homeland, and Saudi Arabia's oil customer/ally/friend America. In this sense, he becomes like most destructive cult leaders. Their deepest motives have to do with power, control, revenge, and overcoming a desperate fear of aloneness and meaninglessness. They do not want a humdrum or ordinary family or vocational life. They have to be legends in their own minds. They gain a sense of power and mastery over their own childhood psychological deformities and feelings of insignificance by becoming overwhelmingly significant and powerful in the lives and destinies of their followers. These Malignant Pied Pipers enter a relentless quest to become strong parental figures for other people in order to finally experience "good parents" within themselves. In Osama's case, he uses the radical, distorted interpretation of the Koran by his mentors/father-figures to mask his inner psychological motivation that really started in his childhood grief, loss, shame, and humiliation. Hopefully Al Qaeda recruiters can be prevented from extensive campaigns in Darfur or among Iraqi youths.

Osama's long search for his father/himself requires a ready supply of child-admirers, whom they find in their cult recruits. Beneath the outward confidence, smoothness, false piety, and swagger of Malignant Pied Pipers is an unconscious sense of shame, rage, and fear of humiliation or aloneness. The terror cult honeymoon is eventually over, and the formerly neglected and abandoned leader now becomes the neglecter and abandoner. Evidence for this occurred on bin Laden's videotape issued after the 9/11 events. He smugly chuckled about his clever strategy of not informing most of the terrorist plane hijackers about the essence of their suicide death missions.

OTHER IDEOLOGUES, THEOLOGIANS, AND THEORETICIANS OF ISLAMOFACISM'S SPURIOUS UTOPIA

We have discussed many theologians and theorists of violent *jihad* besides Osama bin Laden. In addition to Osama and his mentors and immediate colleagues, there are earlier and even more elemental advocates of pure violence as a concrete and political means of achieving freedom for the masses of an oppressed people. Such intellectual leaders are not easily dismissed because of the depth of their experience and ideas. In fact, during any turbulent and rapid social change or revolution, would-be utopian dictators always assassinate intellectuals, academics, and journalists who oppose their views. Throughout history, from Hitler, to Mao, to Pol Pot, and recently Osama bin Laden's minions' assassination of Ahmed Shah Massoud, this heinous point is illustrated.

Frantz Fanon's "Thanatos" and His Tragic Embrace of Violence

Thirty years before Osama bin Laden's advocacy of violence and terror for political purposes, there were dramatic advocates of violence such as Frantz Fanon. I have struggled to moderate my counter-transference anger at Fanon because he was a psychiatrist and psychotherapist like myself. He, like al-Zawahiri, chose to violate his oath of Hippocrates.

Frantz Fanon was born on the Caribbean island of Martinique in 1925. He fought in the French army during World War II, earning medals of distinction. After gaining his credential as a physician, he took the post of chief of the psychiatric department at Blida, Algeria. He resigned his post in 1956 in protest against the brutality of the Algerian war and joined the FNL *(Front de Liberation Nationale)*. Fanon became the permanent ambassador of the All-African People's Congress in 1960 when he tragically learned that he had leukemia. He spent his dying days in Europe in 1961 writing his powerful tirade, *The Wretched of the Earth.* He attacked not only colonialism but the bourgeois regimes that unfairly inherited power in Africa. Fanon maintained that Africa had only obtained "false decolonization" that had left the real power in the hands of foreigners and their "agents" among the ruling elite. True socialism could be established in Africa only by violent overthrow of the entire system. Experts regard Fanon's polemic as a bible for revolutionary enthusiasts around the Third World (Meredith 2005, 146–47).

Fanon brimmed with his angry reaction to clinical work with victims of the Algerian war and maintained that violence is positive and creative. His chilling statement eerily echoes in modern Islamist terrorists' bombs and missiles.

> Violence alone, violence committed by the people, violence organized and educated by its leaders, makes it possible for the masses to understand social truths and gives the key to them. Without that struggle, without that knowledge of the practice of action, there is nothing but a fancy-dress parade and the blare of trumpets. There is nothing save a minimum of readaptation, a few reforms at the top, a flag waving: and down there at the bottom an undivided mass, still living in the middle ages, endlessly marking time. (Fanon [1961] 1963, 147)

We will never know how much intensity of Fanon's *Thanatos* message was driven by his awareness of his rapidly approaching death. He was only 36 when he died and may, like many brilliant people, have matured to have found other nonviolent domains of literary expression and political action to resolve his narcissistic rage at the inevitable scourges of war and injustice.

Kohut (1971) describes the process of resolution of narcissistic rage and woundedness that often occurs towards the end of a successful psychotherapy process of persons with narcissistic problems.

> In evaluating the patient's progress, it is of decisive significance for the analyst [therapist] to ascertain that the patient's devotion to his values and ideals is not that of a fanatic but is accompanied by a sense of proportion which can be expressed through humor. The coexistence of idealism and humor demonstrates not only that the content and psychological locus of the narcissistic positions have changed but also that the narcissistic energies are now tamed and neutralized and that they are following an aim-inhibited course. If on the one hand, the patients values now occupy of greater psychological importance, have become integrated with his ego's realistic goal structure, and quietly give new meaning to his life, while, on the other hand, he is now able to contemplate with humor the very area of the formerly rigidly held narcissistic positions, then the analyst [therapist] may indeed feel that the working-through processes have been successful and that the gains which have been made are solid. (324–25)

I think there are similar domains of genuine resolution of narcissistic rage that occur through creative experiences with Track II diplomacy and genuine intellectual exchanges and benevolent projects with friends and colleagues in other countries. My strong counter-transference wish as I read Fanon is that he might have found a good psychotherapy experience so that his work as a therapist and writer might have found outlets in what Kohut (1971, 197, 299–328) called the "higher transformations of narcissism; i.e. empathy, wisdom, humor, and creativity." As we have seen often in this study, successful political leadership activities and creative accomplishment takes high levels of ego strength, wisdom, empathy, humor, and creative listening. Fanon truthfully describes injustices suffered by oppressed groups that sound exactly like radical Islamist invectives spoken by Osama bin Laden, Ayman al-Zawahiri, et al. When creative and charismatic/messianic men like Osama bin Laden, al-Zawahiri, Rahman, and Fanon, respond predominantly out of their grandiosity and narcissistic rage, we could label their ghastly creations like 9/11—"Lower transformations of narcissism."

Perhaps one of the crucial aspects of modern Western diplomacy and Track II diplomacy is the engagement of African and Mid-Eastern Muslim scholars, intellectuals, theologians, social scientists, and political theorists in respectful dialogue directed toward creative changes in American foreign policy and global economic engagement. Perhaps even the United Nations might move beyond the hypocrisy of its sad scandals and begin encouraging the respectful dialogues mentioned above.

Abu Musab al-Suri: Theorist of *Jihad*

Suri is another theoretician and theologian of the death politics of Islamofascism. Born into a middle-class family in Aleppo, Syria, in 1958, he is described as red-haired and sturdily built. He has a black belt in judo and his real name is said to be Mustafa Setmarian Nasar. Suri studied engineering at the University of Aleppo where like many jihadists he got involved in politics. He moved to Jordan, where he joined the Muslim Brotherhood that opposed the Syrian dictator, Hafez al-Assad. In 1982 Assad killed about 30,000 people in the city of Hama, a Muslim Brotherhood base. Shocked by such violent action, Suri renounced the brotherhood and moved to Europe for several years. After he married and obtained Spanish citizenship, Suri moved to Afghanistan, where he met Osama bin Laden. He was greatly critical of Osama's training camps because they were disorganized and taught no ideology or Islamist doctrine (Wright 2006, 48).

Suri moved back to Spain in 1992, where he established a terrorist cell, and soon moved to London, where he wrote articles for *Al Ansar,* whose editor, the Palestinian cleric Abu Qatada, was regarded as the spiritual guide of Al Qaeda in Europe. Suri and others in their *jihadi* think tank began planning to undermine the despotic regimes in the Arab world and promote attacks on the largely unaware West. The Saudis regarded Suri as far more radical than Osama in the early 1990s, when Al Qaeda was largely an anticommunist organization.

Suri and the very puritanical Salafi *jihadis* used the presence of American troops in the Arabian Peninsula and the Saudi royal family's complicity in that to stoke bin Laden's anger (Wright 2006, 50).

Wright (2006, 50) was told by Peter Bergen, who had spent time with Suri, that Suri is tough, smart, intellectual, and a serious student of history. Suri, who greatly admired the Taliban, told Osama in 1999 that he was endangering the Taliban regime with his highly theatrical attacks on American targets. Suri mocked bin Laden's narcissistic love of publicity (Wright 2006, 50). Suri saw his legacy as the codifier of doctrines that would inspire future generations of Muslim youths for religious war. In 2002, in an Iranian hideout, Suri began writing his 1,600-page magnum opus called "Call for Worldwide Resistance," which was published on the Internet in 2004. Suri writes chilling words about creating the greatest number of casualties for America and its allies. He specifically hates Jews but does not leave out NATO, Russia, China, atheists, pagans, and hypocrites.

Suri regrets the demise of the Taliban, which he and Salafi *jihadis* see as the modern world's only true Islamic government. Suri thinks the next stage of *jihad* will be carried out by small groups or individuals which he calls "leaderless resistance." Later he predicts war on an "open front." Suri cleverly supports the use of democracy to gain broader public support. Hamas in Gaza may be an example of a clever Suri doctrine. Suri does caution against harming other Muslims, women and children, and other noncombatants. Suri saw the American occupation of Iraq as a wonderful rescue of the *jihadi* movement. What an example of how difficult it is for our U.S. president's entourage to spot the paradoxes of our foreign policies and military actions. Clearly one implication of the findings of this study is that American diplomats and politicians need to listen more carefully to our allies and enemies in the Middle East and in the rest of the world. Often our arrogant and narcissistic-sounding American position is presented as if it were some special privilege or reward for Iran's or North Korea's or Syria's leader to speak with our leader or his plenipotentiary. Often we arrogantly demand something from a sovereign enemy country before we will even talk with them or listen to them. To talk to and listen to an enemy is not to be weak or acquiescent.

TURNCOATS: AL QAEDA RECRUITS FROM NON-ARAB AND NON-MUSLIM COUNTRIES

1. Angry or Rebellious Young Idealists and Dreamers

Adam Gadahn—An Angry American Traitor's Televised Voice of Al Qaeda

Adam Gadahn is a 25-year-old American raised in Orange County, California. He calls himself "Azzam the American." Like Osama—Adam searches for his father/himself.

Gadahn is the son of a psychedelic musician, Phil Pearlman, who changed the family name to Gadahn and dropped out of social-climbing society to become a goat farmer in Winchester, South Los Angeles, when Adam was very young. Pearlman is the son of a prosperous Jewish physician and his Protestant wife. While at the University of California, Pearlman was in the counterculture movement and grew long hair and a beard. In an article by Khatchadourian, Pearlman was described by friends as a lovable contrarian, but gentle and almost Christ-like. Pearlman apparently had a spiritual epiphany experience after he found an abandoned Bible on the beach (Khatchadourian 2007, 52). Pearlman felt a divine presence as he read his new-found Bible, and he was affected so deeply that he alluded to it in his music. Phil's 1975 album, called "Relatively Clean Rivers," has lyrics that describe a world that has wandered from divine truth into a Babylon-like confusion (Khatchadourian 2007, 52). In this same album, Pearlman called for peace in the Middle East, with visions of Arabs and Jews cooperating.

Khatchadourian points out that Gadahn refers to the Jewish Biblical warrior Joshua, who, with the aid of trumpets, defeated Israel's enemies as the walls of Jericho fell. I assume Phil denounced American idolatry as Joshua denounced Israeli idolatry, and recently Adam Gadhan's mentors in Al Qaeda denounce American and Western materialism and idolatry.

In his song lyrics, Pearlman clearly regarded the world's governments as too materialistic and hypocritical to achieve peace. Like his son Adam, Phil makes threats in the form of hippie-flavored apocalyptic prophecies in his song lyrics. Adam's threats to America win the oedipal battle with his father by threats of greater violence. I think Adam might have been listening and watching Phil's shifting use of Christianity to adjust to his own spiritual needs. Shifting religious commitments by parents creates precipitous in-betweener issues for teenagers, and this can be associated with involvement with cults and Satanism (Olsson 1980, 173–74). Adam, who also has made dramatic religious shifts, said in an essay after his conversion to Islam:

> My father was raised agnostic or atheist, but he became a believer in One God when he picked up a bible left on the beach. (Khatchadourian 2007, 52)

It is significant that the Gadahns gave Adam the middle name of Yahije, after the Arabic name for John the Baptist. John the Baptist is believed by Muslims to be a prophet. As a boy, Adam was described as shy and very bright. His Jewish physician grandfather Pearlman bragged that Adam could read sections of the encyclopedia when he was six (Khatchadourian 2007, 53).

Adam is one of four children who worked on the family goat farm and was home-schooled in a nominally Christian and religiously eclectic home. According to a September 13, 2005, *Melbourne (Australia) Herald Sun* article, Adam had his first exposure to Islam as a boy through the family business. His father slaughtered the goats according to Islamic law. During his teens Adam began to rebel against his family and society in general. He grew to love death metal music.

In 1993, Adam moved out of the home to live with his grandparents. Significantly, his grandfather is a Jewish physician. He wrote articles for a "death metal" publication called *Xenophobia* and grew to learn about Islam through Internet chat rooms. On a Web site, he wrote,

> I discovered that the beliefs and practices of Islam fit my personal theology and intellect as well as basic human logic. Having been around Muslims during my formative years, I knew well that they were not the bloodthirsty, barbaric terrorists that the news media and televangelists painted them out to be. (Pappsbody 2005, 3)

So, Adam Gadahn drifted rebelliously away from his parents' eclectic religious tastes (the family name had been changed from the obviously Jewish name, Pearlman, to Gadahn) and his grandparents' Jewish home to hang out at the Islamic Center of Orange County. Adam was at that time a classic "in-betweener" who was in between his parents' and grandparents' homes and a job or school. There at the Orange County Mosque, 15-year-old Adam fell under the influence of two naturalized U.S. citizens who were also radical Muslims: Khalil Deek, a Palestinian computer repairman, and Hisham Diab, an Egyptian accountant. These men lived in apartments in an Anaheim area called "Little Gaza." Adam met them at the mosque and Diab's ex-wife said that Diab brought the hungry boy Adam in and asked her to feed him. After that innocent beginning, the two Islamists began indoctrinating Adam with their extremist views. The president of the Islamic Society of Orange County thought that they had such extremist views that he barred them from the mosque. They openly called Islamic Society president Haitham Bundakji an infidel because he reached out to Christians and Jews. At one point Adam assaulted Bundakji. (Did the Imam represent Adam's *repressed* and *displaced* rage and disappointment in his grandfather and father?) In this sense, Adam seems to have a common dynamic with his admired and worshipped mentor Osama bin Laden. Adolescents, though they put down their fathers in their struggles for independence, need strong, caring male role models to help channel their energies towards healthy vocational, ethical, and spiritual development. Even painful narcissistic wounds can be sources of wisdom, humor, and creativity if fathers and family friends or clergy care and connect their care directly with the adolescent. However, the recruitment process of Adam Gadahn sounds sadly like a familiar Malignant Pied Piper tune.

Friends and family members of Deek and Diab say that the two were loyal and avid followers of Omar Adbel Rahman, the blind sheikh. Diab and Deek hosted Rahman, who stayed in Deek's and Diab's apartments during one visit to lecture at local mosques. Saraah Olson, who divorced Diab in 1996, had cooked dinner for Rahman, but says that Gadahn never met the sheikh. Krikorian and Riza (2006, 1) recount how Rahman later would call Deek and Diab from prison so they could record his fiery sermons over the telephone.

Adam Gadahn was a follower of Rahman and, in 1999, he was secretary for Diab's "Charity Without Borders," which according to its charter was founded to "provide an education and humanitarian aid to poor and needy people in the U.S.A. and other countries." The group raised $150,000 that was sent to extremist groups in the Middle East.

Gadahn had gone to Peshwar in Pakistan in 1998. Adam participated in Al Qaeda camps and has met key Al Qaeda leaders, and it has become clear that Osama bin Laden is very interested in "home-grown" American converts. Since 2004 Gadahn has become increasingly open with his articulate and severe threats to the United States and Australia. The detailed study of Gadahn's conversion to radical Islam reveals how vulnerable many adolescent in-betweeners are to the Malignant Pied Piper music of radical Islam. Many in-betweener young Americans are unfortunately not immune to seduction by Al Qaeda's pied piper music. Adam Gadahn, the "American Voice of Al Qaeda," might very well become the master recruiter of rebellious and disaffected young Americans. Father hatred and father hunger go hand in hand in many radical fundamentalists.

John Walker Lindh—The American or Marin Taliban

Walker prefers to be called Hamza Walker Lindh, but was called Suleyman al-Faris during his time in Afghanistan. Twenty-four-year-old John Walker Lindh is currently in a medium security federal prison, having served four years of his plea-bargained 20-year prison sentence for providing services to the Taliban in Afghanistan. John's family and lawyers have understandably given out minimal or selective information, and the information they have given makes John Walker Lindh sound like a sincere, idealistic young California dreamer in search of Islamic identity. A Lindh attorney, Tony West, who has spent many hours with Lindh, says of his devout Muslim client,

> [John] is one of the most sincere individuals I have ever met. I'd describe him as someone with dual qualities. He is on the one hand very naïve—most of what he understood about the world up until 2001 came from what he read in books. He was well read, but not street smart. When you talk to him you realize that you are talking to someone who is very young. At the same time, he has seen things we'll never see. He has experienced horrors of war none of us will ever experience. It gives him an age and wisdom that are very disconcerting. It is an aura that is very familiar to people who live in war-torn areas. (Ashley 2005, 2)

Lawyer Henry Mark Holzer's Web site provides an in-depth, meticulously chronicled account of the charges against John Walker Lindh. Holzer cites data to support the notion that John Walker Lindh in his own words embraced the spirit and plans of Al Qaeda and the radical Islamism of the Taliban to a greater degree than his lawyers would have the public believe. In all fairness, however, John was under stressful, physically painful, and dire circumstances when he expressed devotion to Al Qaeda and criticism or disdain for his country. Holzer describes in voluminous detail the legal conundrums of John Walker Lindh, the U.S. government, and our president and attorney general during the legal maelstroms before a plea bargain was reached to relieve our country from a painful "Solomon cut the baby in half" kind of situation. After 9/11, our country did not seem able to accept that an ordinary U.S. teenager could embrace the evil perpetrators of 9/11 like bin Laden. In fact, John Walker Lindh illustrates some of the key dynamics and in-betweener vulnerabilities of young people to recruitment by terror cult leaders that I have discussed earlier.

If attorney Holzer on his Web site represents one angle of description of John Walker Lindh, and Walker's lawyers another (Ashley 2005, 1–4), then we need to turn to other sources to seek information on John's psychological development and family history. Walker was born in Washington, D.C., to Marilyn Walker and Frank Lindh. John was baptized a Catholic and grew up in Silver Spring, Maryland, until his family moved to San Anselmo, California (Marin County), when he was 10 years old. Walker was sickly as a child with an intestinal disorder and later, after trying several middle schools, his family decided to home-school him after he was 12. He rarely left home and participated constantly in Internet chat rooms, where he became a devoted fan of hip-hop music. He used fake names and sometimes pretended to be black. He saw the Spike Lee film *Malcolm X,* which made a big impression on him and coincided with his interest in Islam. After his health improved, John enrolled at Redwood High School but had trouble fitting in, so he took an independent study program and received a GED at age 16.

John's father, Frank Lindh, is a lawyer for Pacific Gas and Electric Company, and his mother, Marilyn Walker, is an office manager for a small Marin firm. John Walker Lindh's parents' marriage had serious problems throughout his adolescent years and ended in a divorce in 1999. According to Wikipedia, the *San Francisco Examiner* and family friends reported that Frank Lindh was a closeted homosexual. Though controversial, it is said by some observers that discovering his father's homosexuality was traumatic for the teenaged Lindh and might account for disillusionment with U.S. society and his seeking identity elsewhere (Wikipedia). As we have discussed previously, there are often traumatic events in the life history of terrorists, and the issue of homosexual or pseudohomosexual dynamics in radical Islamists or their recruits is often a factor.

Frank Lindh is reported to have moved in with a male lover in 1997, at which time John Walker Lindh, aged 16, dropped his father's name in favor of his mother's name, Walker. He subsequently and officially converted to Islam and began attending mosques in Mill Valley and San Francisco. In 1998, the 18-year-old Walker traveled to Yemen for 10 months to study Arabic so he could read the Koran in its original language. He returned to live with his family in the United States for eight months in 1999. He returned to Yemen in February 2000 and then left for Pakistan to study in an austere Madrassah— al-Iman University. Khizar Hayat, a Pakistani businessman, paid for Walker's Madrassah school. (It is perplexing as to why Walker did not seek financial help for the Madrassah school from his parents, who had both supposedly encouraged his Islamic faith and his study of Arabic. They certainly could afford to have helped him. Was he reluctant to reveal his new radical Islamist leanings and mentors?)

Time magazine reported in October 2002 that Khizar Hayat said that he had a homosexual relationship with Walker. Both John Walker Lindh and his lawyers have denied this report. The *Guardian* magazine reports that the story occurred as a result of confusion in translation of Hayat's broken English. *Time* had said that Hayat had a good knowledge of English and only later changed his story. The homosexual or pseudohomosexual dynamic would be compatible with Walker's passive behavior style and his likely traumatic discovery of his father's homosexual orientation during his stressful adolescent passage. The issue of conflicts about fathers and *Father Hunger* (Herzog, 2001) are recurrent themes among leaders and followers in terror cult groups.

It seems likely that radical Islamist influence led Walker to join the Taliban army in 2001. He purportedly spent seven weeks in an Al Qaeda training camp near Kandahar, where he met Osama bin Laden (Ashley 2005, 2; Henry Mark Holzer Web site). Walker was first captured on November 25, 2001, by the Afghan Northern Alliance forces and questioned by CIA agent Mike Spann, as was repeatedly shown on national television. After the violent prison riot and the death of Spann, Walker was held by U.S. forces and eventually brought to his controversial and legally complex trial, described in vast detail by Henry Mark Holzer on his Web site. Again we see how vulnerable adolescent in-betweeners can be to radical Islamist recruiters.

2. Angry Young Rebels in Search of a Cause

Jose Padilla

Jose Padilla is a 36-year-old man who sometimes calls himself Abdullah al-Muhajir. Padilla's parents moved to the United States from Puerto Rico and he was born in Brooklyn, New York. He became a member of the Latin Kings street gang after his family moved to Chicago, Illinois. Padilla was arrested in Florida in 1991 over a road-rage shooting incident and spent a year in jail. (Again, that prison thing.) A neighbor said his mother was worried about him and one source (BBC 2005) says that he was implicated in a gangland murder when he was 13.

He was arrested several times, and after serving time for aggravated assault, he converted to Islam and, like many new converts of many religious groups, he professed a nonviolent philosophy. He participated in the Masjid Al-Iman mosque in Fort Lauderdale, Florida. His colleague and friend Adham Amin Hassoun was a registered agent for Benevolence International Foundation, a charitable trust that U.S. investigators accused of funding terrorist activities. Accused of consorting with radical Islamic fundamentalists such as Al Qaeda, Hassoun was arrested in 2002 for overstaying his visa (Wikipedia). Padilla traveled to Egypt, Saudi Arabia, Afghanistan, Pakistan, and Iraq. He was tracked as an Al Qaeda groupie and arrested at Chicago's O'Hare Airport on May 8, 2002, because of significant evidence that he had been trained in the making and using of a "dirty nuclear bomb" (Wikipedia).

Significant to this book is the theme of Padilla's prison recruitment and his prolonged adolescent acting out and rebellious search for an exciting identity. Psychopathic and narcissistic character patterns as well as the in-betweener phenomenon are important warning signs among prison populations.

Richard Reid

Richard Reid, the infamous but thankfully incompetent "Shoe-Bomber," is the son of an English mother and Jamaican father who was born in 1973 in the London suburb of Bromley. Richard's father Robin Reid had been in prison for most of Richard's childhood. Robin Reid told the BBC, "I was not there to give him the love and affection he should have had." Richard fell into a life of petty crime and, in the 1990s, was jailed in several youth prisons for assault. In Feltham prison, Reid converted to Islam. (Again that hermetic prison thing.) After his release from prison Richard, like many prison colleagues, went to Brixton Mosque in south London. This mosque is known for attracting and helping ex-offender converts adjust to life in the world outside prison. Initially he did well, calling himself Abdel Rahim. Abdul Haqq Baker, the chairman of the Brixton Mosque, says that at some point Reid was "tempted away" by Islamist extremists. Baker told the BBC that the extremists worked on "weak characters" and that Reid was "very, very impressionable." (A ripe in-betweener, as are so many Al Qaeda recruits.)

Reid began to challenge the peaceful philosophy of his teachers and changed his dress from Western clothes to traditional Islamic robes with a khaki combat jacket on top. Some speculate that he met Zacarias Moussouai, the 9/11 conspirator, during this "father-hungry" period. Moussouai, who attended the Brixton Mosque during the 1990s, was expelled from the mosque because of his extremist views. Reid apparently began travels to Egypt, Turkey, Pakistan, Belgium, the Netherlands, France, and Afghanistan to test security procedures on many airlines. On December 22, 2001, Reid was on Flight 63 from Paris to Miami.

He was overpowered by passengers and crew on the flight after trying to light a fuse connected to explosives in his shoe (BBC 2001).

A fair question raised here is: Are there ways that are minimally intrusive whereby Western intelligence officers can engage in monitoring of in-betweener groups or individuals that have the potential for recruitment of young people for their dangerous and radical causes? More importantly, can specially trained teachers, diplomats, and "peace corps" workers listen to and dialogue with these vulnerable young persons before they are brainwashed, are recruited by Islamists, or seek out Al Qaeda? Reid highlights the extreme level of susceptibility to recruitment by the radical Islamist terror cultists in England.

SUICIDE BOMBERS: PSYCHODYNAMIC PERSPECTIVES ON OSAMA AND COMPANY'S FOOT SOLDIERS

What follows are word snapshots of two ordinary teenagers about to blow up. They are montages the author composed based on his study of many interviews presented in popular magazines and newspapers. They attempt to capture the simultaneous teenage ordinariness and yet a sad, extraordinarily painful, and futile search for identity.

SHIRA

My name is Shira. I am seventeen. I live with my family in Gaza. My ugly, dumb brother is Mohammad. He is fifteen and goes to school taught by Mullahs who are very strong and strict. Mohammad and I were very close when we were little. Now I don't like him anymore because he acts like he is more important than me. My father's smile shines all over my brother. Father seems to not pay as much attention to me anymore. Mohammad prays every morning and every evening. He rocks back and forth like a rocking chair when he prays. I think he is hypnotized. Mohammad says the Koran tells him special things when he reads it. I wish I were special too. The Mullah at Mohammad's school loves him so much that he thinks he will be chosen to be a martyr-bomber of Israelis. My mother and father have already built a shrine to Mohammad's memory after he blows up. Our parents are so proud of Mohammad's study about how to use the bomb-belt. It takes a lot of prayer and study to be a bomber. The prayer is just as important as the special bomb-belt.

My parents and the Mullah don't know that I know as much as Mohammad does about bombs, prayer, and dying with dignity. Tomorrow, before they all wake up— I will be gone to Israel with the bomb belt on. Allah will make me one of his favorite wives because so many Jews will die tomorrow. I feel Arafat and Allah's smile

glowing beyond my morning sky explosion coming soon. I win, Mohammad!!
Love, Shira

(Shira was one of the first female Palestinian suicide bombers.)

ISMAIL

My name is Ismail. I am so scared. I know I will pee my pants before I die. The
bomb men of Emir Zarqawi checked my bomb carefully. It will go off when I crash
this van into the police station. The bomb men are duct-taping my feet to the accel-
erator of the van. That will help me keep my promise to Allah and the honor of my
family. My mother can now easily feed my little brothers and sisters. The Imam will
smile when he hears how many American and Iraqi infidel soldiers have died from
my big bomb blast. My bomb will help get the American soldiers out of my country.
I will be a hero. Now I go faster, faster—I will never stop or slow down. Don't pee,
don't pee. I picture Allah's smile in my mind now.
    BOOOOOM!

The use of terror tactics as military and political tools to achieve positions
of power and control has existed since antiquity. Suicide bombing as a terror tool
is a relatively new tactical phenomenon. The first suicide bombing operation
was performed in Beirut in 1983 (Remnick 2006). These suicide bombing operations increased dramatically during the second Palestinian *Intifada* in the
1990s; the tactic was also used in Sri Lanka and Chechnya during this same time
(Speckhard 2004). The September 11 attacks in the United States were disastrous
and devastating suicide attacks, but suicide attacks have also taken the lives of
thousands of Iraqi citizens and American soldiers since the war in Iraq started in
2003.

Many books and articles are being written about the political, military, economic, religious, and intelligence aspects of terrorism. Let's focus specifically on
psychiatric and psychodynamic perspectives of suicide bombing. What sort of
people are suicide bombers? Do they suffer from a mental disorder or personality
disturbance? What was their upbringing? Are there psychodynamic or psychoge-
netic connections involved with their behavior? Some of these studies reviewed
here involved individuals who were potential suicide bombers but who were
captured and interviewed before they actually committed the act.

PSYCHIATRIC DIAGNOSES?

One surprising finding is that the studies failed to find any severe psychopathology in a traditional descriptive sense among these individuals. None of these
individuals suffered from psychotic disorders or even clinical depression (Post,
Sprinzak, and Denny 2001). Paradoxically, people with significant mental illness

are usually excluded by the terrorist "in-group" from involvement in terrorist groups or acts because they do not tolerate the rigors of training, preparation, planning, or teamwork required for terror bombings.

THE SPIRITUAL-RELIGIOUS DOMAIN

In 2001 a leading Muslim cleric in the Palestinian-controlled territory explained the role of martyrdom in Islamic thinking to Jeffrey Goldberg. He said that a (radical) Muslim embraces death. The Israeli society, he said, is selfish in its love of life, and its people will leave the land rather than die for it. A (radical) Muslim is happy to die. During his visit to Gaza, Goldberg describes a chilling scene involving a game played by the three-year-old, five-year-old, and six-year-old sons of a terrorist leader. The game is called *shuhada* which means martyrs. The youngest played the martyr who pretended to rush an imaginary Israeli bunker. When he pretended to be shot dead, he was carried away to a mock funeral, only to leap up from an imaginary grave shouting "Allahu Akbar" (God is greatest) with giggles (Goldberg 2001, 34, 36).

MORE SUBTLE DOMAINS OF PERSONALITY DISORDER OR PERTURBATION

Sageman (2004, 82–91) is very skeptical about even subtle forms of childhood trauma being found in terrorists' or suicide bombers' personal histories, much less narcissistic, paranoid, or rigid authoritarian personality disorders. My study disagrees with Sageman and advocates a closer look at subtler psychodynamic narcissistic personality patterns that intertwine with social self-psychological and group-self dynamic factors to account for suicide-bombing behavior.

MOTIVATION AND MEANING IN SUICIDE BOMBERS

Despite the terrible nature of suicide bomber behavior, it is nevertheless a human behavior. Theoretically, every human behavior has motivation and meaning. So, what is the motivation for and meaning of suicide bombing?

We will look at two ways of thinking about answers to these questions. One perspective comes from psychoanalytic theories about unconscious motivations for such behavior. The other perspective comes from social psychology, where motivating and causal factors are located in the social, political/community, and family environment of the suicide bomber. Obviously, these approaches have some overlapping elements. For instance, the unconscious of each individual is in part formed in the context of relationships with family members and with the community group of origin.

PSYCHOANALYTIC PERSPECTIVES

Some psychoanalysts emphasize the concept of narcissism and narcissistic injury as a basis for understanding terrorist behavior (Olsson 2005, 12–13, 150–51). Narcissism refers to the domain of self-love, but it is important to remember that narcissism does not necessarily mean selfishness, and a certain amount of narcissism is important to maintain healthy self-esteem and social functioning. But when do problems occur?

Problems occur if narcissistic injury occurs early in individual development. This narcissistic injury occurs because of the failure of caregivers to provide a suitable environment for healthy development. The presence of love, accurate empathy, emotional acceptance, and moral instruction of the child leads to a level of basic trust (Erikson 1950, 249). Such basic trust makes it more likely that a person will be a capable, moral, and peaceful individual. He or she can more readily obtain a genuine love of self and the group-self.

If this love was not available or is massively disrupted by social upheaval or instability, a narcissistic injury or crisis is more likely to occur. Narcissistic injury results in low self-confidence and low self-esteem with subsequent mobilization of narcissistic defenses like grandiose fantasies and reactive narcissistic rage. These inner crises interact with tensions in the family and the community. Recall Volkan's observation:

> Future suicide bombers feel normal, and often experience an enhanced self-esteem. They become, in a sense, a spokesperson [through action] for the traumatized community and assume that they, at least temporarily, can reverse the shared sense of victimization and helplessness by expressing the community's rage. (Volkan 2004, 159)

The author and other psychoanalysts believe the dynamics of these narcissistic injuries are deeply embedded in individuals who organize, lead, plan, and perform suicide operations. Their community of origin may thus participate in the suicide bombing by a vicarious process. Whole communities or countries can be breeding grounds for narcissistic injury and collective woundedness. The volatile Gaza Strip and parts of contemporary Baghdad are hotbeds of narcissistic rage.

We can classify suicide bombing cult groups as 1) leaders and organizers, or 2) followers and performers.

Leaders and Organizers of Suicide Bombers

Here, narcissistic injuries and the consequent anxiety about the self and the external world lead to an unconscious *reaction formation*. Reaction Formation is a *defense mechanism,* operating unconsciously, wherein attitudes and behavior are adopted that are the opposites of impulses the individual harbors either consciously or unconsciously. For example, excessive moral zeal may be a reaction to strong but repressed asocial or antisocial impulses.

Among leaders and organizers, the state of low self-esteem is converted to a sense of unusual self-importance. The leaders come to think they have special abilities; they are convinced that they have special abilities in reasoning and judgment. Such a superiority complex leads to a sense of entitlement about dominating and controlling other people. The terrorist convinces himself that he acts for the benefit of others in his community, even if it includes extremes of abuse and violence. Black-and-white thinking prevails.

This feeling of special status in fact reflects a sluggish self, a self that is unable to feel its genuine significance because of the psychological neglect or distortions via rigid, narrow dogmatic moral teaching during its early development.

Techniques and Circumstances of Terror Cult Recruitment

What kind of ideology or approach do terror cult leaders use to attract followers? In regressed communities that feel victimized, a rigid, moralistic, and fundamentalist ideology is provided to bolster group self-confidence. The unconscious aim of the leader may be to rebel against the early disappointments in his life, but on the surface he becomes a strong and charismatic leader. This dramatic terror-group leadership experience and identity compensates for his inner weakened or injured self. He might have otherwise gone unnoticed by others. This need for a feeling of strength is evidenced by Osama bin Laden's continuous search for strong father figures among men like Azzam, al-Zawahiri, and Turabi. It is also found in his effort to be a great warrior father figure himself (Olsson 2005, 136–41). This rebellion and revolutionary attitude gets expressed in dramatic suicide bombing operations and giant explosions.

Suicide Cult Followers and Performers

The narcissistic injuries to followers in adolescence result in low self-esteem. This affects the developmental processes through which these individuals pass. According to Erik Erikson's psychosocial (epigenetic) model of personality development, individuals develop an ego identity by late adolescence. This identity is assimilated from the emotional, intellectual, and moral standards in the family and community. If this stage of identity formation is passed through successfully, the individual will have a clear identity—i.e., a sense of who he is and where he comes from, as well as his role in society and in life in general.

In other words, the lack of feelings of basic trust (Erikson) and lost self, fragmented self, or false self (Kohut, Winnicott) caused by unresolved early life adversities results in failure to develop a solid identity. Instead, a diffused identity is formed, a vague identity that does not grasp an authentic meaning of existence. This vague identity continues to create cravings for clearer definition and meaning. These individuals may become susceptible to recruitment and brainwashing by charismatic leaders. The low self-esteem of followers leads them to identify with the strong outlook of the leaders. In this way a spontaneously organized network is formed with strong bonds and destructive plans.

I use the analogy of the Pied Piper of a German myth (Olsson 2005, 9, 21–22) to describe the operations of a terror cult leader. In the story, the Pied Piper used his music to lead away the rats and mice that had infested a village. When the villagers did not pay the Piper for his services as they had originally agreed, the Piper got revenge by leading off the village children. They never were returned. The villagers grieved deeply.

A recently deceased contemporary Malignant Pied Piper is Zarqawi, the terror cult leader in Iraq. He sought recruits among Iraqi children as potential future terror performers. The pipers of terror try to convince Iraqi children that their death in a terror bombing gives them immortality and God's smile of greeting in heaven. The mass media provides free publicity for the terror cult and leader, and their grandiose narcissistic affirmation via the terrorist event.

SOCIAL PSYCHOLOGY OF SUICIDE BOMBERS

Against expectations, it was found that most suicide bombers do not come from families of low socioeconomic status. Many of them come from upper middle-class families. Most have high educational achievement, and a large proportion of them had the opportunity to travel to the West to further their education. Problems begin for young immigrants. These individuals start to feel marginalized in the new Western cultures. They feel lonely and devalued. They seek companionship and support at mosques where the charisma of radical Islamist clerics turns them into followers in terrorist cells. The comfort and power found in these groups is accompanied by anger towards Western ways and standards. The domineering leader's charisma draws them into the radical fundamentalist mentality of hate. Western civilization becomes the target of their hatred. Even innocent children and civilians become targets of homicidal bombings.

The Peer Pressure Power of Comrades in Terror and Vicarious Admirers

Aparism Ghosh wrote a psychologically jolting article that appeared in *Time* magazine, July 4, 2005, called "Inside the Mind of an Iraqi Suicide Bomber." Ghosh describes an interview with 20-year-old Marwan Abu Ubeida, who had trained for and was waiting to carry out a suicide bombing mission. Marwan describes his rehearsing of his last prayer in these words:

First I will ask Allah to bless my mission with a high rate of casualties among the Americans. Then I will ask him to purify my soul so I am fit to see him, and I will ask to see my *mujahideen* brothers who are already with him.... The most important thing is that he should let me kill many Americans. (Ghosh 2005, 23–24)

Ghosh's interview with Marwan reveals some important motivations and psychodynamics. Before Saddam's fall, Marwan's father was a prosperous Fallujah businessman. Marwan was an average student in high school but excelled in Koranic studies at the local mosque. He tells Ghosh that his family thinks he has gone too far, but they know they cannot change his mind. Marwan revels in his ferocious pious warrior identity. He quotes frequently from the Koran and he enthusiastically talks about the jihadist ideal of a unified global Islamic state where there is no alcohol, no music, or any Western ideas and behaviors (Ghosh 2005, 25–26).

Marwan describes to Ghosh the "cleansing" process during a suicide bomber's indoctrination. This period seems saturated with brainwashing techniques that Singer, Lifton, and this author describe in destructive cults. Marwan admired Zarqawi as a great Islamic hero. Marwan told Ghosh that he was asked to mentor a friend during his final spiritual preparation for martyrdom and says that his friend was the happiest he had ever seen him. Before this friend blew himself up at a checkpoint manned by Iraqi soldiers in Ramadi, the capital of the infamous Anbar province, they made a pact to meet in heaven. Marwan is pleased to call himself a terrorist. He says that the Koran teaches it is the duty of Muslims to bring terror to the enemy. Marwan expresses some hope that he will not kill innocent civilians with his bomb, but if so, he is sure that they will be asked by Allah in heaven to forgive him. That is an interesting rationalization and projection. Marwan quotes from the surah known as the Spoils of War:

Against them make ready your strength to the utmost of your power, including steeds of war, to strike terror into the enemy of Allah and your enemy. (Ghosh 2005, 29)

For Marwan, the terror cult comrades are like a new family or sibship, not unlike a street gang in Los Angeles or a destructive cult like Charles Manson's "family." For adolescents or young adults in search of an exciting, grandiose, and spurious new noble identity, terror cults fill the bill.

Another aspect of the phenomenon of suicide killing is the presence of a number of populations that consider these acts heroic and sacrificial. The suicide bomber may be motivated by the desire to have the attention of his people, an attention that was not available when he was a growing child or adolescent. If only his countrymen did not encourage such a maladaptive way of behavior, the potential bomber may use other, less destructive, ways of being admired by his people. Community rebuilding efforts, for example, could benefit Iraqi society. If the Arab and Muslim populations do not send messages of acceptance and admiration for terrorist acts, then fewer individuals will commit them. This point underlines the need for vigorous and ubiquitous political and civic participation by as many Iraqis as is possible.

Here we can apply the ideas of Volkan (2001) about societal regression in Islamic and Arab countries. These countries and cultures have been suffering continuous turmoil and instability for centuries. Regression, with all its consequences, is usual in such circumstances. One of the consequences is the need for a strong leader to satisfy needs for dependency and protection. Enter the dictators who make the situation worse by directly preventing societal progression in many Arab/Muslim countries. Individual rights are suppressed to secure "protection," women's rights are ignored, and productive activities of individuation are inhibited. Individual identities are diffused in order to maintain "safe" societal regression and dependency. A rigid fundamentalist religious identity is fostered. Empty rituals are rewarded, while inner values and identity are lost or weak

Even words describing values are emptied of their meaning by continuous abuse. Rigid rules judge intimate interactions, even marital relations. "Big Brother" is watching. Primitive defenses such as projection are commonplace as a result. Conspiratorial thinking ensues. Polarized ideas—"us" versus "them"— are encouraged, and nations in the West easily become enemies. Terrifyingly, these primitive dynamics are rampant recently in Baghdad.

But what makes individuals involve themselves as performers in regressed malignant groups such as suicide bombing cults? The regressive processes discussed earlier, and especially those directed toward women in such countries, affect the quality of care given to children in these cultures. Early developmental emotional disturbances, including narcissistic injuries and defective character structure, are inevitable in such an environment. A constant atmosphere pervaded by the fear of sudden death from a suicide bomb blast is in itself eroding of basic trust and healthy morality and narcissism. These circumstances result in defective identity formation. The group identity based on such regressed societal states will inevitably be marred by the presence of grudges, paranoia, and dishonesty. It can be expected that simplistic and violent solutions will prevail.

The process of identity formation depends on a society's or culture's avenues of educational and vocational pursuits for its young people. If a culture is able to present youth with these opportunities, then young persons do not need to turn to radical causes or fundamentalism for their identity formation.

The West as Father Figure

The West (i.e., Western Europe and the United States) is this era's pioneering location in most fields of endeavor: science, education, and political organization. In addition, the West was involved directly in the modern history of most

Islamic countries through long years of occupation, rule setting, and the establishment of systems of government, administration, and leadership. It is interesting that bin Laden strives to attract the attention of the "Western" media for his purposes. Osama scoffs at modernity but doesn't mind using modern television media for his propaganda. The West, with its democracy and encouragement of human rights, becomes a father figure, the target/victim of displaced narcissistic aggression and explosive, rebellious rage.

It is helpful to remember that idealistic adolescents adore a rebellious cause that allows them to aspire to a noble cause that transcends a mundane existence. Unfortunately, they do not always thoroughly explore and think through the cause they choose.

ACKNOWLEDGMENT

The author is grateful toward and appreciative of the invaluable collaboration and research help of Dr. Uday Khalid of Iraq in writing this chapter.

THE CHILDREN OF TERROR AND MARTYRDOM: THE SELF-PSYCHOLOGICAL SOIL AND ROOTS OF OSAMA AND COMPANY'S FUTURE RECRUITS

THE DEDICATED AND COMPASSIONATE WORK OF DR. RONA FIELDS

Children who are exposed constantly to terror and death show persisting impact on their mental and emotional life. Psychologist Rona Fields has studied the cognitive, affective, and moral development of children in Northern Ireland, the Middle East, and Africa in situations where they have grown up amidst constant violence. Fields's psychological testing and empirical study of kids six to 16 years old reveals the following:

> Children growing up in conditions of ongoing violence, regardless of their age at the commencement of the upheaval, demonstrate a very keen concern with right and wrong. This is quite opposite from the classic syndrome associated with sociopathic personality. However, children traumatized by violence seem to become truncated at the second level of moral development or legal socialization. This is the stage at which an individual views right and wrong in terms of their identity group. (Group-self.) When identification is through a perceived threatened minority group identity, there is a righteous indignation about perceived wrongs and justification for vendetta. (Fields 1986, 5–6)

Fields observes that these children have available a narrow range of role models and a continuing sense of helplessness that is not corrected by observing parental effectiveness in dealing with the terror. There is no feeling of hope that they will ever get out of this powerlessness. Fields (1986, 6) says:

> Personality projectives indicate that these children and adolescents have fixated psychodynamically in impotent rage. The infantile quality of this rage is in concert with basic anxiety and is behaviorally manifested in response to perceived threats of annihilation. Psychic stress [*of this magnitude*] is only experienced when individuals who are thus "set" psychodynamically (emotionally habituated) attempt to face their own freedom and responsibility for action. This is a nearly impossible shift because, for these individuals, the environmental survival threats persist and are exacerbated over time.

It is fascinating but chilling that Fields has found that both Protestant and Catholic youths in Northern Ireland have nearly identical psychodynamics and stunted moral development. Fields concludes that in the above circumstances in which children have been socialized in a climate of constant intergroup violence, fear, and anger about potential annihilation (yet low anxiety about their anger and a higher-than-average curiosity), they will invariably and increasingly become terrorists. In fact, Fields's studies of adult terrorist groups from Northern Ireland, members of the PLO, and South African paramilitary terrorist groups all show a State Trait Personality Inventory that are essentially the same for all terrorists. These otherwise normal personalities have a readiness to commit violence without remorse. Their elevated scores on trait and state anger are matched by their low scores on state and trait anxiety. There is no emotional conflict about expressing or experiencing their anger. Says Fields, "It is the anger of which righteous indignation is construed" (1986, 4).

Fields later retested some of the children she originally examined when they were jailed as young adult terrorists. Again, she found that "these individuals will seek novel and adventurous means for experiencing and expressing their anger"—in other words, "It is the personality dynamics [established over childhood] combined with the individual needs and circumstances that mandate *the conversion of the terrorized into the terrorist*" (Fields 1986, 7). This pattern is frighteningly similar to the multigenerational patterns of child abuse and sexual abuse in societies. An abused child so very often becomes an abusing parent as the sad cycle is perpetuated.

Fields describes in detail a young man named Seamus. His situation provides further data to illustrate our discussion in Chapter 2 about the role of the prison or "closed-space" experience in the formative life experience of terrorists (Shaw 1986, Brennan 1994). Fields presents Seamus's story:

> One fifteen-year-old boy who had been tested in December, 1971, was one of a group of boys who had been lifted and held for interrogation nearly a whole day. At the time he was first tested, he was depressed and confused. He had not been a

member of any group and had been trying very hard to keep up with his schoolwork and prepare for an apprenticeship. He was picked up and beaten five more times between December, 1971, and January, 1973. Once he was picked up by drunken soldiers and beaten, other times he was stopped and verbally abused. His home had been raided a number of times. His father and uncles were interned in the 1940s. Seamus himself had not considered joining any group until after the second beating. He wanted some way to retaliate against his oppressors and felt that this was as good as any. He's still not more politically aware than he was prior to the first lifting and interrogation. He doesn't really care about ideologies or processes, he is only concerned with getting his rights and being left alone. When presented with the blank card [at testing], he gave this story:

"The future of Northern Ireland and perhaps the future of the world—blank—a dead end. There's nothing to do in a dead end but go to Vietnam or something like that. Seems to be a drunk. A shady character. Looks like an IRA man or an American gangster, more like what you see in films. He's waiting for somebody. He'll have a long wait and do whatever he is intending to do: if he doesn't get picked up for loitering he'll wait there the rest of the night."

As for rules and laws, Seamus says:

"Why should people follow rules? Shouldn't always follow them but I suppose it's proper for fear if you didn't follow them you get into trouble. [Why do you follow rules, Seamus?] I follow moral rules because I feel obligated to because I'm a Catholic. If I break them I endanger myself or other people. [If you could change any rule, what rule would you change?] I'd like to change the rule and have justice in Northern Ireland." (Fields 1977, 39–40)

This perceptive young man's experience of cruel, violent, and arbitrary authority in jail by police is a sad but common step down the personal pathway to being a terrorist. The title of Sayyib Qutb's brilliant but troubling book, *Social Justice in Islam,* keeps echoing in my mind.

SAD GURU FATHERS IN GAZA

In a cogent 9/11 anniversary article in the *New Yorker* on September 11, 2006, Jeffrey Goldberg looks in his "Letter From Gaza" at "The Forgotten War: The Overlooked Consequences of Hamas's Actions." He provides good descriptions of the imminent dangers of war between Israel and Palestinians in Gaza; Israel and Hezbollah in Lebanon; and between Israel/U.S. and radical Islamist forces in Syria and Iran, where nuclear club membership is being sought. (In my opinion, only Israeli and American cocoons of denial and intellectualization protect us from constant tension and anxiety. Our current and vastly superior nuclear arsenal is of small comfort if radical Islamist Armageddon worshippers take over in Iran.)

More pertinent to this study is Goldberg's poignant interviews and descriptions with Abu Odeidah (Abu Nasser) and other Hamas militant, rocket-firing leaders. He describes his visit to Gaza as "like breaking into a large beachfront prison." At times Goldberg portrays a grim rivalry Hamas leaders feel for the media attention that Hezbollah has gotten and Hamas does not get. Abu Obeidah brags in an odd, surrealistic way that Hamas is at the vanguard of the anti-Zionist Muslim revolution (Goldberg 2006, 43).

A psychological picture of the sad and defective role models that Hamas leaders provide for their own sons emerges in Goldberg's interview with Abu Hussein, a leader of the Qassam Brigades in Gaza. During the interview, Goldberg poignantly describes the following tragic scene.

> As we sat in Abu Hussein's living room, he pulled his son, Hussein, close to him. Hussein is a spirited ninth grader whose passion, he told me, is drawing. "I want him to finish his studies, but if he happens to die I don't have a problem," his father said, "so long as he dies as a martyr, and on the condition that he takes Jews with him when he dies. I will be happy if he dies this way." (Goldberg 2006, 45)

I have rarely heard in more than 35 years in psychiatry as sad and masochistic a statement from a father as this! Goldberg continues:

> Hussein ran out of the room, and came back with a photograph of himself. "This is my martyr picture," he said, handing it to me. In the photograph, he wore khaki shirt and pants and held an AK-47. "If I die, this is the photo that will appear on the martyr posters in Gaza." All his schoolmates have a "martyr photo," he said, "so when we get killed we'll have the best posters." Hussein said, "I'm his only son, and he wants me to die!" Then he laughed, and put his arm around his father. (Goldberg 2006, 45)

Again, the extreme sadness of this scene of profound child abuse and intergenerational masochism is overwhelming.

At the close of his article, Goldberg interviews Rafig Hamdouna, a former Fatah leader who talks about the temptations of violent death and Palestinian father-son relationships. Hamdouna says:

> My son Basel came to me one day and said he wanted to be a martyr bomber, he told me. I had to keep calm. I said to him, "Basel, do you know what happens when you blow yourself up?" He just looked at me. I said, "You don't go to Heaven. You go into a hole in the ground, and you get covered up with dirt. Every father in Gaza has the same conversation with his sons." Every father faces this. (Goldberg 2006, 47)

What amazes me as a psychoanalyst and psychotherapist is that these self-absorbed Palestinian fathers have not found a way to get their stubborn Hamas leaders to compromise with and live in peace with Israel. This would allow their sons to move beyond their own ignorance and stubborn, rigidly violent positions. The child abuse of these pathologically narcissistic Palestinian fathers is truly sad. They think they are noble and courageous, but they are really stubborn, rigid, and narrow-minded. Allah must weep at their folly!

IRAQ'S CHILDREN OF PRESENT AND FUTURE TERROR

The current conditions in Baghdad and several other Iraqi cities are tragically optimal in terms of the socially and psychologically ideal roots and soil for terrorist formation. In a poignant *Newsweek* article on January 22, 2007, Christian Caryl describes "The Next Jihadists: Iraq's Lost Children." Ammar, the young 17-year-old (going on 47) Shiite militia member, was urged to join by his neighborhood Imam. Caryl describes Ammar's emergence:

> As the grizzly toll of Baghdad's death squads spiked last fall, he helped out in the room at his local mosque where bodies are ritually washed before they are buried. Some corpses had been burned with chemicals. Limbs had been cut off, eyes torn out. One day at the beginning of November 2007, a neighbor of Ammar's, a college student and fellow Sunni, disappeared at an impromptu checkpoint set up by the Mahdi Army. When the neighbor's body finally turned up at the mosque for burial, Ammar saw that he had been beheaded. (He recognized his friend from the clothing.) (Caryl 2007, 1)

Ammar went into the garden and vomited. He then vowed revenge on the Mahdi Army, who he calls "Garbage collectors and robbers." Ammar sounds identical to Rona Fields's young study subjects in Northern Ireland, Palestinian refugee camps, and orphaned South African youths in the black townships. These youngsters are shocked by the violence but eventually fascinated, jaded by, and drawn towards it. As Fields observed, they look readily to violence as a solution and means toward primitive social justice. Al Qaeda and radical Islamist terror cults provide the tools and technology of destruction for these youths. Equally as important to the weapons training are the terror gurus' charismatic spiritual inspiration and utopian transcendent promises of glory.

Caryl in his article notes that Iraq is a young country, with half the population under age 18 (Caryl 2007, 1). With the day-to-day atmosphere of violence in Iraq, and the hangover stress of previous wars and sanctions, the children of Iraq have lost parents and homes, and watch as their communities are torn apart by sectarian fighting. As Fields's studies demonstrated, such children come to believe in force and violence as means to solve problems. The forging of black-and-white thinking and the embrace of force and violence as a solution in Iraqi children is chilling. Caryl conferred with Jonathan Powers, who served as an army captain in Iraq in 2003 and now directs a nonprofit organization that works with Iraqi kids. He notes that the constant violence is leading to a generation of under-educated, unemployed, and traumatized youth and, among the boys, a ripe atmosphere for recruitment by insurgent and militia groups. As we have discussed, Al Qaeda and terror cults hardly have to recruit young people who seek them out and often compete for jihadist positions.

It would be ominous if Iraq joined Pakistan, Waziristan, and Afghanistan as part of the burgeoning recruiting grounds for Al Qaeda and other terror cult franchises with rebuilt and expanding training camps. They would mingle with "Al Qaeda's Western Recruits" (Yousafzai, Moreau, and Hosenball, 2006). Radical Islam provides powerful spiritual energy for metastasizing terror cults. It is not too late to develop our understanding of the individual and group psychodynamics of these people and their groups. The creative application of this understanding has far-reaching importance.

While I have emphasized the defective fathering of fundamentalist fathers, I need to remind the reader of the equally abusive and masochistic fundamentalist mothers who give encouragement to their children about being a martyr.

OSAMA AND COMPANY'S APOCALYPTIC SCENARIOS AND REBELLIOUS GROUP MARTYRDOM IN TERROR CULTS

The terrorist cult leader becomes a "legend in his own mind" and a pseudo-healing legend for the wounded group-self of those who feel rescued. Rebellious charisma in a terror leader meshes with the followers' narcissistic passive-receptiveness to his charismatic influence. The leader-follower pattern in terror cults is remarkably similar to what is seen in apocalyptic cults like those of Jones, Koresh, and Asahara.

The group death or martyr scenario gives the terror-cult group a special, exciting, and dramatically triumphant defining martyr myth. It becomes a source of "underdog" heroism and paradoxical group cohesion and identity. The individual and group will triumph over Evil. These group death myths represent the ultimate *denial of death* as described by Ernest Becker in his 1973 Pulitzer Prize–winning book, *The Denial of Death.*

The sad thing about human nature is that as individuals and groups, we long for good leadership. When we find good leaders, we prosper. Too often, however, this longing allows us to be victims of our dependency and need. It takes a truly independent and strong person to take the road less traveled and vigorously question or oppose the leader. Our leaders, and we Americans, face this issue constantly. The following poem was never read at the White House because Laura Bush canceled the national poetry week readings:

The Emperor's New Duds

He exits jauntily from the helicopter grinning.
His body armor a cocky smile, strut and swagger.

Though pols of polls, have no numbers convincing.
And drums of death, for gasping un-named thousands,
ring from spades of future graves, too soon dug.
"Skulls and Bones" of those who for power grasp,
tempt History's bloody wrong-turns glibly made.
Too little time spent on his and our soul's direction.
Poignant pleas of humble tailors come gently, daily.
Please! Read History and listen to old friends.
"Look! How fine the emperor's shiny new clothes,"
but thoroughly soaked with blood and black gold.
Hold up close that clouded mirror and a microphone.
Can his highness see, pictures of future holocausts?

In the author's opinion, President George W. Bush's sweeping generalization about a tight connection between our invasion and occupation of Iraq and "the global war against terrorism/Islamofascism" is dangerous. In fact this tautology is problematic in terms of whether we are defeating Al Qaeda in Iraq, or sadly only aiding Al Qaeda recruiters and trainers over there. Furthermore, the overgeneralized notion of a war on a tactic (terrorism) can be unduly connected with this administration's notion of preemptive war. There certainly are dangerous groups of radical Islamists around the world who want to kill and harm Americans, but to constantly make dubious connections between every group that uses terror tactics and some apocalyptic war by Islamofascists against the West is suspect. It encourages an impulsive, trigger-happy readiness to use preemptive war doctrine and fosters group war-think. Military action, which ought to be the last resort, begins to creep up to first-resort status.

OSAMA BIN LADEN'S APOCALYPTIC SCENARIO OF MARTYRDOM

For bin Laden, the motivating apocalyptic scenario is his assertion that the West, particularly Americans and Jews, is threatening all Muslims in the world. In a book bin Laden wrote in 1998, he called the faithful to a global *jihad,* a "new vision" that demands the deaths of all Americans and Jews, including children. To attain this religion-perverting and ultimately cynical vision, any violence is justified, from terrorist bombings to suicide missions.

Evil is defined initially by the leader bin Laden via *fatwa,* or decree, but gradually becomes coauthored within the group-self as their group salvation death myth. The codependent leader holds the martyr death myth out to the followers as magical reward. The terror cult leader also holds the death myth over the heads of the followers so as to magnify the special domain of his "mana" power and self-importance. The leader is needed for the dramatic destructive action that is being planned, for which no one individual takes personal responsibility.

The leader experiences the ultimate "celebrity" and fantasized triumph over his lifelong insecurity, hurts, and fear of aloneness.

The codependent followers embrace the martyr/murder death idea because it brings heightened meaning to their otherwise humdrum, mundane, or miserable lives. For example, in the hundreds of hours of recordings of Jim Jones's ranting free-associative "White Night" sermons in Guyana, what is fascinating to hear were the comments of his followers in the background. Those comments extol and reveal the group idealism, excitement, and grandiosity of the group-death scenario via Jim Jones's vintage of "Socialist Suicide." Are not the chanting mobs of Hamas or Hezbollah supporters calling for the obliteration of all Jews and Israelis really joining in a similar call to death? Is it not a form of passive group homicide or suicide if parents allow Hezbollah fighters to hide behind them when they fire their rockets? This seems particularly true when they allow terrorists to fire rockets randomly at Israel from hiding places in their homes, where their children huddle until Israel retaliates. Then when their children die a bloody death, they broadcast the pictures over international television, as if Israel or the United States intended for their children to be killed. Shame, shame on Hezbollah and Hamas for such duplicity about their own child abuse! Hezbollah rockets are filled with buckshot designed to kill civilians. Does Allah value such cowardice in Hezbollah any more than he does in the Israeli's use of "smart" bombs? Group death myths for such grandiose causes are truly terrifying. The inspirational and instructional manuals of the 9/11 terrorist pilots reflect these ultimate denials of death and devotion to the pathetically alleged cause of "Allah," as inserted by bin Laden or his Islamist colleagues. Shame! Shame! Effective diplomacy must prevent the swaggering Islamist espousers of the destruction of evil Israel and evil America to square off with the swaggering accuser of the axis of evil.

OSAMA'S RESEMBLANCE TO HITLER'S PARANOIA AND GRANDIOSE APOCALYPTIC DELUSIONS

Miliora makes the chilling observation that in addition to Osama's grandiose narcissistic states and paranoia, his Manichean view of reality strikingly resembles that of Hitler. (Manichean refers to having stark perceptions of good and evil, black and white, "us" versus "them.") Miliora's cogent argument begins with Osama's murderous hatred of Israel and the United States and its parallel with Hitler's anti-Semitism, and it proceeds as follows:

> Much like Hitler with regard to his claim about the loss of Germanic soil after the First World War, bin Laden stakes a moral claim that his people have suffered injuries perpetrated by the West and avows that it is the sacred duty of Muslims to restore Islamic lands to rightful control. And also like Hitler, bin Laden promotes

his rigid, totalitarian ideology with utter self-righteousness. Moreover, both bin Laden and Hitler imagine that their atrocious mass murders are consistent with the will of God and imbue their sociopathic behavior with religious significance. (Miliora 2004, 134)

Religious zeal and murder or assassination has been a deadly combination throughout history. Miliora applies Kohut's concept of the diseased group-self to the Middle East and bin Laden's manipulative condemnation of the West. Miliora (2004, 136) says:

I propose that the Middle Eastern-Islamic self is "fragmented" and "devitalized." As Hitler, the leader of Nazi Germany, did, so Bin Laden, the leader of the militant Islamic "war" against Americans, focuses on the external sources of his people's fragmentation or "disease": the capitalist system of the West and the "satanic" power of the United States.

Miliora goes on to point out that bin Laden, like Hitler, identifies his own paranoia about the U.S.-Zionist alliance with the fears of his followers and promises a cure via the destruction of America.

Hitler's messianic and apocalyptic visions are well known. Miliora (2004, 135) quotes bin Laden's chilling apocalyptic visions for America:

I tell you, freedom and human rights in America are doomed. The United States government will lead the American people and the West in general into an unbearable hell and a choking life. (November 2001 home video of bin Laden and friends shown on U.S. television, December 6, 2001. Portions found in *New York Times,* December 14, 2001, 1; also see Lawrence 2005, 113.)

Shame on Osama for such distortions of the truth for the sake of propaganda! And, shame on Western leaders who find glib cause for preemptive war!

MARTYR MYTHS OF AMERICAN TERRORISTS WHO KILL IN GOD'S NAME

In case the Israelis or Americans try to grow smug about the killers "out there," we both need to look to our own communities for improvements. We in America are not without fundamentalist countrymen who murder in God's name. Jessica Stern in her important book, *Terror in the Name of God,* describes what she calls the "save the babies movement." The Reverend Michael Bray is the intellectual father of the extreme radical fringe of the antiabortion movement and runs a Reformation Lutheran Church in Maryland. Bray spent four years in prison for conspiring to bomb 10 abortion clinics near Washington, DC. Bray talked to Stern at length about Christian Reconstructionism, which is a movement to turn

America into a fundamentalist Christian state with laws in accordance with the Old Testament (Stern 2003, 148, 163). This notion sounds eerily like Osama bin Laden and al-Zawahiri of Al Qaeda talking about their avidly proposed resurrection of the Caliphate under strict Sharia law for the twenty-first-century world.

Stern describes her interviews with Paul Hill, who is a former Presbyterian minister and regarded by his mentor Michael Bray as a real Christian martyr and good example for Christians to follow. On July 29, 1994, Paul Hill shot and killed Dr. John Britton and his bodyguard. Britton provided abortions in Pensacola, Florida. Hill sees the abortionist's scalpel as the agent of Satan, and that anyone who opposes abortion on moral grounds is obligated to defend the "innocent unborn." In the author's opinion, many antiabortion fundamentalists sense at an unconscious level that if abortion had been readily available to their mothers, they probably would have never existed. Hill told Stern that killing fetuses is like Hitler's killing of Jews in gas chambers, and those who do not take action are like the German clergy who did not stand up against Hitler. Hill enthusiastically sees himself as a Christian martyr. He gives thanks for what he sees as the privilege of his life of imprisonment and suffering. (That prison thing again.) Hill grandiosely compares his suffering with that of Jesus Christ! (Stern 2003, 167–71.) Just as Osama and company identify with the Prophet, so men like Hill identify with Jesus Christ. Peace-loving Christians, Muslims, and Jews need to pray that the true evil of fundamentalist mentality will dissolve or lessen among their brothers and sisters.

An anonymous pilgrim scribbled this in a dusty old prayer book found in an Episcopal Church attic.

Tears At The Earth Project 1-20-07

In the infinite spaces between molecules
An entity pauses to ponder and smile sadly.
HIS earth trial is struggling to survive again.
Mankind's hapless cyclical grand rebellions;
Blood lust disguised as benevolent crusades.
Human clowns faithfully fail to reflect God.
And the sad wonderful fools always forget.
Scientists try to measure the rippling strings.
Changes in energies so proudly measured,
So they can take pride in curiosity satisfied.
Atheists never brilliant enough for proofs.
Agnostics possess tiny flickers of humility.
Poets get sudden inspiration and compose,
with thankful hearts for the Truth's gift.
Kierkegaard's "leap of faith" still possible.
And patience to wait for new Bethlehems.

JEWISH AND ISRAELI TERRORISTS
WHO KILL IN JEHOVAH'S NAME

Jerrold Post in his incisive and insightful 2004 book, *Leaders and Their Followers in a Dangerous World: The Psychology of Political Behavior,* describes the chilling fundamentalist mentality of the followers of the Jewish-American activist Rabbi Meir Kahane. Post describes the 1994 murder of 29 Muslim worshippers by Dr. Baruch Goldstein in the Tomb of the Patriarchs in Hebron. Goldstein was a devoted follower of Kahane who wrote a book to inspire "the fighting Jew." Kahane uses Old Testament scripture and Talmudic writings to encourage Jews to kill their enemies before they can kill them. He also uses scripture to condone killing the enemy of a brother before the enemy strikes. Kahane's murder cult even uses Maimonides's notion of "obligatory war" toward Jewish enemies (Post 2004, 142–43). Here Kahane joins Osama bin Laden and George W. Bush in the impulse toward preemptive war and *jihad.* All in the name of Righteousness, Allah, or Jehovah.

Devoted followers of radical fundamentalists are dangerous. Post concisely describes the tragic assassination of Yitzhak Rabin at a peace rally of thousands of Israelis in Kings of Israel Square in Tel Aviv on November 4, 1995. Rabin, the winner of the 1994 Nobel Peace Prize, was assassinated not by a Palestinian terrorist but by a right-wing extremist, a 27-year-old Orthodox Jewish law student at Bar-Ilan University. Yigal Amir claimed that he acted alone at God's orders and had no regret (Post 2004, 143). Charismatic messianic leaders either use mental splitting or denial to avoid the pain resulting from the violent actions of followers who they inspire, or they consciously get gratification from these murders by association. Every American who saw the smiles and chuckles of Osama bin Laden on videotape as he saw and heard what his Al Qaeda henchmen did on 9/11 needs to be aware that no world community or its leader is above unnecessary and charismatically inspired violence. Military violence or assassination should never creep up from the position of last resort to the top of the list of options for any group. Political structures with many checks and balances form a fine line of protection from group war-think and the violent, irrational side of human nature.

8

HOW A PSYCHIATRIST MIGHT DIAGNOSE BIN LADEN AND COMPANY

DSMS, CLINICAL SCIENCE, AND PSYCHIATRIC POLITICS

In 1952, the American Psychiatric Association's Committee on Nomenclature and Statistics developed *DSM-I (Diagnostic and Statistical Manual — Mental Disorders)*. Periodic revisions of the *DSM* occur in collaboration with WHO (World Health Organization) and its new versions of *ICD (International Classification of Diseases)*. Beginning with *DSM-III* (1974), the committee developed explicit lists of criteria and tried to stay neutral with respect to theories of etiology. But in fact, the *DSM* committee is a political gathering in addition to undertaking scientific efforts.

Since the so-called "Decade of the Brain" in the 1990s, psychiatrists have had less training and experience with psychoanalysis or psychodynamic psychotherapy. Neurochemistry, neurophysiology, and psychopharmacology have provided vast volumes of fascinating and important new information to be learned by a psychiatrist, psychologist, or psychotherapist in training. But psychodynamic psychiatrists feel that psychotherapy and psychodynamic theories have been neglected to the extent that psychiatry has lost its mind. *DSM-IV* in particular was intended (and distorted) to be objective and able to be used for scientific and largely statistical studies. Many psychoanalysts and psychodynamic psychiatrists support the need for objective criteria for psychiatry, but also feel that in psychiatry, so many key factors involved with human behavior and the art of treatment cannot be seen, measured, or quantified (see PDM 2006). Paradoxically, valuable diagnostic labels like "Ego-Dystonic Homosexuality" or "Neurosis," for example, have gradually been dropped from *DSM* for reasons of "scientific" political correctness rather than through careful research.

In this book, *DSM-IV* criteria have been applied to Osama bin Laden. These *DSM* criteria and Kernberg's criteria for malignant narcissism can help us focus and order our thinking about Osama's personality. Strictly speaking, this is not a clinical use of *DSM,* but rather the applied psychiatric use to order the data about bin Laden.

USEFUL DEFINITIONS RELATED TO PERSONALITY DIAGNOSIS AND DYNAMICS

Denial—"A defense mechanism, operating unconsciously, used to resolve emotional conflict and allay anxiety by disavowing thoughts, feelings, wishes, needs, or external reality factors that are consciously intolerable" (*American Psychiatric Glossary,* 41). Dorpat (1985) has written an excellent, detailed, and cogent clinical book about denial. (A key factor about the denial process is that when major emotional issues of grief, pain, and anger are denied, the return of the denied that then erupts into the external world often takes the form of violent action—not just words or thoughts.)

Personality—"The characteristic way in which a person thinks, feels, and behaves; the ingrained pattern of behavior that each person evolves, both consciously and unconsciously, as his or her style of life or way of being" (*American Psychiatric Glossary,* 98).

Personality Disorder—"Enduring patterns of perceiving, relating to, and thinking about the environment and oneself that begin by early adulthood and are exhibited in a wide range of important social and personal contexts. These patterns are inflexible and maladaptive, causing either significant functional impairment or subjective distress" (*American Psychiatric Glossary,* 99).

Paranoid Personality Disorder—"Characterized by pervasive distrust and suspiciousness of others such that their motives are interpreted as malevolent. This distrust is shown in many ways, including unreasonable expectation of exploitation or harm by others; questioning without justification the loyalty or trustworthiness of friends or associates; reading demeaning or threatening meanings into benign remarks or events; having a tendency to bear grudges and be unforgiving of insults or injustices; or experiencing unfounded, recurrent suspiciousness about fidelity of his or her sexual partner" (*American Psychiatric Glossary,* 100).

DIAGNOSING OSAMA BIN LADEN

The conclusion reached in this applied analytic study is that Osama has a mixed narcissistic and paranoid/persecutory personality pattern, with the additional elements of malignant narcissism. Observers can convincingly point to grandiose, paranoid, and delusional qualities in the thinking, pontificating, and teaching of Osama and his mentors. As with all paranoid thinking, there are always some kernels of truth (e.g., the man who says "that secret-service man sure looks constantly paranoid" as the president is giving a speech, is correct.)

On April 9, 2001, Osama recorded an audiotape for the estimated 500,000 delegates to the International Conference of Deobandis near Peshawar, Pakistan. Most of the delegates were from Madrassahs in Pakistan, but others were from Afghanistan, India, Iran, the UK, UAE, Libya, and Saudi Arabia. This widely publicized address by Osama contains clear evidence of grandiose, paranoid, and persecutory content and tone. Osama bin Laden's fundamentalist mentality and overinclusive thinking leads him to accuse even the United Nations (in addition, obviously, to America, Israel, and "the West") of economic and military actions against, and religious persecution of, Muslims, including the sanction of the killing of innocent children (Lawrence 2005, 96).

Observations about Osama's paranoia and that of his colleagues can be supported, but the more pervasive diagnostic pattern is of a personality disorder—"crazy like a fox." In this author's opinion, rather than a paranoid psychosis or paranoid schizophrenic condition, Osama and many of his colleagues seem to have narcissistic personality patterns. They also have a nonpsychotic degree of paranoia found in paranoid personality disorders. People with severe personality disorder (as opposed to anxiety disorder or neurosis, depression, and so on) rarely come to a psychiatrist with the experience of inner pain from guilt or shame. They are usually in total denial about their unresolved childhood conflicts or traumas. Their childhood conflicts or perceived traumas are woven into the very fabric of their personalities. Osama seems to be in massive denial of the connection between his inner life and its possible connections with his childhood experiences. Osama, like all personality-disordered individuals, seems to externalize or blame other people or circumstances outside themselves for their difficulties. The paranoid-persecutory perceptions progress over years, and after 9/11 they crescendo like a symphony of self-fulfilling prophecies.

NARCISSISTIC PERSONALITY DISORDER

The *Diagnostic and Statistical Manual of Mental Disorders (DSM-IV)* of the American Psychiatric Association states the following:

301.81 Narcissistic Personality Disorder. A pervasive pattern of grandiosity (in fantasy or behavior), need for admiration, and lack of empathy, beginning in early childhood and present in a variety of contexts, as indicated by five or more of the following:

1. Has a grandiose sense of importance (e.g., exaggerates achievements and talents, expects to be recognized as superior).
2. Is preoccupied with fantasies of unlimited success, power, brilliance, beauty, or ideal love.
3. Believes that he or she is "special" and unique and can only be understood by, or associate with, other special or high-status people.

4. Requires excessive admiration.

5. Has a sense of entitlement, i.e., unreasonable expectations of especially favorable reatment or automatic compliance with his or her expectations.

6. Is interpersonally exploitive, i.e., takes advantage of others to achieve his or her own ends.

7. Lacks empathy; is unwilling to recognize or identify with the feelings or needs of others.

8. Is often envious of others or believes others are envious of him.

9. Shows arrogant, haughty behaviors or attitudes. (*Diagnostic and Statistical Manual of Mental Disorders [DSM-IV]*. Edition IV. Washington, D.C.: American Psychiatric Association, 1994. These criteria are virtually identical in the [2000] *DSM IV-TR Quick Reference*. Used with permission.)

MALIGNANT NARCISSISM

When a person already suffering from Narcissistic Personality Disorder becomes even more extreme in his or her beliefs and behavior, the condition is diagnosed as Malignant Narcissism. As described by Otto Kernberg, this condition involves four key elements:

1. Paranoid regressive tendencies with "paranoid micro psychotic episodes." These brief episodes of narcissistic rage involve loss of contact with reality and serve the function of punishing external enemies in order to avoid internal pain.

2. Chronic self-destructiveness or suicidal behavior as a triumph over authority figures. The malignant narcissist makes empathic followers or family feel his own hurt by initially seducing but eventually hurting them. Malignant cult leaders do this to their followers and even to their own children. Osama focuses specifically on martyrdom and suicide bombing as forms of "noble" self-destruction.

3. Major and minor dishonesty (psychopathy). Malignant narcissists manipulate and exploit others for profit, for their own satisfaction, or for imagined glory.

4. Malignant grandiosity with overt sadistic efforts to triumph over all authority. This triumph represents a satisfying turning of the tables for a malignant narcissist who, for instance, may have been abandoned without remorse by his father. By killing or vanquishing authority, the malignant narcissist feels as though he has achieved revenge against his uncaring father at an unconscious level.

(Kernberg 1986, 195)

I believe that bin Laden fulfills three of the four criteria for malignant narcissism:

1. In the context of ubiquitous Arab anti-American feelings, I do not see Osama as clinically psychotic, but his pronouncements have a decidedly paranoid-persecutory quality.

2. Osama is chronically homicidal in the context of his bogus *jihad* of hate.

3. I think bin Laden is psychopathically manipulative and dishonest with his followers and with the Arab world. However much Osama believes his admonitions toward the

murder of "infidels," as he so defines them, he is in massive denial of the inner sources of the tragic murderous acting out he advocates.

4. At conscious and unconscious levels, I think bin Laden showed clear evidence of "joyful cruelty" as he watched the suffering he helped create on 9/11.

In one psychodynamic descriptive diagnosis, Osama could be described as being afflicted with Father Hunger (Herzog 2001) or "Father/Brother Hunger."

APPLIED PSYCHOLOGICAL DIAGNOSIS

I also presented evidence (Olsson 2005, 156–58) that bin Laden fulfills eight of the nine criteria for a *DSM-IV* diagnosis of narcissistic personality disorder.

1. Grandiosity and self-importance: bin Laden broadcasts his pied piper "music" via Arab and international television networks in his self-appointed role as wealthy rescuer of oppressed Arabs.

2. Fantasies of success, power, and brilliance: Bodansky describes bin Laden waving his copy of the *Koran* and quotes bin Laden saying, "You cannot defeat heretics with this book alone, you have to show them the fist!" Bodansky goes on about bin Laden, "He also elucidated his vision of the relentless, fateful, global *jihad* against the United States in a book titled *America and the Third World War.* In this book bin Laden propounds a new vision, stressing the imperative of a global uprising. Bin Laden in essence calls on the entire Muslim world to rise up against the existing world order to fight for their rights to live as Muslims—rights he states are being trampled by the West's intentional spreading of Westernization" (Bodansky 1999, 388). No compromises—it is Osama's way or no way. Is there anything more omnipotent and grandiose (and chilling) than Osama's legend in his own mind—and so many Muslims' resonance with it?

    Bin Laden has associated with fugitive Taliban leader Mullah Omar, to whom he married his daughter. Osama's fourth wife is either Omar's daughter or a close tribal relative (Bodansky 1999, 307). Osama has associated with Ayman al-Zawahiri, the head Egyptian terrorist and his terror commanders (Bodansky 1999, 115). Along the road to grandiose splendor, Osama chose father figures like Turabi of Sudan and Azzam, and learned sly tactics as their colleague and acolyte.

3. Specialness: To my observation, bin Laden clearly enjoys the TV spotlight during his performances.

4. Requires excessive admiration: This seems apparent in his dealings with the Saudi leaders, when he proposed to form an army to defend Saudi Arabia and was narcissistically wounded at the Saudis' rejection of his plan. Rather than admire him, the Saudi leaders ignored his offer.

5. Entitlement: see #4. Bin Laden expected instant compliance and admiration.

6. Exploitive of others for his own ends: In my opinion, bin Laden exploited some of the 9/11 skyjackers because he laughed when it was announced that some of the "martyrs" were unaware of the full suicide plans for the hijacked planes. He certainly does not send his own son on such a mission.

7. Lacks empathy: bin Laden shows no empathy for the victims of his bomb attacks or 9/11. Even innocents. Even his own countrymen.

8. Envious: Osama seems too grandiose and malignantly narcissistic to envy anyone.

9. Arrogant: Practically every TV broadcast and public statement by bin Laden reeks of arrogance, grandiosity, and fundamentalist mentality.

As he procures recruits and supporters, Osama becomes the great leader-parent figure to his followers. He becomes, in his fantasies, the strong, devout, and admirable parent that he lacked during his own developing years. He seems to bask in some inner spurious, compensatory fantasy of restitution and revenge. Osama also manifests identification with and grandiose fantasies of merger with the prophet Mohammad (Miliora 2004, 132–33).

APPLYING THE EVIDENCE

Osama bin Laden will never knock on a psychoanalyst's door to seek help. It is worthwhile, however, to apply psychoanalytically informed approaches to understanding, as well as possible, how he thinks, feels, and behaves. We have looked at evidence that Osama bin Laden manifests intense "archaic narcissistic states." Miliora (2004, 132) asserts:

> Because of his grossly inflated grandiosity about having won the "holy" war against the Soviets and his seeing himself as an instrument of divine will, his reactive narcissistic rage was similarly inflated and it may have reached a psychotic level.

While the author does not think that Osama bin Laden is psychotic, he agrees with Miliora about his being deeply identified with the warrior-prophet Mohammad, who he idealizes as a grandiose self-object. Osama bin Laden is consumed by a narcissistic fantasy that leads him to assert himself in a divine mission to achieve a worldwide Islamic revolution. Osama seems to emphasize martyrdom and an Ahab-like violent vengeance, and not a future benevolent utopia under Sharia law.

Osama's unconscious and conscious narcissistic fantasies stem from profound childhood losses (father and best friend); separations (from his mother via parental separation before the death of his father when Osama was 10 years old); and profound ambivalence and disappointment (admiration/identification with his father's devout Wahhabism and ambition, but also unconscious rage and disappointment in his father's devotion to money and Western materialism). These narcissistic wounds have led Osama on a lifelong quest to find, befriend, and incorporate the ideas and philosophy of older father and brother figures (Azzam, Turabi, Qutb and al-Zawahiri, Mullah Omar, et al.). Osama has also attempted to compensate for his ambivalence toward his father by becoming an omnipotent worldwide father-figure warrior/hero for disaffected Arab and Muslim youth.

They adore Osama as a great mythic rebel hero. Osama seems to adore the inner sense of fantasized restitution and revenge he obtains over disappointing Saudi father figures and their Western friends. Nevertheless, the process is endless and incomplete because it requires perpetual external action and destructive acting out.

Osama also experienced *dark epiphanies* (Olsson 2005, 38–39, 148). When Osama returned from Afghanistan a conquering hero, his offer to lead forces to protect Saudi Arabia from Iraq was ignored by Saudi leaders in favor of protection from American forces, whose presence Osama despised. His rage at Saudi leaders and their counter anger at him led to Osama losing his Saudi citizenship and fleeing to exile in Sudan and later Afghanistan. U.S. President George W. Bush, British Prime Minister Tony Blair, and the ruling Saudi dictators are stand-ins for Osama's unconscious narcissistic rage at his long-deceased father, who worshipped at the altar of materialism yet rigidly advocated strict Wahhabism for his sons.

It also is fruitful to undertake the applied self-psychological study of how Osama and other terror cult leaders influence disaffected Arab, Muslim, and even a few American and Western youths. These adolescents and young adults have often suffered themselves while watching their parents being humiliated, oppressed, and impoverished in countries ruled by wealthy dictators who are perceived as puppets of America. They idolize Osama and resonate with the suffering of his life journey and his heroism during the defeat of the Soviets in Afghanistan. Osama's personal rebellious identity and *jihad* of acting out has led to a peculiar celebrity status as an anti-American, anti-Western, anti-Israeli pied piper and Robin Hood–like mythic hero. An understanding of Osama's mind and those of his followers can help with American diplomacy, foreign aid, and education policy formation. It is not that American foreign policy is a direct cause of terrorism, but rather, insensitivities in our policies are magnified and used to fuel hatred of America and to form propaganda against us. Terror cults use this social psychological atmosphere to aid in their recruitment of followers.

9

MORE HOPEFUL WORLD VIEWS AND APPROACHES TO SOCIAL JUSTICE THAN THOSE OF OSAMA AND COMPANY'S ISLAMOFASCISM

HEINZ KOHUT

There are other views that transcend bin Laden and other radical Islamists' tragic fundamentalist mentality. For example, Kohut, in his 1985 "Vein of Hopefulness for Group Selves," made a poignant, heuristic, and prescient statement:

> What moves society towards health is the work of creative individuals in religion, philosophy, art, and in the sciences concerned with man (sociology, political science, history, psychology). These "leaders" are in empathic contact with the illness of the group-self and, through their work and thought, mobilize the unfulfilled narcissistic needs and point the way toward vital internal change. It follows that during crisis and periods of regressive identification of the group-self with pathological leaders, there is an absence of creativity in religion, philosophy, art, and the sciences of man. The absence of experimental art during such periods is a striking phenomenon. Creativity in all fields is choked off. There is no one in empathic touch with the diseased group-self. This points toward the increasingly worsening condition of the group-self (corresponding to the disintegration threat of incipient psychosis in individual psychology) and leads to pathological ad hoc solutions. (Kohut 1985, 247–48)

There is strong evidence of diseased group selves in the Middle East (Israel and Palestinians), in bin Laden's Al Qaeda, and in the frightening American notion of preemptive war. It was not a healthy sign for the American group-self when

Laura Bush cancelled a poetry reading at the White House because she had learned that many poets against the Iraq war planned to read their poetry. (See poem, "The Emperor's New Duds," in Chapter 7.)

"Modern" diplomatic efforts seem to involve speech making, pontificating, the power politics of military or economic threats, and refusal to talk as ways to pressure or manipulate an enemy nation or group. Allowing enemies to remonstrate, ventilate, discuss grievances, and see and hear our leaders face-to-face can, of itself, only help. Withholding is a childish and passive-aggressive approach and almost never helps to create empathy, honesty, or understanding. A smile, a shared lunch or dinner without tasters to detect poison, and firm, clear discussion of views and positions rarely is harmful; for example, the current Iranian president who speaks of the destruction of Israel but probably has never spent time getting to know a Jewish person face-to-face. Our U.S. president will not even respond to a provocative/evocative letter from Mr. Ahmadinejad of Iran. In the letter the Iranian president bluntly criticizes our president's policies and even his Christianity in an "open letter." Mr. Bush could have used the exchange of letters to respectfully and steadily assert some of the seminal ideas about democracy formulated by our founding fathers. Mr. Bush could have sincerely clarified his thoughts about a dialogue between sincere Christians, Jews, and Muslims. In addition to Dr. Billy Graham, George W. Bush could benefit from collaboration with psychologists, psychiatrists, and psychoanalysts knowledgeable about politics like Post, Volkan, Swogger, et al. Sadly, the leaders of America and Iran have never broken bread together. It is much harder to annihilate another country's leader or his country by nuclear blasts if you have had a meal together, listened to each other, and perhaps shared pictures of each other's family. Mr. Bush's pontification about looking into Mr. Putin's eyes and detecting a "good soul" is far less important than the fact that they have spent time together and listened to each other thoroughly. Some psychoanalysts and political psychologists have contributed to an in-depth understanding of diseased selves and the therapeutic leadership processes that help to heal small and large group's hatred and misunderstanding of each other. Let us examine the work of one such psychoanalyst and his associates.

VAMIK VOLKAN

The work of psychoanalyst Vamik Volkan provides hopeful leadership in providing two tools particularly relevant to this study: (1) an approach to the understanding of political leaders and the psychological complexity of how they make decisions (Volkan et al. 1998); and (2) the carefully developed process of "unofficial diplomacy" (i.e., psychoanalytically informed, or "Track II" diplomacy). Volkan's approaches can be a treasure trove of resources for the "leaders" Kohut mentions above. There is hope, but as Volkan says (1999, 266–67, 348), the road is not easy.

A Presentation of Volkan et al.'s (1998) Understanding of Political Leaders and Their Decision-Making Process

The Group for the Advancement of Psychiatry (GAP) has a Committee on International Relations. From 1989 to 1996, while I was a member of this committee, we studied the psychological domains of political leaders and their decision-making process. We interviewed political leaders and experts among diplomats, political scientists, and historians who have written about this subject. Our GAP Committee's study of the literature and these materials led to many conceptions and observations that I will present below.

Every human being is affected by decisions made by other human beings in positions of power, ranging from elected officials to parents or caretakers, and from the line foreman in a factory to the pastor in a church. Yet the process of decision making at either the individual or political level, or within the groups and organizations in between, is not fully understood.

People may tend to not question decision making because they believe, or wish to believe, that important decisions are based on the use of logic and reason to carefully weigh options and make the best possible choice. At the individual level, we like to think that we are generally and primarily rational; those who behave irrationally are judged to be not "normal" and in need psychological help, medication, or incarceration. To an even greater degree, we wish to believe that our leaders, especially political leaders, make objective and rational decisions. Although we may not always agree with decisions made by elected or appointed officials, we presume that there were specific grounds upon which their choice was based. A leader may not have had accurate or appropriate information that caused an error in judgment, but we do not doubt that a logical process was nevertheless engaged in and available data was carefully evaluated.

Even if a leader is in fact prone to irrational or deficient decision making, we further presume that in a democratic country, a formal and informal system of checks and balances involving virtually every layer of government functions is in place to negate decisions that are not in the nation's best interest. Nations or other large political entities are therefore conceived as collective *rational actors* (see Volkan et al. 1998, 172). Given these assumptions, few can tolerate the idea that important domestic or international policy decisions can be heavily tainted by an individual's emotions, personality organization, the psychological impact of previous developmental experiences, and other factors beyond the realm of "reason."

This bias is reflected in the prevalence of "rational actor," "utility maximizing," and "game" theories utilized by many political scientists, economists, sociologists, and others who examine decision makers, their decisions, and the policies that are implemented. Our GAP Committee on International Relations found Barner-Barry and Rosenwein's 1985 book's summary of the Rational Actor Model's seven-stage process very helpful. The Rational Actor Model identifies the problem; clarifies specific goals; ranks relative priorities; specifies alternative solutions; describes costs and benefits of each approach; makes a comparative analysis of alternatives; and selects the best alternative with the hope that his followers will agree with him that "the buck stops there."

Yet, as mental health professionals and behavioral scientists are well aware, "irrationality" pervades human relationships at every level, and our perspectives, perceptions, decisions, and actions derive from a complex intertwining of our internal and external worlds, past and present, reason and emotion, fact and fantasy, and cognitive processes and instinctual drives.

Unconscious, condensed psychodynamic factors and the multiple personal meanings of events almost invariably intrude into the process of decision making. Through the application of psychoanalytic insights, it becomes clear that no matter how strong the wish for a leader to be perfect, without flaw, and unaffected by emotions, such a leader cannot exist. A leader who made decisions without any emotion would be an anomaly and potentially dangerous, since emotion is also critical to good judgment. To truly understand a leader, and to understand the decisions that he or she makes, we must look deeper than the surface. In a leader, we seek and symbolize many things, and leaders themselves seek and symbolize in their own ways. For example, the emotional intensity behind George W. Bush's array of stated reasons for invading Iraq is as strong as Osama bin Laden's about why he ordered and supported 9/11. They both feel they were absolutely right.

Our GAP committee concluded that unlike the nation-state wars that characterized much of the nineteenth and twentieth centuries, recent and ongoing wars have often occurred within, rather than between, states and have involved neighboring large groups that possess many similarities, yet insist that they are inherently and irreconcilably different. The large groups (i.e., ethnic, national, or religious) entangled in these bloody struggles typically have been engaged in an exaggerated process of defining or redefining their identity. As empires and foreign influence disintegrated, the members of various ethnonational groups began to increase their attachment to what they defined as their "own" large group, and simultaneously focused more and more on what differentiates and delineates them from their neighbors. In some cases, this process gained enough strength to greatly influence political, legal, economic, military, and other aspects of domestic and international decision making.

When large groups regress and become preoccupied with the questions "Who are we now?" "How are *we* different from *them?*" and "What will become of *us?*" the result is often a tense and unstable social and political atmosphere in which the group attempts to maintain its sense of a cohesive identity. When a national, ethnic, or religious group perceives a threat or experiences anxiety, both at the individual and collective level, large-group identity often rises to the surface and solidifies into a hard and rigid shell that protects the group and its individual members like a suit of armor. Once the large group puts on this suit of armor, "reality" may become blurred as large-group identity issues are felt more intensely. The possibility for irrational action tends to grow and the potential for violence increases. The seeds of Sunni-versus-Shia civil war long lay dormant under Saddam Hussein's brutal regime. We know that war decisions and civil war decisions, symmetrical and unsymmetrical, are best not made impulsively or out of a leader's unconscious conflicts—but they often are. When Osama bin Laden claims Allah is supporting his *jihad* towards a caliphate, he is no more aware of all his motives and dynamics as George W. Bush is when he speaks of his view of America's sacred promotion of democracy around the world.

Americans, for example, were stunned, enraged, and severely threatened on 9/11. Most all Americans sought to pull together and were ready to support the U.S. president in violent retaliation. The strikes in Afghanistan toward the defeat of Al Qaeda and their protectors among the Taliban was rational and broadly supported by Americans and many in the world community. The far more conflicted and irrational decision to invade Iraq was initially supported by the majority of Americans because of the residual large group identity's suit of armor after 9/11. President George W. Bush's Iraq war decision in retrospect was fraught with irrational dynamics of anxiety, fear, and denial. Among the key blurred realities was faulty groupthink intelligence gathering and interpretation, and poor planning based most tellingly on a shallow understanding of Iraqi religious/political history, society, and culture. The Afghan war decision can be studied as a largely rational and good presidential decision. The Iraq war decision, according to many scholars, can be studied as a poor presidential decision. It has certainly divided our country internally and has fomented distrust and disrespect among even our closest allies. Irrationality in a president and his entourage, no matter what the basis, can be an important area to study and most of all to learn from. The prevention of impulsive and distorted group war-think is of life and death significance in the nuclear age. This effort is vitally important whether in the entourage of bin Laden/al-Zawahiri, or in that of Bush/Cheney.

The Leader's Entourage and The Leader's Decisions

In probing the nature of the leader's decision-making and how it relates to his or her entourage, our GAP committee found the work of Mathew Holden very valuable. Holden (1984, 1988) considers the basic administrative structure of any nation to be tripartite. The three central elements are: (1) the president (general secretary, prime minister, or king); (2) the entourage; and (3) the operating entities that perform the ultimate administrative work (departments, ministries, boards, commissions, etc.). In essence, administration and politics are inseparable; it is impossible to organize or maintain administrative control without the endlessly repetitive decisions and actions that call for discretion regarding force, money, or information. Bargaining and command are alternative modes of giving and reacting to executive direction from the center of power outward. Chief executives have more to do than they can master personally, resulting in the need for an executive entourage with two essential functions: to serve the personal needs of the executive and provide institutional arrangements for extending the power or reach of the chief executive.

The word "entourage" comes from the French word *entourer,* meaning to surround. It generally refers to a leader's personal attendants and circle of subordinates or advisors who protect the leader's political interests. This small group around the leader can help the leader make effective decisions, or the individuals in it can even make decisions for the leader. The personal side of the entourage stems from the chief executive's need to surround himself or herself with comfortable or supportive people who will not cause a disturbance to their leader's core of self-esteem. In his study of the entourages of presidents, Holden (1984) describes three kinds of personal servants who have served U.S. presidents: the "cronies," the ambitious young servants, and the migratory technocrats.

The *cronies* represent persons of senior status who are the president's peers, friends, and trusted personal advisors. President Reagan's "kitchen cabinet" consisted of a group of wealthy Californians who played an important part in his early political nurturing as he moved from being a young Democrat to a conservative Republican leader. President George W. Bush chose conservative or popular cronies of his father's and Reagan's administrations (Rumsfeld, Cheney, Rice, Colin Powell, etc.). Such senior aides and advisors occupy positions and stations that do not allow them to accept the personal subordination that either the practical needs or the self-esteem of a chief may require. The cronies are respected, trusted, and intuitively comprehended by the chief.

The *ambitious young servants* are deeply loyal and passionately dedicated to the chief. They will perform whatever services are required, or imagined to be required, more or less without question. Errand running falls to the young who are equipped with the enthusiasm and zealous obedience born of the ambition to rise in status. Holden (1984) found that seven out of 10 presidential aides have been at least 10 years younger than the president they served. Between 1864 and 1984, three in 10 of the identifiable chief aides have been 35 or under when they initially assumed their responsibilities. George W. Bush's choices of Karl Rove, Mike Brown ("Brownie"), and Alberto Gonzales may have been glaringly poor decisions. Bush's emphasis on political loyalty among his appointees has often trumped basic competence and empathy for the needs of all American citizens.

The *migratory technocrats* provide special advice and complexly integrated information to the leader. This information is neither purely technical nor purely political. The migratory technocrats render their skills to whatever chief executive occupies the office. Henry Kissinger and Zbigniew Brzezinski are good examples. They resemble the seventeenth- and eighteenth-century political technocrats, who migrated from court to court and country to country as opportunity beckoned or necessity dictated. These technocrats are politically skillful and attentive to indicators of power, and they are very aware of media power. David Gergen, for example, has served as a migratory media guru for both Republican and Democratic administrations. The migratory technocrats in the president's entourage usually have more education than the cronies and more status than the ambitious youngsters. Their articulated purpose is service to the nation, and they fill an important need for a modern leader.

Holden (1984) contends that the president of the United States probably cannot appraise, based on his own personal knowledge, more than three or four out of every 100 people he appoints to positions requiring Senate confirmation or who join his own entourage. Holden states that most White House decision making boils down to White House staff members competing for the attention of those very senior staff members who see the president most frequently.

The decision-making group within a president's entourage normally consists of a small group of 8–12 members. Institutional, organizational, and even societal decisions usually come from individual or small-group deliberations. Small-group decisions have both advantages and disadvantages. The advantages include the combined knowledge and experience of the small group members, the potential for contrasting points of view, and the possibility of effectively carrying out the small-group decision. The disadvantages include pressure to conform, the tendency for an individual to try to dominate the process, and time-consuming pontifications in the group. As group size increases, the channels of verbal and nonverbal communication increase exponentially.

Under ordinary or favorable circumstances—when morale is good, political pressures are status quo, and national security is not severely threatened—the decision-making entourage functions as a cohesive task group. Although they theoretically extend the reach of the leader's influence and further his or her program, troubles do occur in this powerful small group.

More Detail About the Ever-Important Notion of "Groupthink"

Janis (1972, 1982) has studied historic decision-making fiascoes and described eight main symptoms of the phenomenon he calls "Groupthink," which can pervade the small-group decision making of the leader and his or her entourage, especially at the time of crisis decision making. The eight symptoms of "Groupthink" are:

1. An illusion of invulnerability that creates excessive optimism and extreme risk-taking by the entourage as a whole. [*Application to Iraq:* Bush/Cheney and their entourage thought the invasion of Iraq and ousting of Saddam would be quick, easy, and relatively inexpensive. They were confident that we would be joyfully greeted as heroes by the Iraqi people. Clearly they were wrong in many ways, and the weapons of mass destruction were an illusion or delusion.]

2. Collective efforts to rationalize away warnings to reconsidered assumptions. [*Application to Iraq:* U.S. generals who thought many more troops and better strategies for the occupation or "the war after the war" were ignored and dismissed.]

3. An unquestioned belief in the group's inherent morality, which inclines members to ignore the complex ethical or moral consequences of their decisions. [*Application to Iraq:* The Wilsonian democratic moral high ground asserted by Bush/Cheney/Rumsfeld/Wolfowitz before the Iraq invasion was breathtaking, but very questionable.]

4. Stereotypic views of rivals and enemies as too evil to warrant genuine attempts to negotiate, or as too weak and stupid to counter mild attempts to defeat them. [*Application to Iraq:* It has taken painful years and the Baker-Hamilton study group to finally stir feeble American efforts towards diplomatic action vis-à-vis Iran, Syria, etc.]

5. Direct pressures on any member who expresses strong arguments against any of the group's stereotypes, illusions, or commitments. Such dissension is perceived as severe disloyalty. [*Application to Iraq:* Bush/Cheney and entourage have been more than subtle in describing Congresspersons, military professionals, media professionals, or statesmen among our allies who vigorously disagree or question their decisions as disloyal, weak, or unpatriotic.]

6. Self-censorship reflecting each member's inclination to minimize to himself the importance of his doubts and counter-arguments. [*Application to Iraq:* Even Colin Powell knuckled under to pressure to be a "good soldier" in the lead-up to the invasion of Iraq. His questions and differing opinions have subsequently been sadly acknowledged.]

7. A shared illusion of unanimity concerning judgments conforming to the majority view, based on the false assumption that silence means consent. [*Application to Iraq:* At a conscious level President Bush sought honest advice about Iraq, but at unconscious levels some observers have questioned his *state of denial*(Woodward 2006). There certainly seemed to be some selective listening going on during the evaluation of "intelligence" before the war.]

8. The emergence of self-appointed "mind-guards" who protect the group from adverse information that might shatter their shared complacency about the effectiveness and morality of their decisions. [*Application to Iraq:* In the author's opinion in hindsight, the dominating personality and administrative/leadership style of Secretary of Defense Donald Rumsfeld and Vice President Cheney would qualify them for the label of "mind-guards."]

In summary, Janis believes that "Groupthink" is a defective pattern of decision making in which members of any small, cohesive group tend to maintain *esprit de corps* by developing a number of shared illusions and group norms that interfere with critical thinking and reality testing. As Janis studied the Bay of Pigs crisis

(1961), he noted the following: A shared illusion of invulnerability that led to excessive risk-taking; a shared illusion of unanimity based on the reluctance of individual members to voice their doubts and the assumption that this silence implied consent; the related tendency of group members to self-censor their own misgivings and in some cases to discourage others from sharing their concerns with the president; and a tendency for John F. Kennedy, acting as a strong group leader, to handle the group's meetings in a way that discouraged discussion of the drawbacks of the emerging plan.

Janis (1972) also observed that Kennedy and his civilian advisers acted in a very deferential way to the authors of the invasion plan, Allen Dulles and Richard Bissell, director and deputy director, respectively, of the CIA. These technocrats had belonged to the Eisenhower administration, and they presented intimidating expertise to an inexperienced Kennedy and his decision-making entourage.

The "bad" decision process regarding the Bay of Pigs experience led Kennedy to set up a system by which he could get information independent of the federal bureaucracy. He expanded the expertise and roles of his most trusted advisors in national security and concentrated more power in the White House staff. Kennedy also became more circumspect about revealing his own thoughts to his advisors so as not to be told only what he wanted to hear. He grew more skeptical of federal agencies and became very wary of the unanimity of advisors' opinions. All of these painful experiences eventually paid off for the Kennedy administration, and he subsequently was able to make "good" decisions after the initial chaos of the Cuban Missile Crisis in 1962.

We can only imagine the range of conscious and unconscious conflicts, groupthink distortions, and power struggles that pervade Bin Laden/al-Zawahiri's entourage. At times it appears that Osama bin Laden and Ayman al-Zawahiri have a definite though layered entourage. For the sake of good public relations, Al Qaeda tries to make it appear that their leadership has solidarity and spiritual harmony. Clearly, such harmony is staged, and they are just as conflicted during stressful times as a U.S. president's cabinet. It takes courageous moderate Muslim scholars and politicians to point out that Osama bin Laden and Ayman al-Zawahiri have no legitimate credentials as Muslim clerics, theologians, or experts in Sharia law. Bin Laden and Al-Zawahiri do not talk about any equitable, socially just political process in the post-*jihadi* society. One can assume that they envision a society where like-minded Islamic fundamentalist judges and authorities will rule. Any interests that differ from theirs will be promptly squelched. In America, the courts and the press eventually bring out our leader and his entourage's dirty laundry. Western democratic checks and balances are imperfect, messy, and at times tedious, but they allow for their societies to struggle towards higher levels of social justice that take into account the vagaries of the irrationality of human nature.

Volkan's TENT Analogy Re: Large Group Identity (Volkan et al. 1998)

Our GAP Committee on International Relations entered many fascinating dialogues with the help of Volkan's TENT analogy and his valuable concepts of Chosen Trauma, Chosen Glory, and Large Group Regression. When thinking about the intertwining of individual and large-group identity, it is useful to consider an analogy of a large canvas tent. Volkan helped us to think in terms of learning to wear, from childhood onward, two layers of clothing. The first layer, which belongs to the individual who wears it, fits snugly. It is one's core personal identity that provides an inner sense of sustained individual sameness. The second layer is a loose covering made of the canvas of the large group's tent (the large-group identity) through which the person shares a persistent sense of sameness with others in the large group—providing comfort, belonging, and protection. But because both are worn every day, the individual hardly notices them under normal circumstances. At times of collective stress, however, such as economic crisis, drastic political change, social upheaval, terrorist attack, or war, the garment made of the tent canvas may take on greater importance, and individuals may collectively seek the protection of their large-group tent. The large group's identity tent is held erect by the group's leader (the tent pole). During such periods of large-group anxiety, a leader may intuitively or calculatedly respond to the needs of the group by employing the large group's "chosen traumas" and "chosen glories." These two concepts are crucial for our understanding of any large group under great stress. This is true for nation-states or subgroups within them. Even Islamic fundamentalist groups like the Taliban in Afghanistan or Al Qaeda in Iraq reflect the operation of these dynamic concepts.

Chosen glories are the shared mental representations of events and heroes, which increase self-esteem among group members when they are activated. Such events and the persons associated with them are heavily mythologized over time, and these mental representations become large-group markers. Chosen glories are passed on to succeeding generations through transgenerational transmissions made in parent/teacher–child interactions and through participation in ritualistic ceremonies recalling past successful events. They link children of a large group with each other and with their group, and the children experience increased self-esteem by being associated with such glories. America may use 9/11 as a chosen trauma, but the Taliban uses it as a chosen glory-by-association with Al Qaeda.

In times of stress or war-like situations, leaders reactivate the mental representation of chosen glories to bolster their group's identity. During the Gulf War, Saddam Hussein depended heavily on chosen glories and even associated himself with Sultan Saladin, who had defeated the Christian crusaders in the twelfth century. Through the reactivation of a past event and a past hero, Saddam aimed to create the illusion that a similar triumphal destiny was awaiting his people and that, like Saladin, he was a hero. It did not matter to Saddam that Saladin was not an Arab, but a Kurd, and ruled from Egypt rather than Iraq. All that mattered was that the foreign invaders had been defeated in the past, and would be defeated again. Narcissistic, paranoid, and grandiose leaders are not concerned with the historical accuracy of their touted chosen glories, they merely make the best possible use of them to compose their Malignant Pied Piper political music.

President George W. Bush and his now-departed secretary of defense, Donald Rumsfeld, often used the American chosen glories from World War II to encourage and mobilize Americans against the Islamofascists and the ruthless Hitler-like dictator Saddam Hussein. Both George W. Bush and his father used such imagery in speeches during their Gulf wars.

Chosen trauma refers to the mental representation of an event that has caused a large group to face drastic losses, feel helpless and victimized by another group, and share a humiliating injury. Although each individual in a traumatized large group has his or her own unique core identity and personal reaction to trauma, all members share the mental representations of the tragedies that have befallen the group. Their injured self-images associated with the mental representation of the shared traumatic event are "deposited" into the developing self-representation of children in the next generation. It is as if these children will be able to mourn the loss or reverse the humiliation. If the children cannot deal with what is deposited in them, they, as adults, will in turn pass the mental representation of the event to the next generation. These useful concepts can be applied to understanding a spectrum of trauma-laden and pain-perpetuating problems such as slavery, genocide, terrorism, and civil or religious wars.

Because they involve attempted resolutions of unconsciously given tasks, chosen traumas influence the large group identity more pervasively than chosen glories. Chosen traumas bring with them powerful experiences of loss and feelings of humiliation, vengeance, and hatred. This triggers within the group's members a variety of shared defense mechanisms that attempt to reverse these experiences and feelings. They therefore differ significantly from chosen glories, in which facts may become embellished or mythologized, but there is no need to attempt to reverse the images of experiences and feelings handed down by ancestors. It is frightening to think about the geometrically developing numbers of future generations of young suicide bombers in Palestine, Iraq, or Iran if it becomes a target of Israeli or American preemptive war.

At times of stress, when the group's identity is threatened, chosen traumas are reactivated and can be used by leaders to inflame the group's shared feelings about themselves and their enemy. In the battle for the minds of contemporary Afghanis, the Taliban and Al Qaeda will use the chosen trauma of invaders like the Soviet Union or alleged invaders like the United States/NATO. They will attempt to present the chosen glory of the defeat of the Soviets, to be repeated against American and NATO forces. A *time collapse* can thus occur, and the chosen trauma is then experienced as if it has happened only yesterday. The associated feelings, perceptions, and expectations associated with a past event and a past enemy heavily contaminate those related to current events and current enemies. This leads to maladaptive group behavior, irrational decision making, and resistance to change. Fortunately, America and NATO have not just invaded with huge numbers of troops like the Soviets did. NATO is helping with strengthening Afghan social institutions, the Afghan economy, and rebuilding the infrastructure. In retrospect, America and NATO should have launched these efforts right after the Soviets left Afghanistan after their defeat.

There are many other recent examples we studied where the rise of nationalistic leaders has occurred when they have responded to their large group's needs by invoking chosen traumas and chosen glories. An example we studied is found in Yugoslavia. Slobodan Milosevic unleashed Serb nationalism and helped to support the Serb's collective identity after the collapse of communism's authoritarian control.

In 1389 the Serbs fought the Ottoman Turks in the Battle of Kosovo (not far from the city of Pristina, where Serbs have recently fought ethnic Albanians). The body of the slain Serbian leader, Prince Lazar, was embalmed, placed in a shrine in the nearby monastery of Ravanica, and he was canonized. Although there may not have been a clear victor at Kosovo, as years and then centuries passed, it evolved as the Serb's major chosen trauma that marked the end of a glorious period of Serbian power and the beginning of their subjugation under the Ottomans. The Ottomans eventually controlled most of the Balkans, and Lazar's body was moved to a site farther north where it would be safe.

In 1889, the 500th anniversary of Kosovo, plans for moving Lazar's mummified body back to Ravanica were discussed, but never materialized. As the 600th anniversary in 1989 approached, Milosevic and others in his circle decided to bring Lazar's body out of "exile." Lazar's mummified remains were placed in a coffin and taken "on tour" to every major Serb village and town, where he was received by crowds of mourners dressed in black and religious leaders dressed in their traditional costumes. They greeted Lazar's body on his triumphant return to his original resting place near Kosovo with tears and wailing, and gave speeches saying that they would never allow such a defeat to occur again. As a result of the time collapse of 600 years initiated by Serb leadership, Serbs began to feel that the defeat in Kosovo had occurred only yesterday, an outcome made far easier by the fact that the chosen trauma had been kept alive throughout the centuries by poetry, epic tales, folk songs, paintings, statues, and other means (Volkan 1997, 66–69).

Sharing this mental representation invisibly connected all Serbs more closely, and they began to develop similar self-images in which they felt a new sense of *entitlement for revenge,* although it is unclear whether this is what Milosevic directly and consciously intended. Some leaders sense these dynamics at a level of unconscious intuition. Nevertheless, Milosevic continued to stir nationalist sentiments. For instance, he ordered the building of a huge monument on a hill overlooking the Kosovo battlefield. Made of red stone, representing blood (Kaplan 1993), it stands 100 feet tall and is surrounded by artillery shell shaped cement pillars inscribed with a sword and the dates 1389–1989. On the tower is written Lazar's battle cry that every Serb man come to Kosovo to fight the Turks. If a Serb fails to respond to this call, Lazar's words warn, "He will not have a child, neither male or female, and he will not have fertile land where crops grow."

On June 28, 1989, the 600th anniversary of the Battle of Kosovo, a helicopter brought Milosevic to the site of the new monument. Riding this wave of nationalism, Milosevic's prominence increased. Destructive/exploitive leaders like Milosevic and Osama bin Laden take advantage of large-group vulnerabilities in precisely this way.

In 1990, the six Yugoslav republics held elections in which the Communists were defeated everywhere except Serbia and Montenegro. In Serbia, the Communists were now called the Serb Socialist Party, and Milosevic was elected as party head. He soon would lead the new "Yugoslavia" against Bosnians and other Muslim Slavs who represented the Serb's former oppressors. The power that comes from the mobilization of strong group emotions can be awesome and irrational.

In times of crisis, a large group will typically seek a leader such as Slobodan Milosevic who influences the group in either a progressive or regressive direction, depending on how they utilize the group's chosen traumas and chosen glories, and whether they create new political ideologies or act as the primary spokesperson for an existing ideology. In this sense, a large group is particularly vulnerable during a crisis, such as America during the aftermath of 9/11. Here, we do not use the term *progressive* in a sense that connotes health or the term *regressive* in a sense that suggests the presence of psychopathology, although the example of Milosevic may reflect the latter at both an individual and group level. Rather, these terms refer to the directions of psychopolitical processes and the ensuing influences on the large-group identity: progression shows the evolution of new social investments, and regression is used to illustrate the recapitulation or renewal of previous strengths or supports for the group's identity.

These concepts from Volkan's work and our GAP committee's discussions help us to begin to understand the bewildering and often violent perturbations among nations, within nations, and between tribes and large groups expressing the vast domains of what we call irrational human nature. We certainly can see how Osama bin Laden, Mullah Mohammad Omar, Ayman al-Zawahiri, and other Islamist terror cult leaders can use their call for the return of the Caliphate and their call for violent *jihad* in terms of these large group dynamic and heuristic concepts.

When President Reagan pulled U.S. Marines out of Lebanon after the U.S. Marine barracks were bombed by Hezbollah, it was touted as a chosen glory by Hezbollah. When President Clinton pulled our American troops out of Somalia,

Osama bin Laden, regardless of all the facts, declared the withdrawal a chosen glory for Al Qaeda and radical Islam. Regardless of whether we should have gone into Iraq after Saddam in 2003, if we leave Iraq in the near future, Osama and company will declare it another chosen glory.

George W. Bush's and Rumsfeld's use of *chosen World War II glories* projected onto the Iraq War can be understood by using Volkan's concepts and this application. The threat of worldwide Islamofascism provides more than a kernel of truth for our American paranoia. George W. Bush has expounded upon parallels between 9/11 and Pearl Harbor. When combined with the threat of mushroom clouds from Saddam's potential aggression, George W. Bush played on our fears of a potential *Chosen Trauma*. Bush also uses our World War II chosen glories in defense of democracy to encourage us towards a new chosen glory—i.e., a safer world for our grandchildren when Islamofascism is defeated.

Track II or Unofficial Diplomacy: Volkan's TREE Model

Volkan (1991) refers to Barston's 1988 work that classified official, modern diplomacy into six broad areas:

1. Providing formal representation. Through its embassies a nation's policies are explained and defended, and the host nation's interpreted or negotiated.
2. Serving as a listening post: An embassy identifies the key issues emerging from the patterns of domestic or external events and sends this information to its own government, especially in the case of developments inimical to its interests.
3. Laying the groundwork for new diplomatic initiatives.
4. Reducing friction in case of conflict, when advisable.
5. Managing change effected by #4.
6. Creating, drafting, and amending many international rules of normative and regulatory kind that give structure to the international system (Barston 1988).

Volkan (1999) describes in detail the history of the field of Track II, or unofficial, diplomacy; its major contributors; and its major developments. The author's summary below tries to capture the essence of Track II Diplomacy:

The CSMHI (Center for the Study of Mind and Human Interaction, founded by Volkan) Tree Model is an interdisciplinary approach to reducing ethnic tensions and promoting peaceful coexistence between opposing large groups. The methodology central to the Tree Model is carried out by a team that includes psychoanalysts, psychiatrists, diplomats, historians, and other social scientists. The role of psychoanalytic insight is central, for it provides the lens through which the team seeks to understand the nature of the conflict at hand and the mechanisms and rituals through which large groups in conflict interact.

The Tree Model is rooted in a psychopolitical diagnosis of the situation including the opposing groups' historically based perceptions of each other, their fears and expectations, and the present-day issues to be addressed. The next stage, forming the trunk of the tree, is a two- to three-year series (longer if necessary) of psychopolitical dialogues between members of the opposing groups, convened and led by the CSMHI team. The dialogues seek to loosen rigid positions on both sides and bring previously hidden aspects of the relationship to the surface where they can be discussed and defused. Once the psychological "poisons"— especially unconscious ones—are removed, dialogue participants design together concrete programs and projects to put into practice the insights gained during the dialogues. With the dialogue participants, CSMHI selects a Contact Group to be given the task of implementing and coordinating the proposed projects. These new institutions and programs become the branches of the tree and extensions of the methods of interacting that evolved during the original dialogues. The neutral facilitating team continues to assist and oversee the developing projects, serving as a catalyst when necessary, and continuing to train the Contact Group members as leaders and models.

The Tree Model thus consists of three phases: assessment, dialogue, and institutionalization. What sets it apart from other methods is its attention to the conscious and unconscious psychology of large groups of human beings and the often overlooked or misunderstood rituals between such groups. The methodology seeks to understand and articulate the identity of each large group involved and how the group relates to its neighbor/enemy group. This understanding then informs and supports efforts to remove conscious and unconscious resistances to adaptive change. The Tree Model is a process; over a significant period of time, it engages individuals who become spokespersons for their respective large groups. By increasing understanding of the conscious and unconscious dynamics at work on both sides, new ways of interacting become possible. By developing programs and institutions that implement and encourage such new ways of interacting, what is experienced at first by a few can be spread and available to many more. With appropriate modifications, this Tree Model approach can be applied to a wide variety of situations to help alleviate tensions, prevent violent conflict, heal traumatized societies, and promote peaceful coexistence (Volkan 1999, 206).

Volkan (1999) provides a poignant description of the "Tree Model Process" in describing a Track II situation he calls "Anatomy of a Dialogue." It highlights how important it is for the Track II diplomacy team to be knowledgeable and clinically experienced with this process. It is presented in detail so the reader can picture the usefulness of this in-depth approach to many tense conflict situations.

> Sometimes, at the outset of a dialogue meeting, a disruptive situation evolves abruptly and absorbs the attention and energy of all participants. Such a situation is usually marked with a sense of urgency, yet the content of this "crisis" is essentially

insignificant in comparison to the salient aspects of the ethnic or national conflict for which the dialogue meeting has been organized. It is reminiscent of the extended debates on who sits where at a conference table that sometimes occur prior to important negotiations between nations. Volkan (1999, 164) calls these *mini-conflicts,* and while seemingly inexplicable and incongruous—much like the masques that precede an Elizabethan tragedy—they provide condensed and symbolically suggestive treatments of what will be explored dramatically later in the play itself. Through the mini-conflict, many of the urgent concerns connected with large-group tensions are reduced to a more local and accessible realm.

Volkan describes the process further.

A mini-conflict occurred at a meeting of Israelis, Egyptians, Palestinians, and Americans that took place in Switzerland a few days after the assassination in Portugal of Dr. Issam Sartawi, then the Palestine Liberation Organization's roving envoy. An argument erupted over whether to hold a moment of silence in Dr. Sartawi's memory. The Palestinians naturally wished to do so, but the Israelis did not want to pay this honor to an associate of Chairman Yasser Arafat. Both sides threatened to leave the gathering, and this crisis had to be resolved before negotiations could begin. (Volkan 1999, 164)

Another mini-conflict at the outset of a later dialogue among Israelis, Egyptians, Palestinians, and American facilitators cropped up as if to "protect" the participants from a heated discussion of a recent troublesome development in the ongoing Arab-Israeli conflict. The "problem" concerned the issue of spouses, for the spouses who had accompanied participants were restricted from participating in the dialogue itself. One Palestinian demanded that his wife be allowed to attend the meeting in an official capacity, and this unexpected development quickly took on seemingly critical importance. The large-group issues were obscured and forgotten for the time being (Volkan 1999, 165).

Such frequent occurrences suggest that mini-conflicts are bound up in the mechanism of displacement. Although individual personalities may be predisposed to causing such disruptions, Volkan helped our GAP committee to see that these early crises also represent a group process in operation. The individual and large-group sense of self are heightened in circumstances of physical closeness, thus threatening the paradoxical equilibrium that is maintained between enemies—they "need" each other yet must avoid perceiving that they are too "close" or similar to one another, and therefore must maintain a degree of distance. By creating mini-conflicts, derivatives of aggression are displaced onto an event that is essentially insignificant in comparison to the magnitude of the national or ethnic conflict at hand. Like intellectualization, a mini-conflict acts as a defense mechanism to cover up the anxiety that is at the heart of the real conflict.

While mini-conflicts appear to derail the dialogue, paradoxically they can actually perform a useful function in the process. They can help facilitators establish or reestablish their leadership role. As stated earlier, there are inherently multiple leaders in such gatherings, but if the head of the facilitating team is able to "resolve" the mini-conflict, he or she establishes authority and can redirect participants to work together, thus turning attention to the large-group conflicts at hand.

The mini-conflict in the first example came to an end when Volkan declared that participants could honor the memory of anyone they wanted during the minute of silence. The Israelis decided to go along with this gesture, but openly declared that they would not honor Dr. Sartawi. They chose instead to honor a recently fallen Israeli, Emil Grunzweig, who had been active in Israel's Peace Now movement. In the second example, regarding a Palestinian's demand that his wife attend the meeting, the mini-conflict was resolved by Volkan's declaring, as leader of the American group, that all spouses were welcome. (None actually attended after that invitation.)

Facilitators of unofficial diplomacy should understand the meaning of mini-conflicts, when they arise, in relation to the psychodynamics of a particular gathering. The leader must approach the crisis seriously, with assurance, and with respect toward the participants' large-group sentiments. Mini-conflicts should not be allowed to drag on, as if they were the main focus of the meeting, for if this happens, the whole meeting can be derailed. Psychoanalysts and psychologists experienced in large-group therapy and large-group process can remain confident and composed in such tense circumstances.

The Echo Phenomenon

When representatives of opposing sides open a discussion, the echo of recent events involving their large groups can often be heard in their exchanges, further igniting emotions that exacerbate resistances to adaptive discussions. During psychopolitical dialogues, Volkan described to us how the shadow of some recent military or political development can fall over the work group. It then becomes necessary to acknowledge and assimilate this shadow and its meaning for the opposing group before realistic negotiation or group work can continue. During work with psychiatric residents learning about group dynamics, we teachers notice examples of such echoes. In a learning group, discussing a patient might bring a recent facet of the patient's situation to life. This identification with the patient and reenactment of his or her psychodynamic aspects is carried out unconsciously within the learning group. The leader of the learning group should therefore bring this to the participants' consciousness so that they may benefit from their identification and reenactment—that is, to have a "firsthand" experience about the patient's perceptions and feelings and develop empathy.

In the opening plenary session at the Arab-Israeli workshop—described to our GAP committee as we studied it with Volkan—we heard that, following the one-minute silence in memory of Dr. Sartawi and Mr. Grunzweig, many aggressive remarks were heard, but the affect was flat. Volkan had noted his own inner anxiety; he shared with us how he pondered how the shadow of the assassinations seemed to inhibit the expression of emotions, especially aggressive emotions related to vengeance and the desire to "get even." Our GAP committee's counter-transference feelings resonated with the emotionally charged events that Volkan shared with us.

The psychodynamics of vengeance in the individual have been studied by Charles Socarides (1977). In the context of the psychopolitical dialogues, Volkan's aim was to focus on the idea that participants' anxiety over their own aggression in the Arab-Israeli conflict might induce in them an unconscious identification with the assassins, or else a hidden anxiety that they might be assassinated themselves. Throughout the years, Volkan has observed that participants who voluntarily become involved in unofficial dialogues with the enemy are seen to some degree as "traitors" by those in their own community who are against all communication with the enemy. These participants may also experience shame, which is intensified if and when the enemy carries out some violent act while the talks are going on. The reader can use his or her imagination about what similar issues might intrude into a Track II diplomacy effort between Sunni and Shiite politicians in present-day Iraq.

In the case of the workshop described above, the echo of the assassinations of Dr. Sartawi and Mr. Grunzweig seemed to have induced a variety of feelings among the participants: vengeance, identification with the aggressor, fear of being a target of aggression, and also heightened shame. When Volkan and the participants at the conference went to a restaurant for dinner in Vevey, Switzerland, where this meeting was held, they were aware of the security measures taken as a precaution. Swiss police patrolled the street outside, and Palestinian participant Elias Frej, then mayor of Bethlehem, was careful not to sit in front of an open window. Volkan was seated between an Israeli psychoanalyst and a Palestinian lawyer. When the latter expressed a desire to learn something about schizophrenia, the Israeli and Volkan replied from their professional perspectives. Then the conversation returned to violence and aggression: the lawyer wanted to know if John Hinckley Jr., the would-be assassin of then-President Ronald Reagan, was schizophrenic, and he bemoaned the impossibility of protecting society from "crazy killers." Volkan noted that the lawyer might be trying to rid himself of aggressive impulses and feelings, in a displaced fashion, by speaking of John Hinckley. (Tragically, not long after this conversation took place, this Palestinian was himself brutally murdered in Gaza. The *Palestinian Weekly* [December 6, 1985] attributed the killing to Abu Nidal or another similar group. It was then clear to Volkan and most other group facilitators that participants' sense of being "traitors" was not just a fantasy. They became more aware of the realities entailed as participants "reentered" their communities after attending such dialogues.)

It seems clear that the potential value of Track II diplomacy is enormous in terms of engaging the authentic emotions beneath the surface of intergroup dialogue, even though many Islamist groups are inaccessible because of the alienation their terrorist actions have created. It seems that it could be used as "preventative dialogue medicine" to engage university students in Muslim countries or foreign students in American universities. Such Track II diplomacy efforts in in-betweener countries and communities within them could perhaps prevent the recruitment successes of Al Qaeda. It is interesting to speculate about how Track II diplomacy might be applied to the contemporary situation in Iraq. The centuries of chosen glories and chosen traumas are overwhelming to ponder vis-à-vis Sunnis and Shiites. It is no surprise to learn how difficult it is for "reconciliation" processes to proceed in Iraq.

LLOYD DEMAUSE

DeMause (2006) describes a study by Palestinian psychologist Shafig Massalha who randomly gave 150 boys and girls aged 10–11 notebooks to record their dreams. Massalha found that 78 percent of the children's dreams were political, and most included physical violence. Half of the children dreamed of becoming suicide bombers. The abusive Palestinian "leaders" and these children's parents tell these children that it is their duty to kill themselves and others "for Allah." The children are often given suicide bomb belts to march around in for practice. An 11-year-old Palestinian girl dreamed that she went into an Israeli market with bombs all over her body and blew herself up in a crowd of shoppers. DeMause says: "And there is a parallel between the sexual submission of young boys to older men in Palestinian society" (2006, 304). These findings correlate closely with Rona Fields's research and my thoughts about radical fundamentalist Muslim child-rearing and pseudohomosexual conflicts in young Muslim men.

DeMause boldly confronts the issue of solutions to abusive Palestinian child-rearing practices in a manner I think Kohut would value:

> Rather than backing military solutions to Palestinian terrorism, America and Israel should instead back a UN-sponsored Marshall Plan for them, designed to reduce the abusive childrearing that is creating the terrorists. Just as the Marshall Plan we created for Germans and Austrians after WWII allowed families to evolve far beyond those that produced Nazism, we put real money and organized effort into a Palestinian Parenting Plan that will help families give better parenting to their children. (DeMause 2006, 305–6)

An existing "Palestine Happy Child Center" in Ramallah was established as an NGO in 1994. It operates with a holistic approach to child rearing and, if more broadly supported by U.S. and Israeli funds, could give the message that Israel and America are not simply against Palestinians.

Robert McFarland set up a Community Parenting Center in Boulder, Colorado, 23 years ago. The center provides lectures for parents, play groups for children with puppet shows that demonstrate parent-child interactions, postpartum depression assistance, support groups dealing with behavior problems without hitting a child, help for unmarried mothers and immigrants, talks on setting limits for toddlers, and even free home visits to new mothers by volunteers to give pediatric and psychological help. It has been demonstrated that for every dollar spent to support this free family center, hundreds of dollars are saved in later costs for social services, jails, and hospitals (DeMause 2006, 306).

DeMause describes helpful models like the one developed by psychiatrist Margaret R. Kind. Dr. Kind taught a course in "parenting" to 30 high school classes. DeMause (2006, 307) comments sardonically that although parenting is one of the most important tasks in any society, there have never previously been courses teaching about it in schools. Of course, normal adolescents will have plenty of vigorous criticism about the job their own parents are doing, but their very focus on the topic will help avoid some mistakes in their own future task of parenting. Hopefully this would also include postponing having children until they are better prepared for the responsibility.

In summary, DeMause (2006, 305–7) proposes unique, idealistic, but possible ideas for troubled regions like Palestine. He advocates a type of psychological Marshall Plan that provides supportive Parenting Education Centers, Home Visiting Programs, and High School Parenting Courses. These primary prevention programs provide guidance, support, and education to parents and future parents in troubled communities. Over the long haul, these programs can reduce rigid, fundamentalist attitudes about men and women and child rearing.

MAHMOUD MOHAMMAD TAHA: SUDAN'S REMARKABLE AND RADICALLY PEACEFUL MARTYR OF ISLAM

Taha was 76 years old when he was executed by Sudan's President Gaafar Nimeiry on January 18, 1985. He was a theologian and leader in the Sudanese Republican party, and had always advocated liberal reform in Sudan and in Islam. Taha had played a prominent role in Sudan's struggle for independence. Packer (2006, 62) astutely observes and summarizes:

Mahmoud Mohammad Taha is the anti-Qutb. Taha, like Qutb, was hanged by an Arab dictatorship; he was executed, in 1985, for sedition and apostasy, after protesting the imposition of Sharia in Sudan by President Jaafar al-Nimeiri. In death, Taha became something rare in contemporary Islam: a moderate martyr. His method of reconciling Muslim belief with twentieth-century values was, in its way, every bit as revolutionary as the contrary vision of Qutb.

Since 9/11, millions of people around the world have heard of Qutb, but Taha is almost unknown. Taha was executed by an Arab dictatorship in 1985. He had been declared an apostate because he protested the rigid imposition of Sharia Law in Sudan by President Jaafar Al-Nimeiri. If Qutb was a martyr for radical Islamism, Taha was a moderate martyr of Islam. Taha valiantly tried to harmonize Muslim belief and twentieth-century values. If more people and their Imams around the world knew about and had studied Taha, maybe television images of Islam would not so often be dominated by masked jihadis and frenzied anti-American mobs (Packer 2006, 62).

Taha was born in 1909 in Rufa'a, a small town on the bank of the Blue Nile in central Sudan. When he was six years old his mother died, and he and his three siblings worked on his father's farm until his father Mohammad Taha died in 1920. Taha's aunt supported his education, and he went on to engineering school at Gordon Memorial College that eventually became the University of Khartoun. He graduated in 1936 and spoke out iconoclastically against the educated elite of Sudan who showed far too much patronage to the colonial powers and traditional religious leaders. Mahmoud helped form the Republican party in 1945 and was imprisoned for a year when he refused to stop his political activities. The British governor pardoned him, but like so many malignant radical "bad guys" we have discussed, this peaceful progressive "good guy" was put in prison again for two years for leading a revolt against the British in his hometown of Rufa'a.

Taha's seclusion continued after his release in 1948. He prayed, fasted, and read widely (Wells, Shaw, Russell, Lenin, Marx) in a hut near his in-laws. While in seclusion, Taha spoke to few people and had long unruly hair and bloodshot eyes. His wife brought him simple food, but her family urged her to divorce her formerly successful professional husband, who many people thought was becoming psychotic. She refused. In this three-year period Taha developed his radically new vision of the meaning of the Koran. After this period of seclusion (1951), he dedicated the rest of his life to teaching it (Packer 2006, 62).

In his most important book, called *The Second Message of Islam* (1967), Taha emphasizes that the Koran was revealed to Mohammad in two phases. The first was in Mecca for 13 years when Mohammad addressed humanity in general and is filled with notions of freedom, equality, sincerity, worship, kindness and peaceful coexistence. In Medina, the verses are full of rules, coercion, threats and "law of the sword." (These two seem a bit like the Christian Old Testament [law and violence] and the New Testament [love and atonement].) The Meccan verses are the ideal Islam of freedom and equality that will be revived when humanity has reached a stage of development or spiritual evolution when it is capable of accepting them (Packer 2006, 63).

Taha used the name "Republican Brothers" for his new spiritual movement, and his disciples recall him as a transformed, saintly presence like Christ or Socrates. He was a "revered teacher" who welcomed argument but with honesty, serenity, intellectual vigor, and charisma. Taha is sometimes compared to Gandhi by some Sudanese and perhaps the twentieth century was not ready for "The Second Message of Islam!" He was constantly condemned by Sudanese and Egyptian clerics and his movement was under attack by the fundamentalist Muslim Brotherhood (Packer 2006, 63).

Taha used his prison (closed-space) experience to urge Muslims to seek liberal reform and extensive modification of Islamic law. He felt that Islam could grow freely in its applied theology toward creative applications to spiritually enrich modern life. Packer observed that Taha's teaching style was not unlike that of Socrates. And I think Taha's style is like Jesus and Gandhi, as well.

Taha's teachings, not unlike those of Socrates, collided with the power politics of the establishment. Sudan's military dictator, Jaafar al-Nimeiri, who seized power in 1969, is an opportunistic tyrant who used one political model after another (Marxism, Arab nationalism, pro-Americanism) to justify his control of Sudan. Turabi, the brilliant political henchman and manipulator, was an enemy of Taha. Taha had once alienated Turabi with a slight by saying "Turabi is clever but not insightful." It is very likely that Taha's execution for apostasy was bogus and engineered by Turabi. Taha was offered a way to repent under Sharia, but he refused and went to his hanging with head held high. He told his Republican brothers, "You back down. As for me, I know that I'm going to be killed. If not in court, the Muslim Brotherhood will kill me in secret" (Packer 2006, 65). If only Muslim political thinkers could fully grasp the dialectic process of democracy that Jefferson and Adams argued within and who never contemplated assassination as a method.

In the decade after Taha's death, Turabi was the political strategist of the Islamist revolution and the reign of terror of Omar al-Bashir. Very recently, Turabi has been declaring that women and men are equal. He now says that women can lead Islamic prayers, and covering their heads is not obligatory. Apostasy is not a crime for Turabi now and Muslim women can marry Christians and Jews. In Khartoum, people were amazed that Turabi sounded exactly like Taha. Turabi seems to be aware of his terrible failures and Sudan's mire of mass death, slavery, civil war, and genocide. Taha would likely chuckle from his grave at his old enemy's attempts to be a newborn "Republican Brother." Taha, if like Socrates he could have many Platos to expound on his ideas, could be like a breath of spiritual fresh air to the Muslim world.

ONE-ON-ONE, PERSON-TO-PERSON, UNOFFICIAL (TRACK II) DIPLOMACY: THE AUTHOR'S REMARKABLE E-MAIL PEN PAL IN BAGHDAD, IRAQ

The almost total worldwide availability of personal computers and the Internet has completely changed the world. Al Qaeda and other practitioners of the so-called asymmetric terror wars have made full and creative use of the Internet.

Osama bin Laden, Al Qaeda spokespersons, and other radical Islamists rail at times against modernity and "the West." Yet, they make full use of the Internet to espouse their ideology, recruit new leaders and foot soldiers, communicate about bomb making, and even transmit their unfolding plans of attack. The author proposes that America should promote a worldwide e-mail pen-pal network to foster friendships, collegial dialogue, person-to-person education/information-sharing, and help create good will. Such a new form of unofficial diplomacy could reinvigorate the spirit of outreach by Americans to Muslim communities and individuals. This network could extend the same spirit that the Peace Corps, college semester-abroad programs, and international student exchange programs have helped to establish. This program would help facilitate dialogue, conferences, and conversations between Muslim clergypersons, physicians, lawyers, businesspersons, merchants, skilled workers, and other individuals with their American counterparts. Such exchanges provide a unique diplomatic dimension because the participants are not professional diplomats or military personnel.

Serendipity Smiles, and the Author Makes a Unique Iraqi Friend

Serendipity: "An aptitude for making desirable discoveries by accident. Horace Walpole named such a faculty in 1754. The word is derived from the Arabic name for Sri Lanka. It was a characteristic possessed by the three heroes of a fairy tale called *The Three Princes of Serendip*."

(Random House Webster's College Dictionary 2001, 1200)

These three free-spirited princes were sent out on missions for the king of Ceylon. But rather than bringing back what they were sent out to find, they brought back other valuable, beautiful, and important things.

On August 4, 2005, I received an e-mail from the editor of a psychoanalytic journal about a young physician colleague in Baghdad. Here is Dr. H's e-mail to the editor:

Dear Editor (August 2, 2005)

I am a psychiatrist from Iraq. I am interested in psychoanalysis and trying to study the subject of motivation for terrorist acts. I think that if we can know the motivation then we can run prophylaxis on long run especially that there is no evidence for phenomenological psychopathology among terrorists.

This subject is important for my country which is injured daily by terrorist acts.

I have the problem that I am not able to find references about the subject. There are many in Medline especially from cites of psychoanalysis but unfortunately abstracts are too short and not enough. I wish I could have your help for how to get whole text articles about the subject—waiting your answer.

Regards, Dr. H.
Baghdad, Iraq

Obviously, Dr. H was interested in more detailed information about psycho-analytic and psychodynamic ideas about group process, large-group dynamics, and psychodynamic theories about terrorism and suicide bombers. He had reviewed the general medical and descriptive psychiatry literature about terrorism and terrorists. Dr. H wanted to deepen his understanding of the psychodynamic, self-psychological, and social psychological roots of terrorism and suicide bombing. Dr. H had read several abstracts and summaries of articles by psychoanalysts, but he was having trouble finding full texts or reprints of psychoanalytic or psychodynamic articles on the subject of terrorism or suicide bombing. Dr. H's inquiry impressed me with its sincerity and poignant relevance.

I immediately sent Dr. H copies of several books and photocopies of articles by Vamik Volkan and myself. Dr. H was very grateful for my efforts and soon read and digested everything I had sent him. Dr. H and I have exchanged thoughts and observations through e-mails once or twice weekly ever since our serendipitous meeting. We have exchanged pictures of our children and ourselves. The dialogue, collaboration, and friendship that developed with Dr. H have taught me many things about the political and social psychology of Iraq. My newfound friend's wisdom and courage in the midst of daily fear and terror has earned my deepest respect. I pray constantly for my friend Dr. H and his family.

E-Mail Exchanges from and to Baghdad

The following section is a selected and annotated chronological account of my correspondence with Dr. H. It contains our exchanges of ideas and Dr. H's insightful descriptions of Iraq's conundrums of terror and exponentially painful changes. Dr. H made major contributions to Chapter 5 of this book. Dr. H's ability to express himself in English is infinitely better than my complete ignorance of Arabic. Direct quotes from Dr. H are unaltered and will reflect some of the language limitations, but the genuine sharing is also clear.

October 10, 2005, 10:16 PM
  Dear Dr. Olsson
  Thank you for your follow up. I need this. I was reviewing the books and papers. My work is slow and I apologize for this because I am doing this work as personal interest in my free time, something that is not easy in our chaotic life in Iraq. Next week I am going to present a review of these papers in a symposium arranged by our Student Scientific Society in my college according to the request by students. I think this will be useful to them and is a way to transmit ideas about the subject to youths. The aspects that I found to be of interest include:
  1—There is a problem of identity to youth who are driven to terrorist cults. The idea of "not me" as presented by Kohut is of importance here.

Actually, as Dr. H and I discussed, Kohut (1971, 8, 11) refers to "the fragmented self"; Winnicott (1986, 65–70), "the false self"; and Erikson (1964, 97–100), "negative identity formation." Any one of the three might be very applicable here.

Dr. H continued:

> *I think that the Islamic and Arab identity is living in crisis. This identity is not strong enough now to give youth a chance to be identified with in a healthy way. If you look to artistic productions in Arab countries. If you look at satellite channels of Arabic countries—You find a senseless copy of Western style. This is one way to see that there is no unique identity for Muslim youth or adults nowadays. That's why some individuals shift into radical Salafi movements in their craving for identity.* [A profound observation!]
> *2—The problem of identity not only affects potential terrorists but the whole society and as a result we find that the mass acceptance and sympathy of Arab citizens occurs towards the terrorist acts. This creates a reinforcement factor for the terrorists because their acts are perceived as heroic and gain fame for them through the modern mass media.*
> *3—The cause of this identity confusion is because Islamist teachings are not able to stand for the new developments in civilization and modern democratic life. So the youth is faced with conflicts about obeying the strict* fundamentalist *teachings, or expressing free self-motives and ideas. These are some of the aspects I am thinking about.*
> V.H.

I was impressed with the thinking and searching of this young Iraqi psychiatrist, who clearly grasped quickly the notion that simplistic ideas that would label terrorists as merely psychopathic criminals or psychotic individuals is inadequate. He was hungry for psychodynamic ideas about the self, the group-self and social psychological concepts to be applied to terrorism prevention and suicide bomber recruitment prevention. It is a moving experience to sense such a kindred spirit and resonance of ideas with a young colleague who is so far away but yet at a terrifying vortex of raw terror cults' evil presences.

November 1, 2005, 3:22 PM

Dear Doctor H,

I am pleased that your presentation about the psychology of suicide bombers has the enthusiastic support of your dean. Congratulations on the publication of your monograph. You are wise to be mindful of political issues because of the turmoil and uncertainty in your country.

If I understood you correctly, many thoughtful, feeling, and compassionate people like yourself must have felt like you were in moral and spiritual hibernation or a limbo of fear—during Saddam's brutal autocracy. Just because he is gone may not mean that the troubles are over. The hangover from Saddam must be great and the uncertainty still enormous. America as you know has struggled with freedom and democracy and it got so messy that we had a horrible, bloody and spiritually draining civil war. One of our early American political leaders James Madison said,

"First a good government must have order and control over its citizens, then, it must have control of the government."

You, in my opinion, are showing great depth of what Erik Erikson called generativity. In his famous book, Childhood and Society, Erikson describes the "Eight Ages of Man" that occur in each person's life development. According to Erikson's Epigenetic Principle, normal personality development requires accomplishing the critical psychosocial tasks of each childhood and adult life phases in sequence. They are (1) Basic Trust vs. Mistrust (Freud's Oral Phase); (2) Autonomy vs. Shame and Doubt (Freud's Anal Phase); (3) Initiative vs. guilt (Freud's Phallic/Oedipal Phase); (4) Industry vs. Inferiority (Freud's Latency Phase); (5) Identity vs. Identity Diffusion (Adolescence); (6) Intimacy vs. Self-absorption Young and Middle Adult); (7) Generativity vs. Stagnation (Late Middle Age); (8) Integrity vs. Despair, (Old Age). Many variables can affect these phases—war, illness, an occupation, rapid political/social change, etc.

Keep up your good steady work. (I do not think you are slow working at all.) Let's keep in touch.

Sincerely, Peter Olsson

November 1, 2005, 3:22 PM

Dear Dr. Olsson

The meeting with the students was postponed till December, but the Dean liked my monograph about the psychology of suicide bombers and is very supportive and enthusiastic despite the delicate political issues that the topic touches on. My monograph published in the student scientific community journal is in Arabic. I preferred Arabic because though we all speak English, we are not as able to think and feel in English. [This is an interesting point for Iraqi physicians, psychiatrists, and psychologists in dialogue with Westerners.]

I hope I am doing generativity. Really, I feel that I should be responsible to deal with this subject in face of what my country and my nation is facing. But I am still slow. I hope I can do better. Do you think I am doing generativity? I am now 33 years old and I feel myself part of my young students regarding this whole subject. I feel that the problem with Identity is deeply suited to my generation. I hope I can help my students regarding this subject because of the nature of my psychiatric specialty. In reality my training period was accompanied by profound changes in my moral standards or lets say moral development that were both associated with deep changes in my country—especially the war and its subsequent moral "Quake." Fortunately I had the benefit of being in psychotherapy at the time otherwise I might have had a mental breakdown. I hope I can be mature, resilient and strong for the sake of my students and colleagues. I am grateful for your enthusiasm and support.

Yours, V.

November 10, 2005, 11:20 PM

Dear V.,

My thoughts have been with you as you prepare that important talk to the young colleagues. I have re-read your thoughts about identity formation and the crisis in identity searching among Arab, Iraqi and Muslim youth that you describe. I believe that your thoughts are right on target. It is sad that terror acts of Zarqawi/Osama bin Laden et al. are perceived as "Strong" or "Heroic" by many Muslim and Arab young people; especially when such acts are in conflict with or a perversion of all of the world's major religions' teachings about the unacceptability of violent solutions. The harsh reality however, is that early in the formation of democracies there is often a lot of turmoil, vagueness of boundaries, and such uncertainty that even a brutal dictator seems often to be preferred by many citizens.

Traditional Western philosophers, political scientists and academics look to education as the long term answer to most political dilemmas and questions. However, many young people who are not inclined towards academics or artistic pursuits search for other anchors for their identity. Any thriving democracy and particularly a capitalistic economic system need civil order and effective laws for their effective operation. In Western societies the ranks of the police and the military are as important to safeguard democracy as are the ideas of the academics. In Iraq and other Mid-East countries the military and police have usually been tied into the retention of power for tribal, religious, and political figures. It seems vital for young persons in the military and the police in Iraq to gain identity as protectors of citizens and their freedoms. I notice that Zarqawi and Al Qaeda target judges, lawyers, policeman as well as academics and rival clerics. Iraqi soldiers or policemen who have a strong identity as ethical and a protective community consciousness are a profound threat to Al Qaeda and psychopaths like Zarqawi.

November 14, 2005, 3:52 PM
  Peter
  To my knowledge there is no communication between psychiatry or public health officials and our police or security people. After the U.S. invasion and the fall of the previous regime, there was a rapid recruitment of soldiers and policemen. A lot of these recruits are not truly concerned with the quality of life of citizens or defending our homeland. Religious and ethnic loyalties dominate the commitments of our security people. Though the loyalties are to Kurdish or Shiite groups, they do see terrorism as an enemy to all Iraqis. Sunni Arabs are finally joining the political process and the ranks of the security forces. A lot of the soldiers come from poor families and primarily are in need of money to support their families. Corruption is also a major problem. Eventually we psychiatrists will need to meet with policemen about many issues that certainly include the obvious public health problem created by suicide bombers.
  Sincerely, V.

November 15, 2005, 3:27 PM
  Dear V.
  I had further thoughts about you last night and our exchange about Iraqi security forces. Please be careful about conversations you have with police or security people. As you pointed out to me—some of them might be dangerous, unscrupulous people! Forgive my protective thoughts about you.

November 15, 2005, 3:52 PM
   Dear Peter
   I will be careful. I need to confer with colleagues about the idea about consulting with security people. Do not be worried about me. Really, I am cautious to the degree that I feel too passive. Thank you for the concern about my safety.
                                                            Yours, V.

December 10, 2005, 12:31 PM
   Dear Peter
   Through the reading materials you sent and our exchanges I am beginning to understand psychodynamic concepts. During my medical school years, 2 years of internship and 4 years as a psychiatric resident, I had very little training in psychotherapy or psychoanalytic therapy though I continued reading about psychology and psychotherapy.
   I want to talk to you about a painful subject. Before the war I had excellent grades in high school and was selected to attend Saddam College of Medicine. My studies were purely scientific and we were not contaminated by Saddam's regime's influence. In fact, corruption was less prevalent than in other universities. Dictators can do good things not because they are good but in order to deceive people to think that they are good. [Fascinating observation.] *During my undergraduate medical studies I was introverted and did purely scientific things.*
   After the fall of Saddam we were considered part of the previous regime. It is very painful for me to be considered as such. I feel filled with guilt about these accusations. I want to share in rebuilding my country, but the psychiatric authority does not welcome my efforts. This may account for my efforts to work with on our project about understanding and preventing terrorism.
   When I chose psychiatry it astonished my dean because psychiatry in our country is neglected; it does not allow for the earning of much money; and is chosen by students who cannot find opportunities in Medicine or Surgery. I liked psychology and psychiatry and had hoped to gain the respect of my father figures [mentors?] *by continuing in an academic psychiatry career. I refused to participate in corruption to advance myself. An academic spot did not work out for me, so my wife who is also a psychiatrist and I do basic clinical work. We enjoy poetry and music, and we spend much time with our 2.5-year-old son who is active and curious.*
   I apologize for this long letter but I wanted to be frank with you. It is now up to you to consider me to be part of the previous regime or not.
                                                            Yours, V.

Wow! This new colleague trusts me with such personal issues over such a long distance. He and his young family breathe the atmosphere of terror daily. I contemplate it from afar. What can I say? Here goes.

December 11, 2005, 2:02 PM
   Dear V.
   I am struck with the harmonic convergences of our lives. My wife Pam is also a psychiatrist. In America, some colleagues in medicine and surgery have always

subtly devalued psychiatry. I think part of the devaluing of psychiatry by some of our medical colleagues has to do with various levels of fear, superstition and obsessional neurosis, even among well-educated medical colleagues. My philosophy has always been to try to do steady and reliable clinical work with patients and communicate as clearly and as helpfully as possible with our physician colleagues. It usually works out OK, but if necessary, I stand up against colleagues by firm clinical discussion on the behalf of our patients' best care.

Pam and I have a seventeen-year-old son who is a senior in high school. I would be proud for my family to meet you and your family.

My experience with you as a colleague finds me feeling the utmost of respect and admiration for your tenacity, integrity, and courage. If I had been "In your Shoes" (as our English saying goes), I would have done the very same things you have done. I would have poured myself into my work and stayed as far away from politics as I could. During our foolish, failed and deeply sad American war in Vietnam, I was called to serve in our military as a Navy psychiatrist. I hated that war! What I did was work as best I could with my patients (young Navy and Marine heroin addicts); wrote professional papers; did research; and prayed for the day when the war would be over.

I am enjoying our work together on trying to understand the mentality of suicide bombers and possible ways for preventing their formation in Iraqi and America.

Yours truly, Peter

Dr. H comments on the Iraqi elections:

December 17, 2005
  Dear Peter
  Thank you for your New Year gifts. Happy New Year and Merry Christmas to you all. Last Thursday me, my wife, and her sister went to participate in the Iraqi elections. We voted for Liberal characters. We hope that Liberal people will take responsibility within the next few years. The election succeeded and Iraqis are happy for democracy.
                                                                                          V.

December 31, 2007
  INTERNET CHRISTMAS/NEW YEARS CARD from Dr. H—Thank you for the warm voice from beyond the seas. Santa gifts arrived. My wife and son are sitting beside me and they send you and your family greetings. V.

December 31, 2005, 8:49 PM
  Dear V and Family
  Thank you for the Holiday card. My family and I enjoyed its arrival from 8000 mi away. We pray for your safety in what we hope will be a prosperous new Iraq.

January 19, 2006, 4:37 PM
  Dear Peter
  Silence means resistance doesn't it? I was thinking about what to say next. Work with you has made me re-live periods with my first father figure in psychiatry (1995). He was

my personal psychiatrist first when he treated me for mild depression and obsessions. He then became my supervisor. He had a warm fathering character. He like you had very well organized knowledge, and was a very good listener. I think by adopting a boyish (infantile?) position with him I was trying to attract him as his little kind son. I felt these experiences reoccurring with you. I always felt like I was apologizing toward you and feeling forced to express respect.

Now, I have run out of words. Yours, V.

January 19, 2006, 4:37 PM

V. You mention silence as a resistance. Of course it can be so, but it also allows for quiet self-reflection, self inquires, and meditation. After an appropriate period of testing as we work together as colleagues—I think trust has developed between us. I feel that process of trust steadily developing in our collegial friendship. I have been impressed that you thought through your own ideas and observations. You did not just parrot my ideas or those of Vamik Volkan who is my mentor and after many years my close colleague and friend.

I think you readily and accurately spotted your positive and negative paternal transference feelings and thoughts about me. Transference is inevitable and ubiquitous. Hopefully you will learn from this self-knowledge and awareness, and not be limited by unresolved transferences. I wanted to share a poem I wrote after I learned of my analyst's death. We had spent 7 years together—4 days per week.

IN MEMORY OF R.G.

A graceful combination of empathy and insight.
He provided wings for many minds to fly freely.
His rapier wit, punctured pompous balloons,
Of pseudo-scientific psychoanalytic sanctimony.
If wisdom and compassion could form a science,
R.M.G. was their founder and leader.
His wry humor held sway in work and play,
Rising to a genuine new art form.
That wonderful, gleaming, nodding smile,
A beacon light in our collective memory
Mirroring Bob's presence in our hearts.

V.—I look forward to our work together.

Yours, Peter

In addition to sharing some of my poetry with Dr. H, I sent him a copy of my book, *Malignant Pied Pipers,* and we exchanged research and ideas about the dynamics of suicide bombers and the prevention of their destructive actions. See Chapter 5, which includes in part the result of our collaborations on that subject. I have also consulted with Dr. H about his study group on the subject of long-term programs for the prevention of suicide bombers. The group includes public health nurses, school teachers, moderate Muslim clergy, and physicians.

January 27, 2006, 12:51 PM
  Dear Peter
  In terms of the formation of suicide bomber personalities, I think narcissistic injuries can occur even when there are no obvious traumas found in the personal histories of suicide bombers. It would take a long time in psychotherapy for these issues to appear in the individual's psychotherapy. Now that we know that childhood temperament has a strong biological basis we can see that what for one child may not be so for another. For example, some have said that rather than suffering trauma, Atta of 9/11 infamy was over-protected by his mother. I ask as to whether over-protection by his mother was a crucial form of neglect?
  I think that in Muslim countries there is more possibility for narcissistic injury than in other cultures. In Muslim cultures rigid rules are obeyed. Marriage is a contract than involving an emotional attachment or collaborative intimacy. Muslims believe in the proverb, "Marriage is a matter of fate and chance." Only low probability can predict when emotions such as love or intimacy occur. Usually there exists no premarital sex or romance. Marriage is considered a Holy duty and an obligation. Bringing children into the world is considered as a matter of pride and has little to do with the children's emerging feelings or emotional stability. There is severe competition for marriage partners and the basis for conflict is over economic survival. In such situations it is quite possible for pathological dynamics to prevail so there is improper child care even when there are no obvious traumatic events.
  Peter, you sent me that article about Iraqi doctors fleeing the country. Many are fleeing the chaos because they are wealthy and are often attacked because they seek status with religious political groups.
  My wife and I as psychiatrists, try to avoid strictly financial status positions. Life is difficult but we hope that Iraq can overcome this difficult and critical period in its history. Many of our colleagues adopt our modest principles and I think it is through us Iraqis living in the shadows that Iraq will stand up again. The situation is not free of risk but we are cautious. Thank you for your concern. V.

February 17, 2006, 2:33 PM
  Dear Peter
  Violence in Iraq has escalated in the last few days. A wave of bombed cars and mine explosions spread over our Baghdad and our neighborhood was not an exception. Also, another wave of assassinations of doctors occurred. We are well physically but not psychologically. We are taking extreme precautions and not leaving home except for work or shopping. We forget trips, we don't go out for dinner, and we don't even go to parks or visit friends.
  My wife is not well. She is thirty-seven-years-old and is on one antidepressant (Imipramine). She suffers a relapse whenever there is a stressful event. She has recently gotten pregnant and last time in her post partum period she required ECT at the

insistence of her psychotherapist. Her therapist has left Iraq. A second antidepressant (Paroxetine) may help her to avoid ECT, but it is unavailable in our hospitals. Sorry to bother you with my problems. I wish you the best. V.

I contacted some colleagues and drug company representatives and I was touched by the quick and compassionate response. Within two weeks, Dr. H's wife had her supply of Paroxetine and was able to avoid ECT and began to be less depressed. Dr. H knew about my follow-up tests for a stomach tumor, for which I had been operated upon in the previous year. Dr. H has faithfully inquired about my health and that of my wife.

Dr. H brought up the idea of his moving his family to Syria. Dr. H's father had moved to Syria quite a while ago after he and Dr. H's mother had divorced. I had worked with a Syrian psychiatrist at our community mental health center and this friend and colleague was helpful in providing names and phone numbers of Syrian psychiatrists who could help Dr. H find employment in Syria if he chose to move there. Other American colleagues and I researched information about possible emigration to America, and several of us wrote recommendations for Dr. H and his wife for the Fulbright program through our American embassy in Baghdad. Dr. H and his wife were expecting their second child soon, and they had many relatives in Baghdad who were very financially dependent on them.

March 16–17, 2006, 1:35 PM, 3:04 PM

Dear Peter

We are well. We are so grateful for your concern. Our son's name is Asal and he is now three years old. We will keep safe. I will be in touch so do not be worried if sometimes we answer late because we sometimes have internet connection and electricity problems.

My wife asks me to thank you and says that you are very caring persons. Caring people are very few here. Violent aggression is the prevalent way of interaction even within families here. My wife's mood swings are still present and the current situation is also affecting her. She has panic attacks and when we go to work she is afraid that we won't return to our son. She gets very anxious when I leave home. These fears and anxieties are exhausting.

The situation in Iraq is not well. Life just goes on and the psychopaths are not able to get agreements that please them. After the fall of Saddam we were filled with hope that our country would be better. Before psychopaths' aggression was predictable from Saddam's regime sometimes but now many forms of psychopaths are fighting and causing even more harm. We still do not lose hope but there seemingly will be a period in which violence and aggression will prevail before the emergence of a new Iraq.

The paper you and I collaborated on about Suicide Bombers is at the printing stage at the Journal of Students Scientific Community. It will be distributed to the teaching committee and I am eager to get their responses. The students are hesitant about arranging a meeting to discuss the paper because they are concerned about the risks. Sometimes I feel guilty because I am not able to transmit the ideas that may be beneficial in our country's situation but it is best to be quiet and careful for the sake of safety.

Yesterday there was a program on Al Arabia satellite channel about psychodynamic aspects of suicide terrorism. I think it was originally from the BBC program about the July 5 suicide bombings in London. It is interesting that many of the ideas presented we had already covered in our discussions and in our paper. It seems important that the subject is being presented to an Arab audience. Our dream is that someday our homeland and nation will mature and prosper.

It is interesting that you read and enjoy T. S. Eliot. I read the poems of my favorite poet Badr Shaker Sayab. He is the founder of the new modern Iraqi and Arab poetry. He is well known and was influenced by his reading of Western poetry especially Eliot. Al Sayab freed Arabic poetry from the old traditions and his school is called free poetry.

I wish you and your family the best. V.

In late March 2006, I sent V. a copy of an interesting report that a psychoanalytic colleague had recently sent me: "Iraqi Immigrants in the United States," by Elizabeth Grieco of the Migration Policy Institute, dated April 1, 2003. It states that the 2000 census reported 90,000 immigrants born in Iraq were residing in the United States (less than 1 percent of the foreign-born U.S. population; the number had doubled over the last decade). In 2000, the states with the largest Iraqi foreign-born populations were Michigan (31,927), California (20,532), and Illinois (9,634). The remaining seven states with the largest Iraqi immigrant populations were Tennessee (2,766), Texas (2,752), New York (2,721), Arizona (2,456), Virginia (1,841), Missouri (1,275), and Pennsylvania (1,209). Beyond the consequential but narrow concerns about "winning" in Iraq, it would seem crucial to the author that America and Western democracies be welcoming to Iraqi students, immigrants, and friends over the next decades.

April 16, 2006, 2:22 PM
Dear Peter

I hope you and family are well. I hope that you are not disappointed about our "helplessness" regarding emigration. I will be frank. We are hesitant and afraid of the stress involved in making such great changes even though we are constantly anxious as our lives go on. I think that the exams and credentialing to become doctors in the USA would take too long before we could have an income to support us and relatives back here in Iraq. My wife thanks you, Dr. White, and the other kind colleagues for the Paxil. (Her illness and pregnancy is also a factor.) We are so grateful for your help and concern.

Happy Easter, (I am going to send you a translation of "Rain Song" by Badr Shaker Al Sayab.) V.

April 29, 2006, 7:34 PM
Dear V,

Thank you for the Al Sayab poem, "Rain Song." It moved me to tears as I read it. The mingling of history's seldom-recognized lessons with the natural features of the land, the trees, and the hopes and fears of children are painted in the striking pictures and music of his words. Al Sayab reminds me of Boris Pasternak of Russia, Gabriela Mistral of Chile, and Carl Sandburg of America.

Thank you, Peter

May 6, 2006, 3:45 PM
  Dear Peter
  I am sorry for moving you to tears while reading the poem. Yes it is true that Al Sayab works have depressive content and he has been criticized for that. But, the truth and precision through which he expresses his feelings are unique. His works also contain a bit of delicate hope within the pessimistic background. This makes for a true expression for the Iraqi individual while we are passing through difficult periods in modern Iraqi history, and especially in the current situation. It helps me much to read his poems nowadays while looking at our country through the window of that delicate hope.
  Best, V.

May 6, 2006, 6:42 PM
  Dear V
  I think you misunderstood my comments. My tears in response to Al Sayab were the tears of strong feelings, sadness yes, but not depression. Wars and violent fights between individuals or groups always bring sadness. I also shed tears when my two sons were born, when I listen to great opera, in 1962 when I heard T. S. Eliot read his poems in Chicago, and when brave American and Iraqi soldiers die. Al Sayab's poetry is emotionally moving, and beautifully expressive of the most beautiful music of the virtuous human soul—a rare entity in a world where violence is too seldom a last resort.
  I like your term used in describing Al Sayab's work, "Delicate hope." I join your hopes that your country will transcend this difficult period. I highly value our friendship.

Sincerely, Peter

FRIENDSHIP SONG

Sounds and sights of everything important,
And wandering close to the heart of Meaning.
Condensation of Life's essence in memories.
Soothing, self-other melodies that last for
decades, and stir long nostalgic soul-dances.
Surprised again and again by reunion joys.
Prayers of thanksgiving offered for Friendship's
Special soaring song for all seasons of Life.

May 25, 2006, 3:58 PM
  Dear Peter
  At last our government is formed only six months after the elections. Our country still has a lot to do. There are bad people ascending into the Parliament through sectarian

competition rather than democratic process or ideals. We hope that they will be removed over the next few years.

Thank you for your recent elaboration about your "joyful tears." Peter, when I read your poems I felt as if I was taken to a world of calmness and the tranquility of nature. Those meanings are seldom thought about under our torrent of daily life.

Best, V.

In June 2006, I had major surgery for a tumor that turned out to be benign. V was aware of a mildly malignant tumor that I had had removed two years previously. V and his wife faithfully asked about my progress and sent me e-mail "get-well cards." We have continued to exchange e-mails every 10–14 days and occasional phone calls up till the present time. V and I have shared intimate information about problems in our families of origin, our childhoods, our marriages and our valued psychotherapies. The following e-mail arrived after a lengthy series of exchanges about both of our failures, fears, and frailties. The details of this shared material is too personal for this venue.

July 21, 2006, 8:58 AM
Dear Peter
I do highly appreciate your support, understanding and patience at your reading of my last letter. I felt great comfort as you touched on and understood points I wished to communicate. I am so grateful for your sharing your experiences in life and your psychoanalysis to help me. For a long time I have been feeling sad because things are no longer the same in my friendships as they were when I was younger. For example, I have my school friends who I have "Known" since my childhood. They are nice and we used to support each other but I feel that they have remained stagnated to the rules and norms of our old society. When I communicate ideas such as those I communicate with you, they just make fun.

Upon reading that, I felt sudden pangs of guilt and anxiety—brief doubts about my influence? Then came the following:

What I really want to say Peter, is that I feel that I am able to sail in life more freely than my old friends. I am experiencing more opportunities for more varieties of experience in life; opportunities to have new quality friendships that are the source of intellectual and spiritual continuity with the universal. I feel this in our friendship as I had with my early mentor in psychiatry and with my psychotherapist.

Sincerely, V.

I try to touch base with V every week, and my friend responds whenever he can do so safely. The e-mail below is typical of recent contacts with V:

March 4, 2007, 1:26 PM
Dear Peter
Today I went to central Baghdad to get the medicine for my wife sent by Dr. White. Baghdad center was so crowded. It is the central market for the whole of Iraq. That

location has been targeted many times for assassinations of major merchants or explosions—before the recent U.S./Iraqi Secuurity Plan. A question came to my mind. What makes these people continue to work inspite of what they have faced? Then I laugh to myself and say, "What makes me go to work every day inspite of all the threats?" My answer was that we don't have any other choice but to continue living. The power of life is still stronger than terrorism here. Our hope that things will get better is increasing. Al Sadre Mehdi ran away to Iran so kidnapping and killing stopped. Al Qaeda is now alone and we hope the Iraqi-American forces can defeat them.

Best wishes, V.

I continue to be moved to tears at hearing the hopes of my friend V. Unlike the spirit of Americans after the onset of World War II, we Americans seem to be too-soon forgetting 9/11. Despite our government's mistakes, we still are at war with a new form of fascism that makes Hitler look like an amateur.

My friendship and collegial relationship with Dr. H is one of the most important experiences of my life. I am totally convinced that networks of e-mail pen-pal relationships of the quality demonstrated above could not only counteract Al Qaeda's evil network, but would contribute substantially toward the struggle for a more peaceful world.

10

CONCLUSION

PREDICTIONS AND SUGGESTIONS

In light of some of the findings about Osama's mind, it is possible to list speculative predictions about his behavior and by implication some other terror cult leaders.

First, the CIA, Homeland Security, and military intelligence experts would do well to keep track of Osama's potential "anniversary reactions." For example, Mohammad bin Laden, Osama's father, died when his airplane, flown by an American pilot, crashed on September 3, 1967. (September was the chosen month for 9/11.) Osama's older half-brother Salem died in a plane crash near San Antonio, Texas, on Memorial Day, 1988. There were some suspicious aspects about Salem's death because he was an experienced pilot and had business connections with George W. Bush's oil business (Mill 2001).

Interpol says that Osama was born on March 10, 1957. The U.S. State Department says July 30, 1957. The Prophet Mohammad arrived in Medina on July 16, A.D. 622. Osama strongly identifies with the prophet. (In this vein, July and September are key times for the United States to be particularly alert. The August-September months have often found our presidents to be on vacation. Terrorists do not take vacations.)

Second, Osama will never surrender and will be difficult to capture. Osama consciously extols and seems obsessed with martyrdom. At an unconscious level, he is filled with hate, rage, guilt, and shame that massive denial and projection can barely contain. Dorpat (1985, 44, 144–47) presents an elegant summary of Freud's, Waelder's, and his own cogent thinking about the psychodynamics of and mental consequences for a person that uses massive denial and projection as a mental defense. An impending return of the "denied" truth for a person like Osama usually results in delusional and paranoid thinking and action. Such delusions often contain a kernel of truth, albeit distorted and magnified. For example, Americans and Israelis *do* want Arab oil (a kernel of truth), but it is not their evil intention to occupy and dictatorially control Arab land without yielding fair profits.

The partial content of truth in such delusions creates a tenacious conviction that inevitably slides down the slippery slope of projection, suspension of self-reflection, paranoid thinking, splitting, and symptom formation. Whole stressed Muslim communities are susceptible to regressive yearning for a savior.

Osama's symptoms involve severe personality disorder (malignant narcissism) and violent acting-out behavior. Osama's statements have clearly revealed his paranoid thinking and violent intentions toward America and the West. Episodes of delusional thinking and violent acting out do not necessarily mean that Osama has a psychosis. As we discussed earlier, he is "crazy like a fox." His thinking and lack of logic should be vigorously challenged, especially by moderate Muslim scholars and politicians. Osama bin Laden has absolutely no credentials as a theologian or clergy person. He has a master's degree in business and engineering. He is a wealthy renegade warrior, amateur poet, and recruiter of murderers. Osama bin Laden should be denounced by credentialed Muslim clergy and declared an amateur in Sharia law and Muslim theology. Osama bin Laden pronouncing about the theological basis for *Jihad* is like the author pronouncing about and offering to perform cardiovascular surgery because his professor of surgery in medical school was Michael DeBakey.

Third, if Osama were captured, it would be valuable for a public and detailed trial to take place in the World Court in The Hague. It is absolutely imperative that his trial be speedy and very public. A long, drawn-out prison stay would only magnify his lust for the paradoxical power of martyrdom.

Reprimands of America's impulsive "going it alone" in Iraq, and our treatment of prisoners taken in the "war on terror" (Abu Ghraib), would need to be as vigorously presented as the prosecution of Osama's horrendous murder of innocents. The so-called war on terror dramatically underlines the need for worldwide respect for international law and the World Court. So far, neither our country nor the world community has been able to take the gigantic step towards unwavering social justice. UN and U.S. "politics as usual" must be avoided. Defiance of international law is totally inappropriate for Osama bin Laden and Al Qaeda, or George W. Bush's administration and Israel.

Fourth, Osama will be likely to order an attack if a brother figure like Mullah Omar or al-Zawahiri is killed or captured. If Osama is still alive, his late midlife crisis and the Eriksonian life challenge of Generativity versus Stagnation are upon him. This may lead him to suicidal despair if he grasps the implications of where his theology is leading the next Muslim generation, or he may become withdrawn. In other words, one of Osama bin Laden's major psychological problems is a total failure in generativity.

Fifth, Osama's mother might have a slim chance of influencing him toward moderation if she could take firm and effective stances theologically (see Bergen 2006, 151). Hamida will, of course, have no influence with the other Malignant Pied Pipers of Al Qaeda.

Sixth, as Lawrence astutely observes (2005, xxii), Al Qaeda differs from other terror groups such as the Red Brigade, Hamas, or other radical Islamists. Osama and Al Qaeda propose no positive political or social structures to be established after the *jihad*. One could assume that they would favor a government with the moral rigidities of their pals among the Taliban. But Osama's main focus is on the glories of martyrdom and his politics of death. Osama's dark obsession with such *Thanatos* needs to be extensively and bull-doggedly presented in the media.

Seventh, Mahmoud Mohammad Taha's inspiring ideas need to be studied and publicized worldwide. His ideas can prevent more Islamist terrorism than thousands of "smart bombs." He could become a profoundly important spiritual and intellectual hero for future generations of Muslim youth. He should become as well known and important to the modern world as Einstein, Gandhi, Shakespeare, Locke, Hobbes, Adams, Jefferson, Jay, Madison, Hamilton, Franklin, Marx, and Freud. If read and followed thoughtfully, Taha's vision could prevent a huge amount of future bloodshed and terrorism, and promote more peace in the world.

Eighth, the notion of "Collateral Damage" (civilian casualties) and the abusive child rearing involved with hate speech by parents, clergy, or national political leaders should become the topic of research, discussion, and reform. Hateful rhetoric by national leaders toward other countries or their leaders is as polluting as carbon emissions and radioactive fallout.

CONCLUSIONS

"This is the ideological battle, *everything* is the Battle of Ideas."

—Fidel Castro (Anderson 2006, 47)

Fundamentalist mentality of whatever ilk involves, at its rigid, black-and-white core, profound deficiencies in knowledge, humility, wisdom, empathy, and sense of humor. The future generations of Osama bin Laden's terror cult and similar franchises seem unlikely to be eliminated by bullets, missiles, or "smart bombs." America has put $50 million on the heads of Osama bin Laden and Dr. Ayman al-Zawahiri. Paradoxically, Osama bin Laden's status as media celebrity and Robin Hood–like folk hero for many millions of Muslim youths is thus elevated. Would it not be more valuable if these two Malignant Pied Pipers were found out and transcended, psychologically speaking? Rather than a hail of bullets or a hellfire missile blast to render them martyrs, perhaps an exciting new Arab or Muslim application of Gandhi's ideas could make bin Laden and Zawahiri seem like two tired old terrorists, and Bush's notion of "preemptive war" seem like some forgotten nightmare. Taha's moderate view of Islam seems like a good place to start. The minds of radical fundamentalist Muslim men like Osama bin Laden, Ayman Al-Zawahiri, Nasrallah of Hezbollah, Omar Abdel-Rahman, and Abu Hamza Al-Masri will never be changed by dialogue. However, there is hope that the creative ideas of men like Taha and Swogger can be used to dialogue with Muslim young people around the world, and especially those who study in our country. Such psychoeducational approaches hold some promise for reducing the vast pool of recruits that radical Islamists seek to reach with their false doctrines of violence, hate, and martyrdom.

Groupthink can afflict American councils of preemptive war-making as readily as it does bin Laden's councils of jihadists. The future foreign policies of America need to be informed about the social-psychological origins and dynamics of terrorist groups and their leaders. It would be helpful in this regard if our State Department would support "Unofficial"/Track II diplomacy (Volkan 1988, 225). Social-psychological and psychobiographical intelligence can be applied with equal vigor to that of military intelligence when confronting Osama.

As we have seen, an important part of Osama's charisma and influence in the Muslim world stems from his literary self-presentation (Lawrence 2005, xvii). Intelligent and knowledgeable confrontations need to be launched in the Arab media to dispute and refute Osama's distortions of Muslim theology, teaching, and law. As we discussed earlier, Taha's approaches to Islam should be used to dispute Osama's *Thanatos*. The accuracy of Osama's historical pronouncements also need to be studied seriously and briskly challenged or agreed with. Agreement with the truth about historical events, if it occurs authentically, does not imply support of Osama or Al Qaeda's violent actions.

Devastated communities, families, and wounded group-selves in poverty-stricken and war-torn nations continents away are ignored at our peril. It is helpful for the United States to be aware of the notion of the "in-betweener." Billions of foreign "aid" dollars given to Middle East dictator "friends" that seldom helps ordinary citizens may not be worth the enemy-accumulating consequences. Nation building, the "preventative medicine" of "unofficial diplomacy," and common-people-friendly American foreign aid may be difficult, but we cannot just walk away from in-betweener communities as we did in Afghanistan after the Soviet defeat. Genuine foreign aid could help impoverished and wounded world communities find ways to rebuild their dignity and group-self confidence. Legitimate efforts in this regard seem underway in Afghanistan.

It seems futile to try to terrify terrorists into submission, just so we might feel safe. It seems important to thoroughly understand the psychology of an enemy like Osama bin Laden as well as the complex social psychology of his followers. Such study may help us spot future Osamas early in their gestation, or even prevent the social psychological circumstances that fertilize the soil in which they take root.

American and Western democracies' efforts to win the support of Muslim and Arab countries are likely to fail unless there are massive political and educational efforts towards a dialogue in contemporary Islam about changing values and attitudes toward marriage, the rights of women, and child rearing. As the 9/11 Commission indicated (Kean et al. 2004, 376), this progress can ultimately only come from within the Arab/Muslim culture.

President Musharraf of Pakistan calls for a process of "enlightened moderation." Musharraf said:

> The Muslim world, should shun militancy and extremism; the West—and the United States in particular—should seek to resolve disputes with justice and help better the Muslim world. (Kean et al. 2004, 369)

Books, not bullets and bombs, will end the terror wars. Islamic scholars made some of the finest modern intellectual, scientific, artistic, and theological/philosophical contributions. Genuine and empathic foreign aid helps wounded or foundering world communities to find ways to be liberally educated and able to build equality and dignity between men and women. This progress promotes child-rearing practices that do not find mothers fearing or fostering rigid ideas of masculinity in boys and subservience in girls.

EPILOGUE

Our new century often seems to be plunging relentlessly and exponentially into a worldwide worsening pathology of the group-self and between group-selves. Misunderstandings between East and West, moderate Muslim and radical Muslim, neocons and pacifists in America, Republicans and Democrats, are growing. Destructive, polarizing fundamentalist mentality often pollutes the group-self and seems to be leading deeper into the maelstrom of *jihad*, preemptive war, and the so-called "war on terror." (A war against a tactic?) There seem to be no world leaders in tune with what Kohut called "empathic touch with the diseased group-self." Groupthink seems to afflict both the leaders of *jihad* against America, and our American leaders in the "war on terror." Without creative, empathic leaders, group war-think can spread exponentially to Western electorates and the mushrooming followers of worldwide radical jihadists. It seems possible for the world's collective unconscious to be dominated by fear, distrust, and group war-think.

Our search should be for empathic leaders who reach out to the healthy group-self and all its potential. Unfortunately, soon after 9/11, American politics steadily returned to the character assassinations of political opponents and the devaluing rhetoric and negative campaigning that is not seen abroad as healthy disagreements among respectful persons of differing ideas. Rather, it is seen as

"Ugly American" arrogance, and a mean-spirited division of America. We need to pull together steadily without the necessity of stark stimulations like 9/11. Perhaps we need what Barack Obama has called *The Audacity of Hope*?

In closing, the irrational domains of humanity will never be completely eliminated. However, the contribution of psychodynamic thinking and therapy applications to the study of politics, government, and international relations can make an important contribution towards controlling human irrationality and violence. It would be ironical, paradoxical, but laudable if this study of Osama and company would help terror cults to become extinct like dinosaurs. Genuinely mature, empathic, and wise leaders can help national character/large group identity to shift from an asymmetrical terror war identity or insecure notions of preemptive war to an identity of peace, prosperity, and democracy. The process is long, arduous, and fraught with many perils.

POETIC RESPONSES TO THIS RESEARCH—THREE POEMS BY PETER A. OLSSON

Young Lions Too Soon Old

Osama looked to Afghan mountains where he grew strong.
Israel's David also knew a hilly strength of Psalm 121, 1.
Two paradoxical poets, longing to save their people.
Sad leaders too soon choosing violence as last resort.
Their poetry would have been a longer-valued legacy.

Eagle Wounded (9–11–01)

Bizarre flying Trojan Horses. Souls engulfed by fire.
"Pilots, give them what they want and we are safe.
Negotiators,come to relieve our plight on landing."
My God! throats of fragile freedom cut, painfully.
Horror decades envisioned for angry revenge seeking.
Listening, now paralyzed by greedy gulps of hatred.
Forgiveness blurred, in scared scenes scarred by loss.

Eagle Healing (9–19–01)

Searching tirelessly in the rubble shedding love-tears.
Respected and beloved first-responders extolled.
Transformation of pain and rage with healing prayer.
The light of ideals fighting Hatred's endless night.
Destruction's curse transcended by long listening.
Healing Eagle reaching out, embracing new friends.

GLOSSARY

Many of the definitions in this addendum expand upon and refer to terms and concepts used within the book. Definitions are based on those in the American Psychiatric Glossary (APG), *1975 and 1994, and Moore and Fine's* Psychoanalytic Concepts (PC), *1990, as well as other sources cited.*

Ambivalence The coexistence of two opposing drives, desires, feelings, or emotions toward the same person, object, or goal. These may be conscious or partly conscious; or one side of the feelings may be unconscious. Example: Love and hate toward the same person (APG 1975, 13–14).

Anniversary reaction An emotional response to a previous event occurring at the same time of year. Often the event involved a loss and the reaction involves a depressed state. The reaction can range from mild to severe and may occur at any time after the event (APG 1994, 10).

Applied Psychoanalysis Use of insights and concepts gained from clinical psychoanalysis to enlarge or deepen the understanding of various aspects of human nature, culture, and society. Most prominent have been studies in the fields of history, biography, literature, art, religion, mythology, and anthropology. The application of psychoanalysis to biography and history has given rise to the terms *psychobiography* and *psychohistory,* which suggest an artificial and misleading compartmentalization in the recording of human history (PC 1990, 27).

Collective Unconscious In Jungian theory, a portion of the unconscious common to all people (APG 1975, 33).

Conscious The content of the mind or mental functioning of which one is aware (APG 1975, 36).

Counter-transference "The psychiatrist's partly unconscious or conscious emotional reaction to his patient" (APG 1975, 38).

Doppelganger A ghostly double or counterpart of a living person (Webster's New Collegiate Dictionary, 393).

Ego "In psychoanalytic theory, one of the three major divisions in the model of the psychic apparatus [mind]; the others being the **id** and the **superego**. The ego represents the sum of certain mental mechanisms, such as perception and memory, and specific *defense mechanisms*. It serves to mediate between the demands of the primitive instinctual drives (id), of internalized parental and social prohibitions (superego) and of reality. The compromises between these forces achieved by the **ego** tend to resolve intrapsychic conflict and serve an adaptive and executive function" (APG 1975, 45). [*Note:* Psychiatric usage of the term should not be confused with common usage, which denotes self-love or selfishness.]

Ego Ideal "The part of the personality that comprises the aims and goals for the self; usually refers to the conscious or unconscious emulation of significant figures with whom one has identified. The ego ideal emphasizes what one should do or be in contrast to what one should not be or not do" (APG 1975, 46).

Externalization "A general heading for mental processes that result from the individual's attributing inner phenomenon to the external world. It can be viewed as the counterpart to **internalization**. Instinctual wishes, conflicts, moods, and ways of thinking (cognitive styles) may be projected" (PC 1990, 70).

Faction A key term defined by James Madison, "By faction I understand a number of citizens, whether amounting to a majority of the whole, who are united and actuated by some common impulse of passion, or of interest, adverse to the rights of other citizens, or to the permanent and aggregate interests of the community" ([1787] 1987, 123, quoted in Swogger 2001, 354).

Fascism A system of government marked by centralization of authority under a dictator, stringent socioeconomic controls, suppression of the opposition through terror and censorship, and typically a policy of belligerent nationalism and racism (Wikipedia).

Fundamentalist mentality "Fundamentalists, no matter how sweet, kind, or pious they behave on the surface, are convinced that they have *the* superior moral, ethical, theological, epistemological, political, and spiritual truth. Fundamentalists (Christian, Jewish, Muslim, Sikh, Hindu, even some anti-war pacifists) experience in a delusional way their own way of thinking and believing as '*the* one and only way.' Fundamentalist mentality is more prevalent and seems more readily embraced at times of severe social turmoil, rapid social change, economic hardship, and related oppression of minority groups. The radical fundamentalists of any religious or political group are willing to confidently condemn to hell and or kill those who do not believe exactly as they do. They are the final judges, juries, and 'holy' executioners. There is no room for honest discussion, doubt or debate. They are their own gods themselves" (Olsson 2004, 1).

Generativity "Mature man needs to be needed, and maturity needs guidance as well as encouragement from what has been produced and must be taken care of. Generativity, then, is primarily the concern in establishing and guiding the next generation, although there are individuals who, through misfortune or because of special and genuine gifts in other directions, do not apply this drive to their own offspring" (Erikson 1950, 266–67).

Group-self There is a parallel process by which an individual's sense of himself as part of a group is formed. In essence, inner representations of our self and our self-in-a-group are parallel and conjoined early in developmental and maturational experiences

(Olsson 2005, 150). In 1976, Heinz Kohut first described the group-self (Kohut 1978, 2:837–38n21).

Groupthink Irving Janis (1972, 35–36) described the "Groupthink Hypothesis" in explaining the Bay of Pigs mistake early in John F. Kennedy's presidency. Janis said, "Members of any small cohesive group tend to maintain esprit de corps by unconsciously developing a number of shared illusions and related norms that interfere with critical thinking and reality testing." A contention of this book is that radical Islamist leaders and Western leaders can become victims of this process.

Identification "A defense mechanism, operating unconsciously, by which one patterns oneself after some other person. Identification plays a major role in the development of one's personality and specifically of the superego. To be differentiated from imitation or role modeling, which is a conscious process" (APA 1994, 67).

Identity "Think of identity and personality as two sides of the same coin: when an individual perceives him or herself, it is called 'identity'; when another person observes the outward expressions of this identity, it is called 'personality.' Whereas identity is the individual's subjective sense of his or her own inner sameness, personality comprises an individual's habitual behavior, thinking and feeling patterns, modes of speech, and physical gestures: the observable and predictable patterns that an individual uses regularly—consciously or not—to maintain harmony in relationships with others and to create a routine and stable existence. In order to understand how a person perceives his or her own consistent internal sameness (**identity**), one needs to develop an intimate and meaningful relationship with the person" (Volkan 2004, 177).

In-Betweeners A term to describe Margaret Singer's observation (1995, 21) that any normal person is vulnerable to recruitment and exploitation by a cult group during periods of rapid change in their life. Or, who are at "in-between times" or key transitions in their lives. "In-betweeners" are in between relationships, in between divorce and remarriage, in between high school and college, in between jobs, and so on. I contend (Olsson 2005, 113) that nations, tribes, and societies can become in-betweeners and are more vulnerable to terror cult recruitment during rapid social, economic, and political change.

Incorporation "A primitive defense mechanism, operating unconsciously, in which the psychic representation of a person, or parts of the person, is figuratively ingested" (APA 1994, 68).

Interest According to Swogger (2001, 353) this term goes beyond an economic concept to intangible but very important domains such as "ownership" that can include intense involvement with a person, thing, idea or ideological or religious commitments. Swogger feels that the concept of *interests* can be reformulated in psychoanalytic terms to deepen our understanding of political behavior.

Internalization "In its broadest sense, a process by which aspects of the outer world and interactions with it are taken into the organism and represented in its internal structure. In the psychoanalytic frame of reference, the process is intrapsychic and usually object-related, taking place by three principal modes: **incorporation, introjection, and identification. Projection** and action are correlated externalizing phenomena" (PC 1999, 102).

Introjection "A defense mechanism, operating unconsciously, whereby loved or hated external objects are taken within oneself symbolically. The converse of projection. May serve as a defense against conscious recognition of intolerable hostile impulses" (APG 1975, 92).

Islamism An Islamic revivalist movement, often characterized by moral conservatism, literalism, and the attempt to implement Islamic values in all spheres of life (Spencer 2006, 6–7).

National character/large-group identity "Besides focusing on an individual's identity, Erikson also showed interest in large-group identities. He defined a process he called *pseudospeciation,* in which, at the outset of human history, each human group developed a distinct sense of identity, wearing skins and feathers like armor to protect it from other groups who wore different kinds of skins and feathers. Erikson hypothesized that each group became convinced that it was the sole possessor of the true human identity. Thus, each group also became a pseudospecies, adopting an attitude of superiority over other groups" (Volkan 2006, 15). In Volkan's work he deals in depth with ethnic, national, religious, and ideological large-group identities that all are formed in childhood.

Negative Identity Erik Erikson, who wrote so eloquently about adolescents, described young people who have lost respect for their parents' values and ethical standards as experiencing negative identity formation. They join a throng or worldwide community of adolescent rebels who in their tragic disappointment in their parents' generation mock and devalue their fallen and shallow role models. They often also limit their own potential satisfaction or accomplishments (Erikson 1964, 99).

Object (intrapsychic) The internalized representation, in the mind of one person, of another person's mind and its function in the perceived interpersonal relationship (Olsson 2005).

Object relations "The emotional bonds that exist between an individual and another person, as contrasted with his interest in, and love for himself: usually described in terms of his capacity for loving and reacting appropriately to others" (APG 1975, 110).

Overdetermination "The concept of multiple *unconscious* causes of an emotional reaction or symptom" (APG 1975, 95).

Personality *See* Identity.

Preconscious "Thoughts that are not in immediate awareness but that can be recalled by conscious effort" (APG 1975, 122).

Projection "A *defense mechanism* operating unconsciously in which what is emotionally unacceptable in the self is unconsciously rejected and attributed to others" (APG 1975, 108).

Psychiatry In our "modern" times we are not as sophisticated as we think we are. The definition of the profession I love has been remarkably trivialized. So, all the more pressing reason for the following eloquent definition of psychiatry. The medical specialty that studies and treats a variety of disorders that affect the mind—mental illnesses. Because our minds create our humanity and our sense of self, our specialty cares for illnesses that affect the core of our existence. The common theme that unites all mental illnesses is that they are expressed in signs that reflect the activity of the mind—memory, mood, and emotion, fear and anxiety, sensory perception, attention, impulse control, pleasure, appetitive drives, willed actions, executive functions, ability to think in representations, language, creativity and imagination, consciousness, introspection, and a host of other mental activities. Our science explores the mechanisms of these activities of the mind and the way their disruption leads to mental illness. When disruption occurs in syndromal patterns in these multiple systems in the mind, we observe disorders that we diagnose as dementias, schizophrenias, mood disorders, anxiety disorders, or other mental illnesses. Our patients, our science, and our history define our specialty, not by the form of treatment provided (e.g., psychotherapy, medications), nor by the presence or absence of known mechanisms of illness. Its province defines psychiatry: the mind (Andreasen 1997, 592).

Psychodynamics "The aspect of psychoanalytic theory that explains mental phenomena, such as thoughts, feelings, and behavior, as the results of interacting and opposing goal-directed or motivational forces. The theory focuses on the interplay of such forces, illuminating processes, developments, progressions, regressions, and fixations. The concept of the psychic apparatus as a tripartite structure of the mind (Ego, Id, and Superego) aids in understanding the dynamics postulated" (PC 1990, 152–53).

Psychogenesis Attempts to understand "psychogenetics" are based on the premise that what happens in the mind in the present is influenced or even determined by events and processes that happened in the past (i.e., psychic determinism). Discontinuities and phenomena that appear random and unexplainable can be understood by following a chain of causation in the sequential relationship of psychic events arising from a complex interplay of conscious and unconscious forces (PC 1990, 153). See, for example, sections dealing with Osama's "dark epiphanies" via the Saudi rulers' rejection of his offer to protect Saudi Arabia from Saddam Hussein.

Rationalization A defense mechanism, operating unconsciously, in which an individual attempts to justify or make consciously tolerable by plausible means, feelings or behavior that otherwise would be intolerable (i.e., radical Islamists like Bin Laden's pronouncements about the murder of Western women, children, and noncombatants during Al Qaeda's terror attacks).

Reaction formation A defense mechanism, operating unconsciously, wherein attitudes and behavior are adopted that are the opposites of impulses the individual harbors either consciously or unconsciously, e.g., excessive moral zeal may be a reaction to strong but repressed asocial or antisocial impulses (APG 1975, 133).

Repression A defense mechanism, operating unconsciously, that banishes unacceptable ideas, fantasies, affects, or impulses from consciousness or that keeps out of consciousness what has never been conscious. Although not subject to voluntary recall, the repressed material may emerge in disguised form. Often confused with the conscious mechanism of suppression (APG 1975, 135).

Self psychology An elaboration of the psychoanalytic concepts of narcissism and the self, developed by Heinz Kohut and his colleagues. Self psychology is characterized by emphasis on the vicissitudes of the structure of the self; the associated subjective, conscious, preconscious, and unconscious experience of selfhood; and the self in relation to its sustaining self-objects (PC 1990,174–79). "The basic premise of the psychoanalytic psychology of the self is the defining position it assigns to empathy and introspection" (Kohut 1985, 73).

Self-object transference In the self psychology of Kohut, a transference relationship in which the therapist serves as a self object for the patient by providing needed self-enhancing and self-regulatory functions and emotional stability, which can subsequently be internalized and transformed into the structure of the patient's self (APG 1994, 136).

Splitting "A mental mechanism in which the self or others are viewed as all good or all bad, with failure to integrate the positive and negative qualities of self and others into cohesive images. Often the person alternately idealizes and devalues the same person" (APG 1994, 128).

Sublimation A defense mechanism, operating unconsciously, by which instinctual drives, consciously unacceptable, are diverted into personally and socially acceptable channels (AGP 1994, 129).

Thanatos (Death Instinct) "In Freudian theory, the unconscious drive toward dissolution and death. Coexists with and is in opposition to the life instinct or **eros**" (APG 1975, 34). Many modern psychoanalysts such as myself would be skeptical of Freud's strictly dualistic theory here, but some of us would use it to describe clinical situations where for various reasons there is excessive destructive aggression towards another person or the self (Olsson 2005).

Topographic model of the mind Freud's model of the structure of the mind, first described in terms of the conscious-preconscious-unconscious and a simple conflict theory of the conscious opposing the unconscious (APG 1994, 134).

Totem and Taboo Freud's 1913 allegorical essay based on anthropological sources. Freud uses psychoanalytic formulations to describe the period in primitive man's development when despotic father figures led small tribes where the leader considered all the women in the tribe his exclusive property. The young men (sons) grew jealous and rose up to kill the father and consume him in a totem feast. The sons' guilt, conflict and remorse made them impotent with the women of the tribe. The powerful ghost of the father was displaced onto a fierce animal or totem. Freud connected these totems with primitive tribes' use of human sacrifice, cannibalism, and totemic prohibitions except for special festivals or occasions. Without effective and ethical leadership even some modern groups and tribes can regress and resort to what the psychoanalyst Bion called basic or primitive assumption groups called (1) Fight-Flight, (2) Dependency, and (3) Pairing agendas. Postwar Iraq is replete with examples of these dynamics.

Transference "The unconscious assignment to others of feelings and attitudes that were originally associated with important figures (parents, siblings, etc.) in one's life. The transference relationship follows the pattern of its prototype. The psychiatrist utilizes this phenomenon as a therapeutic tool to help the patient understand emotional problems and their origins" (APG 1994, 135).

Twinship Transference One of the three major types of self-object transferences—mirroring, idealizing, and alter-ego (twinship) (APG 1994, 136).

Umma Islamic global community or supernation (Lawrence 2005, xviii).

Unconscious That part of the mind or mental functioning of which the content is only rarely subject to awareness. It is a repository for data that has never been conscious (primary repression) or that may have been conscious and later repressed (secondary repression). (APG 1975, 151)

Working Through "Exploration of a problem by patient and therapist until a satisfactory solution has been found or until a symptom has been traced to its unconscious sources" (APG 1975, 154).

REFERENCES

Abt, L.E., and S.L. Weissman. 1965. *Acting out: Theoretical and clinical aspects.* New York: Grune & Stratton.

Akhtar, S., S. Kramer, and H. Parens. 1995. *The birth of hatred: Developmental, clinical, and technical aspects of intense aggression.* New York: Jason Aronson.

Anderson, J.L. 2006. Castro's last battle. *New Yorker,* July 31.

Andreasen, N. 1997. What is psychiatry? *American Journal of Psychiatry,* editorial, 154 (5): 592.

Ashley, B. 2005. Silent treatment: New details are emerging about John Walker Lindh's volatile time in Afghanistan. *Marin Independent Journal,* November 21, 2005.

Barner-Barry, C., and R. Rosenwein. 1985. *Psychological perspectives on politics.* Englewood Cliffs, NJ: Prentice Hall.

Barston, R.P. 1988. *Modern diplomacy.* London: Longman.

BBC News. 2001. Who is Richard Reid? *BBC.co.uk,* December 28, 2001, world edition. http://news.bbc.co.uk/2/hi/uk_news/1731568.stm/.

———. 2005. Profile: Jose Padilla. *BBC.co.uk,* November 22, 2005. http://news.bbc.co.uk/1/hi/world/americas/2037444.stm/.

Becker, E. 1973. *The denial of death.* New York: Free Press.

Berman, P. 2003. The philosopher of Islamic terror. *New York Times,* March 23, 2003.

Bergen, P. 2001. *Holy War, Inc.: Inside the secret world of Osama bin Laden.* New York: Touchstone, Simon and Schuster.

———. 2006. *The Osama bin Laden I know: An oral history of al Qaeda's leader.* New York: Free Press.

Bernfeld, S. 1923. Uber eine typische form de männlichen pubertät. *Image* 9.

Bin Laden, O. 1998. America and the Third World War. MS draft, in Arabic and South Asia languages, circulated among key Islamist leaders.

Bodansky, Y. 1999. *Bin Laden: The man who declared war on America.* New York: Prima Publishing, Random House.

Brennan, J.G. 1994. *Foundations of moral obligation: The Stockdale course.* Novata, CA: Presidio Press.

Carlile, J. 2006. Islamic radicalization feared in Europe's jails. *MSNBC*, July 7. http://www.msnbc.msn.com/id/13733782/.

Carter, J. 2006. *Palestine: peace not apartheid.* New York: Simon and Schuster.

Caryl, C. 2007. The next jihadists: Iraq's lost children. *Newsweek, MSNBC*, January 22. http://www.msnbc.msn.com/id/16610767/site/newsweek/.

CNN. 2006. Ayman al-Zawahiri: Egyptian doctor emerges as terror mastermind. *CNN.com,* People in the News, October 4. http://cnn.com/.

Coll, S. 2005. Young Osama: How he learned radicalism and may have seen America.*New Yorker,* December 12.

DeMause, L. 2006. If I blow myself up and become a martyr, I'll finally be loved. *Journal of Psychohistory* 33, no. 4 (Spring): 300–17.

Dennis, A. 2002. *Osama bin Laden: A psychological and political portrait.* Lima, OH: Wyndam Hall Press.

Diagnostic and statistical manual of mental disorders (DSM-IV). 1994. 4th ed., ed. A. Francis. Washington, DC: American Psychiatric Publishing.

Dorpat, T. 1985. *Denial and defense in the therapeutic situation.*New York: Jason Aronson.

Edgerton, J., and R. Campbell III, eds. 1994. *American Psychiatric Glossary.* 7th ed. Washington, DC: American Psychiatric Press.

Erikson, E. 1950. *Childhood and society.* New York: Norton and Company.

———. 1964. *Insight and responsibility.* New York: Norton and Company.

Fanon, F. [1961] 1963. *The wretched of the earth: The handbook for the Black Revolution that is changing the shape of the world.* Trans. C. Farrington. New York: Black Cat, Grove Weidenfield.

Fields, R. 1977. *Society under siege: A psychology of Northern Ireland.* Philadelphia: Temple University Press.

———. 1986. Psychological profile of a terrorist. Paper presented at the American Psychological Association Convention, Washington, DC.

Fornari, F. 1966. *Psychoanalysis of war.* Bloomington: University of Indiana Press.

Freud, A. 1936. *The ego and the mechanisms of defense.* New York: International Universities Press.

Freud, S. [1900] 1958. Preface to the second edition of *The Interpretation of Dreams,* xxvi. *Standard edition of the complete psychological works of Sigmund Freud.* Ed. J. Strachey. Vol. 14. London: Hogarth Press.

———. [1913] 1958. Totem and taboo. *Standard edition of the complete psychological works of Sigmund Freud.* Ed. J. Strachey. Vol. 13. London: Hogarth Press.

———. [1919] 1958. The uncanny. *Standard edition of the complete psychological works of Sigmund Freud.* Ed. J. Strachey. Vol. 17. London: Hogarth Press.

———. [1921] 1958. Group psychology and the analysis of the ego. *Standard edition of the complete psychological works of Sigmund Freud.* Ed. J. Strachey. Vol. 8. London: Hogarth Press.

———. [1933] 1958. Why war? *Standard edition of the complete psychological works of Sigmund Freud.* Ed. J. Strachey. Vol. 22. London: Hogarth Press.

Friedman, T. 2002. The 2 Domes of Belgium. *New York Times,* January 27, 2002.

———. 2005. *The world is flat: A brief history of the twenty-first century.* New York: Farrar, Straus, and Giroux.

Ghosh, A. 2005. Inside the mind of an Iraqi suicide bomber. *Time,* July 4, 23–29.

Goldberg, J. 2001. Letter from Gaza: The martyr strategy: What does the new phase of terrorism signify? *New Yorker,* July 9.

Grieco, E. 2003. Iraqi immigrants in the United States. Migration Policy Institute, April 1. http://www.migrationinformation.org/feature/print.cfm?ID=113

Gunaratna, R. 2002. *Inside Al Qaeda: Global network of terror.* New York: Berkley Books.

Hamilton, A. [1788] 1987. Federalist No. 71. *The Federalist Papers.* Ed. I. Kramnick. New York: Penguin.

Herzog, James. 2001.*Father hunger.* New York: Analytic Press.

Holden, M. 1984. Bargaining and command in the administrative process: Chief executives and the executive entourage.Paper presented at the Institute of Government,University of Virginia.

————. 1988. Bargaining and command by heads of U.S. government departments. *The Social Science Journal* 25:255–276.

Holzer, H.M. Taliban John. http://www.henrymarkholzer.citymax.com/talibanjohn.html/.

Horner, A. 1992. The role of the female therapist in the affirmation of gender in male patients. *Journal of American Academy of Psychoanalysis* 20:599–610.

Janis, I., and I. Mann. 1972. *Victims of groupthink: A psychological study of foreign policy fiascoes.* Boston: Houghton Mifflin.

Kaplan, R.D. 1993. *Balkan ghosts: A journey through history.* New York: Vintage Books.

Kean, T.H., L.H. Hamilton, R. Ben-Veniste, F.F. Fielding, J.S. Gorelick, S. Gorton, B. Kerrey, J.F. Lehman, T.J. Roemer, and J.R. Thompson. 2004. *The 9/11 commission report: Final report of the national commission on terrorist attacks upon the United States.* New York: W. W. Norton.

Kernberg, O. 1986. *Severe personality disorders: Psycho-therapeutic strategies.* New Haven: Yale Univ. Press.

Khatchadourian, R. 2007. Reporter at large: Azzam the American: The making of an Al Qaeda homegrown. *New Yorker,* January 22.

King, M.L., Jr. 1963. Letter from Birmingham Jail. The King Center, Atlanta, GA.

Kohut, H. 1971. *The analysis of the self.* New York: International Universities Press. Used by permission of International Universities Press, Inc. © 1971 by International Universities Press, Inc.

————. 1978. Creativeness, charisma, group psychology. In *Search for the self: Selected writings of Heinz Kohut: 1950–1978.* Ed. P. Ornstein. Vol. 2. New York: International Universities Press.

————. 1985. *Self-psychology and the humanities.* New York: W.W. Norton.

Krikorian, G., and H.G. Reza. 2006. Orange County man rises in al Qaeda: "Azzam the American," or Adam Gadahn, has moved from translator to propagandist. *Los Angeles Times,* October 8, 2006, Sunday home edition.

Langer, W. 1972. *The mind of Adolf Hitler: The secret wartime report.* New York: Basic Books.

Lawrence, B., ed. 2005. *Messages to the world: The statements of Osama Bin Laden.* Trans. J. Howarth. London: Verso.

Leaderer, W., and E. Burdick. 1958. *The ugly American.* New York: W.W. Norton.

Lifton, R. 1989. *Thought reform and the psychology of totalism: A study of "Brainwashing" in China.* Chapel Hill: University of North Carolina Press. (Orig. pub. 1961, W.W. Norton.)

Madison, J. [1787] 1987. Federalist No. 10. *The Federalist Papers.* Ed. I. Kramnick. New York: Penguin.

Mahler, J. 2006. The Bush Administration vs. Salim Hamdan. *New York Times Magazine,* January 8, 2006.

Mandela, N. 1995. *Long walk to freedom.* Boston: Little, Brown and Company.

Meredith, M. 2005. *The fate of Africa: From the hopes of freedom to the heart of despair.* New York: Public Affairs of the Perseus Books Group.

Miliora, M. 2004. The psychology and ideology of an Islamic terrorist leader: Osama bin Laden. *International Journal of Applied Psychoanalytic Studies* 1 (2).

Mill, R. 2001. Bush and Bin Laden. *American Free Press,* October 7, 2001, 1–5.

Moore, B., and B. Fine. 1990. *Psychoanalytic terms and concepts.* American Psychoanalytic Association. New Haven: Yale University Press.

Morgan, R. 1989. *The demon lover: On the sexuality of terrorism.* New York: W. W. Norton.

Obama, B. 2006. *The audacity of hope: Thoughts on reclaiming the American dream.* New York: Crown Books.

Olsson, P. 1980. Adolescent involvement with the supernatural and cults: Some psychoanalytic considerations. *Annual of Psychoanalysis,* vol. 7, 171–196.

———. 2004. Fundamentalist mentality and the Iraq War. *Academy Forum, American Academy of Psychoanalysis and Dynamic Psychiatry,* 48, no. 1 (Winter).

———. 2005. *Malignant pied pipers of our time: A psychological study of destructive cult leaders from the Rev. Jim Jones to Osama bin Laden.* Baltimore: Publish America.

Ovesey, L. 1969. *Homosexuality and pseudohomosexuality.* New York: Science House.

Packer, G. 2006. Letter from Sudan: The moderate martyr: A radically peaceful vision of Islam. *New Yorker,* September 11.

Pappsbody, N. 2005. The man behind the mask: Terror target Melbourne. *Melbourne Herald Sun,* September 13.

PDM Task Force. 2006. *Psychodynamic Diagnostic Manual.* Silver Spring, MD: Alliance of Psychoanalytic Organizations.

Pipes, D. 1983. *In the path of God: Islam and political power.* New York: Basic Books.

Post, J. 2004. *Leaders and their followers in a dangerous world: The psychology of political behavior.* Ithaca and London: Cornell University Press.

Post, J., E. Sprinzak, and L. Denny. 2001. Terrorists in their own words: Interviews with 35 incarcerated Middle East terrorists. (Preliminary research under support of the Smith Richardson Foundation.)

Psychiatric Glossary. 1975. Ed. S. Frazier. Washington, D. C.: American Psychiatric Association Publications Office: Subcommittee on Public Information.

Qutb, S. 1953. *Social justice in Islam.* Trans. J. Hardie. Oneonta, NY: Islamic Publications International.

Rashid, A. 2001. *Taliban: Militant Islam, oil and fundamentalism in Central Asia.* New Haven: Nota Bene Publications, Yale University Press.

Remnick, D. 2002. Letter from Jerusalem: Rage and reason: Will anyone listen to the P.L.O.'s voice of restraint? *New Yorker,* May 6.

Robinson, A. 2001. *Bin Laden: Behind the mask of the terrorist.* New York: Arcade Publishing. © 2001 by Adam Robinson. Electronic permission courtesy of Mainstream Publishing.

Rohde, D. 2002. Al Qaeda—verses from bin Laden's war. Wielding the pen as a sword of the Jihad: Of exile and betrayal. Arabic language poem found with Al Qaeda documents in an abandoned house in Kabul. Written half by poet Dr. Abd-ar-Rahman al-Ashmawi and one half by Sheikh Osama bin Laden. *New York Times,* April 7, 2002, 16.

Rubin, E. 2006. Taking the fight to the Taliban: The experience of American soldiers on the ground in Afghanistan shows what a counterinsurgency can, and cannot, do. *New York Times Magazine,* October 29, 2006.

Sageman, M. 2004. *Understanding terror networks.* Philadelphia: University of Pennsylvania Press.

Said, E. 1986. *After the last sky: Palestinian lives.* New York: Pantheon Books.

Shahrokh, N., and R. Hales, eds. 2003. *American psychiatric glossary.* Arlington, VA: American Psychiatric Publishing.

Shaw, E. 1986. Political terrorists: Dangers of diagnosis, an alternative to the psychopathological model. *International Journal of Law and Psychiatry* 8: 188–89.

Singer, M. 1995. *Cults in our midst: The hidden menace in our everyday lives.* San Francisco: Jossey-Bass Publishers.

Socarides, C. 1977. On vengeance: The desire to "get even." In *World of emotions: Clinical studies of affects and their expressions.* Ed. C. Socarides, 403–25. New York: International Universities Press.

Speckhard, A. 2004. Understanding suicide terrorism: Countering human bombs and their senders. Paper presented at Atlantic Council's conference, "Topics on terrorism: Toward a transatlantic consensus on the nature of threat," November 29–30, Brussels, Belgium.

Spencer, R. 2006. *The truth about Mohammad: Founder of the world's most intolerant religion.* Washington, DC: Regnery Publishing.

Stern, J. 2003. *Terror in the name of God: Why religious militants kill.* New York: Harper-Collins.

Stockdale, J. and S. 1984. *In love and war: The story of a family's ordeal and sacrifice during the Vietnam years.* New York: Harper and Row.

Strachey, J., ed. 1958. *Standard edition of the complete psychological works of Sigmund Freud.* 23 vols. London: Hogarth Press.

Sun Tzu. [500 BCE] 2002. *The art of war.* Minneola, NY: Dover.

Swogger, G., Jr. 2001. The psychodynamic assumptions of the U. S. Constitution. *Journal of Applied Psychoanalytic Studies* 3, no. 4 (October): 353–80.

Volkan, V. 1988. *The need to have enemies and allies: From clinical practice to international relationships.* Northvale, NJ: Jason Aronson.

———. 1997. Experiment in Estonia: "Unofficial diplomacy" at work. In *Bloodlines: From ethnic pride to ethnic terrorism.* New York: Farrar, Straus, and Giroux.

———. 1999. The tree model: a comprehensive psychopolitical approach to unofficial diplomacy and the reduction of ethnic tension. *Mind and Human Interaction* 10, no. 3, 142–206.

———. 2001. September 11 and societal regression. *Mind and Human Interaction* 12, no. 3, 196–216.

Volkan, V., S. Akhtar, R. Dorn, J. Kafka, O. Kernberg, P. Olsson, and R. Rogers. 1999. Psychodynamics of leaders and decision-making. *Mind and Human Interaction* 9, no. 3, 129–81.

Volkan, V., and M. Harris. 1993. Shaking the tent: The psychodynamics of ethnic terrorism. *Center for the Study of Mind and Human Interaction* Monograph no. 1.

Volkan, V., J. Montvale, and D. Julius, eds. 1991. *The psychodynamics of international relationships, Volume II: Unofficial Diplomacy at Work.* Lexington, MA: Lexington Books.

Wikipedia. Abu Musab al-Zarqawi. http://en.wikipedia.org/wiki/Abu_Musab_al-Zarqawi/.

————. Fascism. http://en.wikipedia.org/wiki/Fascism/.

————. John Walker Lindh. http://en.wikipedia.org/wiki/John_Walker_Lindh/.

————. Jose Padilla. http://en.wikipedia.org/wiki/Jos%C3%A9_Padilla_%28prisoner%29/.

————. Mahmoud Mohamed Taha. http://en.wikipedia.org/wiki/Mahmoud_Mohammad_ Taha/.

Winnicott, D.W. 1960. Ego distortion in terms of true and false self. In *The maturational process and the facilitating environment*. New York: International Universities Press.

————. 1986. *Home is where we start from: Essays by a psychoanalyst*. Ed. C. Winnicott, R. Shepherd, and M. Davis. New York: W.W. Norton.

Wintrob, R. 1978. *Self-involvement in the Middle East conflict*. Monograph 103, vol. 10. New York: Group for the Advancement of Psychiatry, Committee on International Relations.

Woodward, B. 2006. *State of denial*. New York: Simon and Schuster.

Wright, L. 2006. Annals of terrorism: The master plan: For the new theorists of jihad, Al Qaeda is just the beginning. *New Yorker*, September 11.

Yousafzai, S., R. Moreau, and M. Hosenball. 2006. Al Qaeda's Western recruits. *Newsweek, MSNBC*, December 25–January 1. http://www.msnbc.msn.com/id/16240565/site/ newsweek/page/4/print/1/displaymode/1098/.

INDEX

Note on Arabic names: The prefixes "al-" and "el-" have been retained but ignored when the entry is alphabetized, so that al-Zarqawi is listed under Z. "Bin" is treated as a primary element and appears under B.

ABOUT THE AUTHOR

PETER ALAN OLSSON, M.D. is a Psychiatrist at Monadnock Community Hospital, an Assistant Professor of Psychiatry at Dartmouth Medical School, and an Adjunct Clinical Professor of Psychiatry at Baylor College of Medicine. He practiced Psychiatry and Psychotherapy in Houston for twenty-five years and in New Hampshire for eight years. His training and residency was completed at Baylor College of Medicine.